Bertrand Russell   KARSH

BERTRAND RUSSELL

THE

PASSIONATE SKEPTIC

A Biography by

ALAN WOOD

I heard the beat of centaur's hoofs over the hard turf
As his dry and passionate talk devoured the afternoon.
'He is a charming man'—'But after all what did he mean?' ...
T. S. ELIOT, *Mr. Apollinax*

He left ...
To seek strange truths in undiscovered lands.
SHELLEY, *Alastor*

SIMON AND SCHUSTER · NEW YORK · 1958

LIBRARY OF CONGRESS CATALOG CARD NUMBER: 58–6266
MANUFACTURED IN THE UNITED STATES OF AMERICA
PRINTED BY MARK H. HERMER, LITHOGRAPHY, NEW YORK, N.Y.
BOUND BY AMERICAN BOOK-STRATFORD PRESS, NEW YORK, N.Y.

Dedicated to
Norman S. Wood

PREFACE

FOR access to unpublished letters and documents, or for help in other ways in writing this book, I wish to express my grateful thanks to Lady Allen of Hurtwood, Miss Elizabeth Anscombe, Dr John Baker, Mr Bernard Berenson, Mr H. N. Brailsford, Professor C. D. Broad, Mr Fenner Brockway, Miss Catherine Brown, Mr T. S. Eliot, Professor John K. Fairbank, Professor C. P. FitzGerald, Miss Mary Fletcher, Mr John Fletcher, the Hon R. Gathorne-Hardy, Mrs Mary Agnes Hamilton, Sir Ralph Hawtrey, Dr and Mrs Julian Huxley, Mrs Harold Laski, Professor J. E. Littlewood, Mr and Mrs E. M. H. Lloyd, Mr Ralph Lyon, the Warden of Merton, Professor and Mrs G. E. Moore, Miss Louise Morgan, Mrs Bernard Muscio, Dr Gilbert Murray, Professor E. H. Neville, Madame Thérèse Nicod, Miss J. E. Norton, the Trustees of the Late Lord Passfield and Mrs Webb, Professor W. V. Quine, Mr Anthony Quinton, Miss Diana Russell, Miss Flora Russell, Professor P. Sargant Florence, Dr D. S. Schwayder, Mr James Strachey, Sir Charles and Lady Trevelyan, Mrs R. C. Trevelyan, Sir Stanley Unwin, Mrs Julian Vinogradoff, Sir Ralph Wedgwood, Mr W. H. Werkmeister, Professor Morris Weitz, Professor J. H. C. Whitehead, Mr G. Woledge, and Mr Leonard Woolf.

In particular, my work would have been impossible without the great help and kindness I have received, over a period of several years, from Lord and Lady Russell.

I have had throughout the collaboration in research of my wife, Mary Seaton Wood, but not her concurrence in all my opinions.

Chapters V and VI originated in a series of lectures prepared for the Oxford University Delegacy for Extra-Mural Studies, to whom I should like to make the appropriate acknowledgments.

This book is intended mainly for the general reader. In some cases, however, it has seemed better for those who are not philosophers to pass over passages with technical terms, rather than divert the argument for the lengthy definitions and discussions which would be needed to explain them, and which can be found easily accessible in Russell's own works. Only four chapters are concerned solely with philosophy.

References to sources of quotations will be provided in great detail, together with a bibliography, in my *Russell's Philosophy: A Study of its Development*.

London, 1956   A.A.W.W.

CONTENTS

I want to stand at the rim of the world and peer into the darkness beyond, and see a little more than others have seen, of the strange shapes of mystery that inhabit that unknown night.... I want to bring back into the world of men some little bit of new wisdom. There is a little wisdom in the world; Heraclitus, Spinoza, and a saying here and there. I want to add to it, even if only ever so little....

Bertrand Russell, in a letter
written from Brixton Prison, 1918

Bertrand Russell
as a young man.

Bertrand Russell
at the age of
seventy-seven.
PHOTO BY
H. W. LEGGETT

Alys Russell

Alfred North Whitehead

G. E. Moore as a
young man.

Group at Garsington, 1915. Left to right: (behind) Lytton
Strachey, J. M. Keynes, Bertrand Russell, J. H. Whitehouse,
Edward Daws; (in front) Lucy Silcox, Lady Ottoline Morrell,
Mary Agnes Hamilton, Marie Juliette Baillot (later Mrs.
Julian Huxley).

Cambridge Moral
Science Club, 1915.
Left to right:
(standing)
G. E. Moore,
Mary Fletcher,
H. T. J. Norton,
Bertrand Russell,
Prof. G. Dawes Hicks;
(seated)
Prof. W. R. Sorley,
Karin Stephen
(formerly Costelloe),
W. E. Johnson,
Mrs. McTaggart,
J. M. McTaggart.

Parliamentary
Candidate
for Chelsea,
1924.

With some of
the children at
Beacon Hill
School.

"A voice that was heard . . ."
Before the microphones at the Caxton Hall. (see p. 239)
PICTURE POST

Bertrand Russell
in 1931.
UNITED PRESS

Russell and a Koala bear. (see p. 212)

As William James
Lecturer in
Philosophy at
Harvard University,
1940.
WIDE WORLD

With Edith Russell.

With Mary and Alan Wood. A photograph taken by Godfrey Cake in 1955, when Russell was 83.

CHAPTER I

The Boy in the Garden

PHILOSOPHERS exist to ask questions, not to answer them. The more unsolved problems they have on their hands, the better they are doing their job; so the gibes at them by the practical men completely miss the point. Though philosophy can claim no great advances in knowledge compared with the sciences, the sciences might never have got started without philosophy first awakening wonder. When the scientists give answers, often it is only because philosophers have asked.

The philosophers speculated about atoms long before they were discovered; and they may have given the scientists the idea of what to look for. Philosophers questioned the common sense view of matter, and the scientists later agreed with them that matter is not what it seems. To the practical man a tree is a tree, and common sense is common sense, and life is a dull prosaic affair. But one day in the history of the human race, some pioneer first asked a philosophical question—perhaps a completely impractical and useless question—such as 'Does this tree continue to exist if there is nobody here to see it; and, if so, how can I *know* that it does?' On that day philosophy was born, and men became more than automatic animals. And the achievement of the first philosopher to ask this question is not lessened in the least by the fact that, from that day to this, no subsequent philosopher has yet found a satisfactory answer to it.

Other questions first considered by philosophy, having been answered, have become part of science or mathematics or physiology. Bertrand Russell once put it that 'Science is what you know, philosophy is what you don't know'. But the finest minds will still be attracted by the unsolved residue of problems which remain, because to see the universe through the eyes of a philosopher is the most exciting way to look at it. To the scientist it is a monotonous fact that the sun rises every morning. But the philosopher suddenly discovers the problem of induction, and asks 'How do I *know* that the sun will rise tomorrow?'; and he finds, with a new interest in life, that nobody can tell him. To be a philosopher is to leave the commonplace realm of dull certainties, and always to be aware of the magic and mystery of the universe and of existence. It is to keep alive throughout life the eager wonder of a child.

Bertrand Russell was a child who began asking penetrating questions as soon as he could speak—in fact, three days after he was born, his mother wrote that 'He lifts his head up and looks about in a very energetic way'. He was still looking about him in an energetic and inquiring way when he was over eighty. To many of his questions he found answers; because that, of course, is the point of asking questions. He had a contempt for those philosophers who tease themselves with conundrums for their own sakes. He was a passionate sceptic because he wanted to be a passionate believer; he questioned everything because he craved for *certain* knowledge, in the same way that some men crave for religion. But, like all great philosophers, he ended up by asking more questions than he could answer: and it is because he was frank about his failures that he ranks as one of the greatest philosophers of all. He is certainly the leading questioner of our times. He started by asking questions about mathematics and religion and philosophy, and he went on to question accepted ideas about war and politics and sex and education, setting the minds of men on the march, so that the world could never be quite the same as if he had not lived.

The three days' old baby, who lifted up his head and looked about so energetically, represented as cogent an argument as can be found for a hereditary aristocracy. His lineage occupies some complicated columns in Burke's *Peerage*, without a commoner in sight. To save space I will only go back three generations—to the sixth Duke of Bedford, who married the daughter of Viscount Torrington. Their third son, the grandfather of Bertrand Russell, became famous in English history as Lord John Russell. (He was later created the first Earl Russell.) Lord John Russell's first wife was the widow of Lord Ribblesdale; his second wife was a daughter of the Earl of Minto. The eldest son of this second marriage, with the courtesy title of Viscount Amberley, married Kate Stanley, daughter of Lord Stanley of Alderley.

The Amberleys' eldest boy, Frank, was born in 1865, and became the second Earl Russell. Their daughter Rachel was born in 1868: she was, as her grandmother said, 'as sweet a little bright-eyed lassie as I ever saw'. Their youngest child, Bertrand Arthur William Russell, was born at a quarter to six on the evening of May 18, 1872, in a house near the banks of the Wye. 'It's a very fine boy,' said the doctor, Mr Audland, adding that not one baby in thirty was so big and fat. Kate Amberley wrote to her own mother, Lady Stanley: 'The baby weighed 8¾ lbs, is 21 inches long and very fat and ugly . . . Very like Frank, everyone thinks—blue eyes far apart and not much chin. . . . I have lots of milk now, but if he does not get it at once, or has wind or anything, he gets into such a rage and screams and kicks and trembles till he is soothed off. . . . He is very vigorous, and Mr Audland says he is an out of the way strong muscular child.'

What name should the baby be given? One grandmother, Lady Russell, suggested 'Galahad' as appropriate; but the other grandmother, Lady Stanley, retorted to her daughter: 'Pray do not inflict such a punishment on your child as to call it Galahad.' So the boy was named, and was to be known ever after in the history of philosophy, as Bertrand Russell; except when he also became known by the title he inherited and the honours he earned—as the third Earl Russell, OM, FRS.

All mothers think their children are marvellous; but the whole family thought this about the merry and irrepressible boy called Bertrand. Grandmother Russell described him as 'full of fun and merriment'. His uncle William Russell noticed that he had 'a perpetual smile on his face'. His Aunt Agatha Russell recorded in a letter that 'Yesterday he insisted on lifting all alone an enormous book out of the shelf to a little stool, where he sat down with it open before him—in a fit of laughter at his own wisdom!' When he was a year and ten months old, he was able to talk with such words as 'spoon', 'excuse', 'all gone', and 'don't'. He began to share in the social life enjoyed by a family of such aristocratic standing. One day Queen Victoria came on a visit when Bertrand was staying with his Russell grandparents, and Aunt Agatha reported that 'Bertie made such a nice little bow—but was much subdued and did not treat Her Majesty with the utter disrespect I expected'.

Tragedy came upon the young parents of the merry Bertrand, and clouded the rest of his boyhood. The year after he was born his father, Viscount Amberley, had an illness which was diagnosed, probably inexpertly, as epilepsy. The next year Amberley's brother William became insane, remaining so till his death in 1933; and Bertrand's elder brother Frank was ill with diphtheria. Frank, robust and strong-minded—he remained so throughout life—threw the illness off; but his sister Rachel, now six years old, caught the disease. Nursing her, Kate Amberley got diphtheria herself. Both she and Rachel died.

Bertrand, just two years old, was sent to a neighbouring farm and escaped infection.

Amberley did not long survive the loss of his wife and daughter, dying himself some eighteen months later, when only thirty-three. Chance has preserved a description of his death, in a letter written by one of the family:

'Frank remained sobbing and crying, so that his father's hand was wet with tears. The doctor lifted Bertrand up, and he kissed him gently and softly and said "Goodbye my little dears, for ever". He then lay perfectly quiet with a smile.'

Frank Russell was now ten years old, Bertrand less than four—too young to understand fully what had happened, but already too keen-minded and sensitive not to have a sense of loss and tragedy. In after years he was to write, inaccurately, that 'I was born unhappy'—so completely had periods of later unhappiness effaced in his memory the cheerfulness of his early infancy. He could remember calculating gloomily, when he was five, that if he lived till seventy he still had to endure all except one-fourteenth of his life.

Amberley, a vigorous free thinker, had appointed two atheists as guardians for his sons, but the will was set aside. The orphans were made Wards in Chancery, and sent to be brought up by their grandparents.

Lord John Russell, as a former Prime Minister of august eminence, had made his home at Pembroke Lodge, Richmond Park, a house in the gift of the Queen. (In these more prosaic days, the Ministry of Works has turned part of it into a café for tourists and trippers in the park.) When Frank and Bertrand went there, Earl Russell was eighty three; and he died two years later, leaving Bertrand with nothing but vague memories of a nice old man in a bathchair, 'full of kindly jollity, fond of children, and quite undisturbed by their noise'. Frank succeeded to the Earldom.

The dominant influence in the children's upbringing was to be their grandmother. Lady Russell, often known as 'Lady John', came from a strict Scottish Presbyterian family. Though austere and Puritan in her views, she enjoyed fun and merriment; she was also younger and much more radical than her husband (whose more cautious Cabinet colleagues, fearing her influence, had called her 'The Deadly Nightshade'). She shocked conventional opinion by becoming a Unitarian at the age of seventy, supporting Irish Home Rule, and opposing British Imperialist wars. The two boys were thus brought up under an affectionate but rigid régime which combined old-fashioned Puritanism and advanced Liberalism, with the traditional Scottish porridge for breakfast as austere food for the body, and a series of German and Swiss governesses to provide radical enlightment for the mind. (At this time British Liberals preferred Germany to France, a country which seemed addicted to dictatorship and militarism under the Napoleons.) Bertrand learnt German almost as soon as he learnt English.

The ménage at Pembroke Lodge was completed by Bertrand's unmarried Aunt Agatha, who always wore a white shawl and black velvet slippers whatever the weather; and by his unconventional Uncle Rollo, who was small and shy and had few social graces. Rollo Russell was probably the first to awaken Bertrand's interest in science. He wrote modern psalms in praise of God, using the biblical psalm metres, but bringing in scientific references to atmospheric pressure, 'contending' atoms, and the nineteenth century ether which 'beareth messages from matter through all creation'.

It was not an exciting household for two lively boys. One published description was given, in *A Victorian Childhood*, by Annabel Jackson: 'They all drifted in and out of the room like ghosts, and no one ever seemed to be hungry.' The same visitor also recalled that Frank used to tie her up to trees by her hair; whereas 'Bertie, a solemn little boy in a blue velvet suit with an equally solemn governess, was always kind.'

This account is confirmed by two other small girls who used to play at Pembroke Lodge—Flora and Diana Russell, cousins who afterwards remembered Frank as 'very violent'. A nurse-maid once came into a room to find that Frank, having lost his temper with Flora, had chased her round the room and was apparently trying to throw her on the fire. Bertrand, on the other hand, was marked by precocious courtesy and precise diction. Once Lady John told him to take one of his young guests into the garden and entertain her.

'Yes, Granny,' he replied. 'Or, at least, I shall endeavour to do so.'

Another visitor, Santayana the philosopher, commented that the atmosphere at Pembroke Lodge was exactly like old-fashioned Boston. (This was when Bertrand had taken Santayana to tea in later years, at a time when Lady Russell 'never went to London except to dine with Mr Gladstone'.)

The political tradition at Pembroke Lodge was strong. Lady John told of her husband's fights for electoral reform; and of one other particular family hero, William Lord Russell, executed for his resistance to Charles II. At a very early age Bertrand was inculcated with the ideas that Russells have a duty of public service, and that rebellion is sometimes justified. His grandmother wrote on the Bible she gave him on his twelfth birthday: '*Thou shalt not follow a multitude to do evil.*' And his Uncle Rollo wrote in one of his modern scientific psalms:

> *A strong will is above all to be desired. . . .*
> *To contend against every ill will that*
> *pleaseth a company, to oppose the*
> *cry of the multitude;*

> To drive the goodwill of princes before us
> like chaff, if the right offendeth
> their pleasure . . .

As he grew older, Bertrand also saw something of his mother's family, the Stanleys. If the Russells were scholarly introverts, the Stanleys were vigorous extroverts; and meeting them only increased Bertrand's natural shyness. Lady Stanley was a lady of caustic speech who hated humbug, and who announced that she was leaving her brain to the Royal College of Surgeons, 'because it will be so interesting for them to have a clever woman's brain to cut up'. One of her daughters was the Countess of Airlie, whose granddaughter married Winston Churchill.

Frank Russell took after the Stanleys in temperament, rebelling robustly against the confinement of Pembroke Lodge. He ran away, and got himself sent off to boarding school by threatening that otherwise he would go on running away. Bertrand, at this period, was more like the Russells; years were to elapse before he fully recaptured the Stanley inheritance of high spirits and gaiety. Frank Russell wrote of him, with the kind of robust overstatement by which elder brothers will disparage younger brothers:

'Bertie, whom they caught younger and was more amenable, did enjoy the full benefit of a home education in an atmosphere of love, with the result that till he went to Cambridge he was an unendurable young prig.'

Bertrand himself said afterwards that 'Like others who had a Puritan education, I had the habit of meditating on my sins, follies and shortcomings.'

Regular churchgoing, of course, was part of the Pembroke Lodge régime: and so was hymn singing on Sunday evenings, with Lady John playing the piano. The effect of the hymns on Bertrand is evident enough from the way they impressed themselves on his memory. Some eighty years later he would still claim 'I know *thousands* of hymns by heart'; and he would proceed to recite, for instance:

Days and moments quickly flying
Blend the living with the dead;
Soon will you and I be lying
Each within our narrow bed . . .

Thoughts of his sinfulness filled his head in some of his solitary rambles through the big neglected garden of Pembroke Lodge. He was growing up a young recluse, silent and shy for lack of company of his own age.

Partly from shyness, and partly from training in the aristocratic tradition that it is wrong to display private emotions, he soon developed diffidence and difficulty in expressing any personal affection or feeling. Once his Aunt Agatha was away ill—she often seemed to be ill—and Lady John told Bertrand that he should write to her. He asked what he could put in the letter, and his grandmother told him: 'Say how much you hope she will be better when she comes back'.

'It would make me hot all over to say that,' replied Bertrand.

Apart from shyness and loneliness, however, Bertrand was not an abnormal child in any way; he had a boy's natural delight in games and adventure, and Lady John did her best to find him companions. There was one boy who stayed at Pembroke Lodge for nearly a year. He and Bertrand tied a rope high up an oak tree on a slope. With practice and skill, they could swing out on the rope and get back to where they started; any error of judgment meant they would be bashed against the trunk of the tree. When other unsuspecting small boys came on visits, they liked persuading them to try the rope.

Bertrand also had a passion for skating, and climbing trees for birds' nests. The Duke of Cambridge owned the pheasant shooting rights in a plantation in Richmond Park, and Bertrand drove the park keepers frantic trying to stop him trespassing.

In his rambles he thought of other things besides his sins; his head was full of imagination and speculation. The first recorded instance of his career as a questioner of orthodox beliefs came as early as the age of five. Informed that the earth was round, he refused to believe it, but began digging a hole in the garden to see if he came out in Australia. About the same time he was told that angels watched beside him as he slept. He retorted that he never saw them, and was told that they went away the moment he opened his eyes. So he decided to trick them by keeping his eyes tight shut, but making a sudden grab; and he caught nothing.

Further reinforcement of his scepticism arose from Mother Shipton's prophecy that the world was coming to an end in 1881. In that year there was one very dark overcast day, and he was quite sure that it meant the end; but the year came to a close with the world still in being.

Any scepticism was always directed at finding true facts; once again, there is an instance when he was only five. Taken to the seaside at Broadstairs, he was annoyed to find the limpets defeating his efforts to get them off rocks. He asked his Aunt Agatha: 'Do limpets think?'

'I don't know,' she replied.

'Then,' said Bertrand, 'you must learn.'

His interests soon turned to mathematics: in fact he said afterwards that it was 'the desire to know more mathematics' that saved him from suicide during adolescence. His eagerness was caused largely, I think, by his almost mystical yearning for some truth that was absolutely certain.

It is some consolation to ordinary people to know that he wept bitterly over his first efforts to learn the multiplication table, and began with a great dislike of algebra. (He wanted to know what x and y really were, and thought his tutor knew but would not tell him.) But he made rapid progress, and the major event in his intellectual development can be dated precisely.

On August 9, 1883, when Bertrand was eleven, his brother Frank recorded: 'I gave Bertie his first lesson in Euclid this afternoon. He did very well indeed, and we got half through the definitions.' On September 9: 'Bertie successfully mastered the Pons Asinorum this evening.'

At first there had been a hitch. Bertrand was bitterly disappointed at finding that geometry started with axioms which had to be taken on trust, and could not be *proved*. He continued his career as a questioner by startling evidence of philosophical genius. It occurred to him to question Euclid's axioms, beginning by questioning whether two things which are equal to the same thing are equal to one another.

Frank could only reply: 'If you don't accept the axioms we can't go on.' So they proceeded on this working basis; but the doubts raised in Bertrand's eleven-year old mind about the validity of the foundations of mathematics were to dominate his life from that day to the completion of *Principia Mathematica*.

After mathematics, his greatest interest was in history, then literature; he discovered Shelley with delight. He could vividly recall first reading *Alastor*, an early romantic poem. 'As I read, the world left me . . . I forgot where I was.' He was told not to read most of the books in his grandfather's library, and did so avidly as a result: 'I can scarcely imagine a more effective method of instilling literary culture.' He also laid the foundations of an extraordinary store of knowledge on almost every subject, which even his voluminous writings never fully reflected; for he would not introduce an irrelevant fact just to show his erudition.

When he was about sixteen, he overstrained his eyes so badly that for a time he was ordered neither to read nor write. He occupied himself learning poetry by heart, including two volumes of Elizabethan lyrics.

One of his grandfather's books, called *The Annals of Ireland*, told about men who had gone to Ireland before the Flood, and had all been drowned in it. His sceptical mind immediately questioned how the authors could have known about the adventures of these men, and he put down the book in disgust.

Russell's next step as a questioner was to examine the arguments for different tenets of religion, writing his musings in Greek letters in a secret journal. He was determined to ignore what he *wanted* to believe, and to be guided only by reason.

His uncle Rollo thought that scientific determinism could be reconciled with free will. Rollo wrote that 'Not an atom, nor a galaxy of suns, dares lift itself against the word. . . . In the universe there is no corner void of Law'. At the same time he thanked God for 'the glorious freedom of will in man'. Bertrand decided that this was a contradiction. Living bodies were just as much subject to the laws of dynamics as any other matter; therefore the motions of a human being were as predictable, given sufficient knowledge, as those of the planets.

He went on to reject personal immortality. For a long time he accepted the 'First Cause' argument for God's existence, but rejected it after reading J. S. Mill, and gave up all belief in God.

Mill, who had been a close friend of Bertrand's father, was the writer who had most influence on his developing ideas. Mill was the leading nineteenth century exponent of British empirical philosophy—the common sense matter-of-fact philosophy which believes that all knowledge comes from experience.

To this, the most obvious apparent exceptions are mathematical propositions; it seemed that $2+2=4$ was an eternal *a priori** truth, and whole philosophies had been constructed on an almost mystical regard for mathematics. Mill, in so far as he did not simply ignore the problem, held that mathematical knowledge consisted of generalizations based on experience. This was something which young Russell could not accept: he thought that once you had seen that $2+2=4$, you knew it in a way which was not made more certain by any added experience of different pairs of couples. Once more he found himself wondering, in his lonely walks in the garden, about the real nature of mathematics.

There is interesting evidence in Russell, then, for those who believe that the early years are decisive in any man's career. His writings on morals, education and religion seemed partly evoked by a reaction against his Puritan upbringing. But while rejecting this aspect of his grandmother's teachings in Pembroke Lodge, there were other things which remained; in particular, the idea that there are few higher virtues than moral courage in an unpopular cause. Finally, his mind was already bent on those speculations which led to his main permanent achievement as a philosopher—the way he added to empirical philosophy a tenable theory of mathematical knowledge, and reinforced it with the rigour of new logical techniques.

On the personal side, his youth was also all-important.

Someone once remarked that we all spend our lives looking for the things we have missed in our childhood. Russell himself, writing of Abraham Lincoln's early days in the woods, said that 'He loved human beings, partly, perhaps, because in the forest

---

* *A priori* knowledge can be roughly defined as knowledge which has a basis other than experience. To provide a precise philosophical definition would involve a whole book, if not a whole philosophy.

they were rare'. Russell's loneliness left him with a craving for
ordinary human affection, as well as a lack of knowledge about
ordinary human beings; he was often mistaken in his first
judgments about men and women, though later he became a
perceptive judge of character. It was one of the oldest and most
understanding of his friends who suggested to me that perhaps
the worst thing lacking in his boyhood was a sister, and that his
life might have been very different if his sister Rachel had not
died.

On the other hand, his loneliness may well have fostered his
intellectual development. He himself once wrote: 'I sometimes
think—though this goes much against much that I wish to believe—that greatness is more likely to be achieved by those who
have been solitary and somewhat neglected in their childhood,
than by those who have received sympathetic encouragement.
. . . Without the capacity for mental solitude, none of the
supreme achievements of human genius would have been
possible.' And he quoted Wordsworth's description of Newton
as 'voyaging through strange seas of thought alone'.

It was this combination of supreme intellectual achievement
in abstract thought, with a rather belated understanding of ordinary human beings, which led T. S. Eliot to describe him in
middle-age as 'permanently precocious'.

We must add that, however much about Russell we may
explain by way of upbringing and circumstances, there remains
the one random and inexplicable element which we can only
label, for short, as genius. One of his later friends, Charles
Sanger, was to put it:

'His admirable and lucid English style may be attributed to
the fact that he did not undergo a classical education at a public
school; his religious views and moral character may be due to
the wise exercise of the paternal jurisdiction of the Court of
Chancery; but his wit, his love of truth, and his capacity for hard
work seem to be innate.'

One thing was needed to complete his preliminary education.
In order to matriculate at Cambridge, Bertrand had to bring his
Latin and Greek up to standard; and it was also decided that he

should try for a scholarship—not because he lacked money, but to give him a chance to see how he would get on in competition with other boys. For this purpose he was sent to a 'Crammer', an institution mainly concerned with coaching would-be Army officers for Sandhurst. Apparently Lady John decided on the Crammer because of her dislike of public schools.

When he first arrived at the Crammer, one of the tutors came out to meet him. He was so paralysed with shyness that he could not even pay the cabman his fare, and was overcome with shame on hearing the tutor whispering to a servant to pay it.

Russell explained afterwards that his shyness made him 'just the sort of boy that other boys make fun of'; and his fellow pupils were stupid and loutish. Nearly seventy years later he could still recall, with horror in his voice, his feelings at finding a boy who was so ignorant that, when told that $\mathrm{Tan}\ x = \dfrac{\mathrm{Sin}\ x}{\mathrm{Cos}\ x}$, he thought he could cancel out the x's above and below and get $\dfrac{\mathrm{Sin}}{\mathrm{Cos}}$.

Russell acquired, in eighteen months, the knowledge of the classics which takes the average schoolboy six years or more, and he won his scholarship to Cambridge. But he never had the thorough knowledge of defunct languages enjoyed by many contemporary British philosophers. At an age when G. E. Moore, for instance, was translating English verses backwards and forwards into Greek verses and Latin verses, Russell had been discussing scientific problems with his uncle Rollo; and, with the new advances in science which lay ahead, I think the advantage was on Russell's side. So was the fact that he could read German or French or Italian mathematicians and philosophers in their own languages. Both his grandmothers would speak English, German, French or Italian with equal fluency when distinguished foreign visitors arrived; and he was familiar with the inheritance of European culture as a matter of course.

CHAPTER II

'He was Always Talking'

RUSSELL entered Trinity College Cambridge in October 1890, at the age of eighteen, and found himself in 'a new world of infinite delight'.

It is hard to deny the intellectual supremacy of Cambridge during the half century or more which followed. F. H. Bradley at Oxford was regarded for many years as the leading British philosopher; but his reign was to be overthrown by a revolt inspired firstly by Cambridge, and secondly by the American 'realists'. One college alone in Cambridge—Trinity—could boast of McTaggart, Whitehead, Russell, Moore, Broad, Ramsey and Wittgenstein, together with Eddington, Rutherford and J. J. Thomson. To these we may add such other Cambridge names as W. E. Johnson, Marshall, and Keynes.

No one has yet explained this extraordinary conglomeration of talent; perhaps it can only be ascribed to chance. But one reason for the Cambridge philosophical renaissance may be that Cambridge was far ahead of Oxford in mathematics and science, and the main advances in philosophy were destined to come from this direction. It was because he wanted to study mathematics that Bertrand went to Cambridge, whereas his brother Frank had gone to Oxford.

From the start Russell made friends with an outstanding group of men. One examiner for his scholarship had been A. N. Whitehead, who had entered Trinity as an undergraduate ten years earlier, in 1880, and became a Fellow in 1885. Whitehead was so impressed by Russell's scholarship papers that he made a point of asking senior students to call on Russell and get to know him.

One of the new philosophical friends who had most influence

on him was McTaggart, the Hegelian philosopher. He had some of Russell's wit and more than Russell's shyness; he would walk along the cloisters in Trinity with a shuffling sideways gait, keeping as close to the wall as possible. He was unusual among Russell's friends in being a Conservative in politics. A younger friend was G. E. Moore, who came to Cambridge two years after Russell.

There were other friends, some of whom I will be referring to again later, and some of whom became well known in England and abroad. There was Lowes Dickinson, the classical scholar. There were Theodore and Crompton Llewellyn Davies, and the three Trevelyan brothers—Charles the politician, Robert the poet, and George M. Trevelyan the historian. Charles Trevelyan lived to become the last surviving member of the first Labour Government in Britain; and G. M. Trevelyan—in his distant undergraduate days—was regarded as even more of a radical.

An undergraduate friend and exact contemporary, with whom Russell shared rooms for a time, was Charles Sanger, exceptionally gifted as a mathematician, as a lawyer, and a linguist. One description is still preserved, written by Lowes Dickinson, of Sanger and Russell together. Sanger, said Dickinson, was 'very small, face all alert, bright complexion, eager movements'; while Russell 'looked like a French abbé of the eighteenth century crossed with an English aristocrat'.

The gentle Lowes Dickinson was one of the first to protest against Russell's life-long habit of truthful candour, once calling him 'Cordelia'. Even when he was an undergraduate, many people already found Russell rather a frightening person. Charles Trevelyan, who was some years older, went down before Russell, but he sometimes came back to Cambridge to see his younger brothers. Many years afterwards he recalled that 'Russell was much too clever for me, and I was inclined to keep out of his way. . . . I felt he was a great man who would see through me'.

These were the days before a University education in England had become part of the professional class's struggle for existence, with most students grimly concentrating on getting good degrees as the means to a job. Russell and his friends worked hard at their particular academic subjects; but they also read and

talked about philosophy, politics, literature, religion, and anything else which interested them. A mathematician like
Whitehead, for instance, recalled afterwards that he had spent
so much time studying Kant's *Critique of Pure Reason* that he
almost knew parts of it by heart. For Whitehead and Russell,
as undergraduates, Cambridge conformed almost exactly to the
Platonic ideal of education; they divided their time between the
study of mathematics and the free discussion of diverse subjects
with their friends. In fact, according to Whitehead, these talks
almost amounted to 'a daily Platonic dialogue'.

The centre of the discussions was the small exclusive group
known as 'The Society' or 'The Apostles'—so exclusive that its
existence was supposed to be secret. On Saturday evenings they
would meet in each other's rooms to talk far into the night, meet
again for a late breakfast on Sunday, and then go off for a whole
day's walk, still talking as they went.

In these discussions Russell was soon a shining figure. He
was no longer living under the shadow of his grandmothers. He
found, still with something of a feeling of surprise, that the
cleverest men of Cambridge were delighted to listen to him. In
character and in wit he developed rapidly, as though he were a
new being in a new world. When in congenial company his
shyness was forgotten. He took to smoking—at Pembroke
Lodge, Lady John had frowned on tobacco as 'sinful'—and he
was ready to puff his pipe and talk all day and all night.

Sixty years afterwards I was pressing G. E. Moore for any
recollections he might have of Russell as an undergraduate.
After such a lapse of time, memories were growing dim; but
there was one thing he remembered quite definitely about
Russell. 'He was always talking,' said Moore.

As for Moore himself, he was usually silent, except when
roused by an argument about philosophy, when he would forget
everything else in the intensity of his feeling. His hair would flop
down over his forehead, and he had a characteristic way of
recovering it by drawing his hand back over his head, while
expressing passionate disagreement. Where another man
would say 'I don't agree with you,' Moore would say. '*My God*,
you haven't understood *one word* I've been saying!!'

One of the remarkable things about Russell, quite apart from his own work, was the way that he brought others to the study of philosophy. When Moore first came to Cambridge he had no greater ambition than to go on learning the classics, and to teach them in turn as a schoolmaster. But one day Russell invited him to tea to meet McTaggart; and McTaggart produced his celebrated theory that Time is unreal. Moore thought this nonsense; and his skill in argument, on this and other occasions, made Russell persuade him to abandon the classics for philosophy. He soon showed such brilliance that there came a period later when Russell probably learnt more from Moore than Moore did from Russell.

For some years most people in Cambridge regarded Moore as a greater man than Russell; and Moore had much more influence on younger students. The profusion of Russell's wit could be mistaken for mere cleverness, leading him into picturesque over-statements which Moore would never indulge in. Moore was always marked by a luminous passion for literal truth; and, judging by his early articles and the impression he made on his early contemporaries, his books do not do full justice to his influence.

So far as Russell's academic work was concerned, he studied mathematics for his first three years at Cambridge. In those more carefree days, University teaching staffs still had their share of eccentrics, and Russell's coach in mathematics eventually became insane. There was a Fellow of St John's who sometimes attempted (according to Russell) to slay his guests with a red-hot poker, but was fortunately handicapped in pursuit by a bad leg. There were also such pleasant figures as the elderly don who kept a coffin in his room, and delighted in prodding the worms in the garden with his stick when they came out after rain, exclaiming 'You haven't got me yet!'

Russell was bracketed Seventh Wrangler in 1893. It was a good, but not outstanding, result: his friend Charles Sanger was bracketed Second Wrangler in the same year. Russell actually did rather better than his tutors expected. In later life he once remarked that he owed his subsequent achievements to 'pertinacity and obstinacy'; and he would say that when he and Sanger were working on mathematics together, Sanger was much quicker. But there is a more important reason why he only came seventh in his year. Owing to the need for placing students in the Tripos in a definite order, most Cambridge mathematics consisted in working out problems. Russell regarded many of these as futile exercises, which had nothing to do with the fundamental difficulties in the philosophy of mathematics which really interested him. He questioned the ideas of his tutors, and decided (rightly) that what he was taught about the Binomial Theorem and the Infinitesimal Calculus was full of fallacies.

His disgust was so great that, having got through his Tripos, he sold nearly all his mathematics books, and vowed he would never do mathematics again.

He then, in his remaining year at Cambridge, studied philosophy. The first result was to turn his thoughts round in the wrong direction; for he was persuaded by his tutors and McTaggart that the British empirical tradition he had accepted from J. S. Mill was wrong, and that there was superior wisdom in Kant, Hegel and Bradley.

At the time, the main excitement in the British philosophical world was the publication of Bradley's *Appearance and Reality* (1893); which, according to one hostile critic, should have been called 'The Disappearance of Reality'. For Bradley took everything commonly considered as making up the everyday world— Things and Qualities, Time and Space—and ruled them out in turn as involving relations, in which he claimed to have found an inherent contradiction. The realm of Appearance was fragmentary and contradictory; the only true Reality was a single timeless all-embracing whole, known as the 'Absolute'.

The Absolute was in some sense spiritual or soulful, quite different from the things of everyday life. In other words, Bradley was a kind of 'idealist', as opposed to a 'realist'—a philosophical realist may be defined roughly as a man who believes that real things are really there, in a more or less common-sense way, irrespective of whether any mind is aware of them. Following the 'subject-predicate' logic, Bradley wrote that all judgment 'predicates its idea' of the Absolute.

Russell, after considerable persuasion, became a follower of Hegel and Bradley; and it seems obvious that he owed less to his academic tuition at Cambridge than to talks with his friends.

His mathematics tutors told him nothing of such developments as the work of Weierstrass, while his philosophy tutors diverted him from empiricism. In each case, it was only after graduation that his original work began: and, in each case, it was his dissatisfaction about the foundation of mathematics which led to his eventual rebellion against Cambridge orthodoxy. He returned to mathematics with a Fellowship Dissertation on *The Foundations of Geometry*, but this still reflected the philosophy he had learnt at Cambridge, and was dedicated to McTaggart.

Even when Russell and Moore came later to reject McTaggart's views, they still shared at least two things which he professed. Firstly, a hatred of what McTaggart called 'woolliness', and an insistence on getting the meaning of words clear; secondly, a conviction that the greatest intellectual crime was to try and steer a philosophical argument towards an emotionally desirable conclusion.

It is interesting to mention here one criticism of Russell made by his Cambridge philosophy tutors. They used to say that his essays and replies to examination papers were too short. He always kept this capacity for conciseness; though he subsequently left no cause for complaint about the smallness of his output.

Any great thinker, however original, is bound to be influenced by the intellectual atmosphere of his times; and something must be said about the pre-suppositions shared by Russell and his undergraduate friends. He arrived at Cambridge just before a transition began, in moods of thought, from the hopeful and creative nineteenth century to the cynical and critical twentieth century. Everywhere was bright optimism about the future of the world, which was quite independent of national or political divisions. It could draw its inspiration from Hegelian philosophy in Germany, or from Darwin's theory of evolution in Britain. The Conservative Imperialist, the Liberal Free Trader, and the Marxist revolutionary were all alike certain that they would get the kind of world they wanted.

Russell wrote afterwards of himself and his contemporaries: 'We all felt convinced that nineteenth century progress would continue, and that we ourselves should be able to contribute something of value.'

As for war, it was a barbarous anachronism belonging to the past, only fit for the kind of dullards whom Russell had known at the Crammers on their way to Sandhurst; there was no need for any sensible person to bother his head about it. There might be minor skirmishes against remote savages on the outskirts of Empire; but it was usually hard for any intelligent person to believe, right up to 1914, that there would ever really be fighting again between civilized nations in Europe.

This prevailing belief about the inevitability of progress was rudely shattered in practice by wars and dictatorships, and in theory by the rejection of Hegelianism or any other evolutionary philosophy. Russell was to point out more than once that, though the transition from amoeba to philosopher represented progress from the point of view of the philosopher, it was not known whether the amoeba felt the same. But the ingrained belief in progress still remained in Russell's subconscious, influencing his thinking in one respect. If human society was continually changing and improving, it followed that moral codes should be changed with it; there was a presumption that any ethical precepts based on past tradition were likely to be wrong, and that any new ideas about morals were more likely to be right than old ones. Russell made this point in one of his earliest undergraduate essays; it encouraged his later delight in annoying the conventional and challenging traditional morality. He wrote that 'In ethics, as in every department of human thought, there are two kinds of opinions, those based upon tradition on the one hand, and, on the other hand, those having something in their favour'.

As an undergraduate, Russell's rebellious rationalism was still tempered by traces of the Puritan asceticism in which he had been brought up. When he first discovered the intellectual delights of Cambridge, he was so happy that he almost felt there was something wrong about it, and he decided that it was his duty to make himself do one unpleasant thing every day. And Russell was at this time orthodox in his views on sex: he is reported to have reproved one girl for flirting with a man she did not love.

Feminine infiltration into Cambridge in those days was still slight, but occasionally a don would give a dinner party and invite some young ladies from Newnham or Girton. There is early testimony of the fascination which Russell had for women: a subsequent recollection, by a fellow undergraduate, of a girl sitting beside him at dinner gazing intensely with shining eyes, as he discoursed to her on some moral or philosophical problem.

After his lonely boyhood, Russell grew up with little knowledge of the other sex. To a man of his eager temperament it was therefore more or less inevitable that, when he fell in love, he did so completely. He fell in love with Alys Pearsall Smith, the beautiful daughter of Evangelical Quakers from Pennsylvania who had settled in England. Her brother was Logan Pearsall Smith, the writer. Her sister married Bernard Berenson, the distinguished art critic; and many years later Berenson was to give me his recollections of Russell's early visits to the Pearsall Smith's in the capacity of Alys's suitor. Russell, said Berenson, was 'frightened, timid, shy, slight, rather dark, and said very little'. Alys herself once described taking him to see some friends: 'I don't know what they thought of Bertie Russell. They were most kind to him, but he was too shy with them.'

It was regarded as rather a strange match for an English aristocrat. Some of Russell's friends were against it; and so was his grandmother, Lady John. She arranged for him to be made an honorary attaché at the British Embassy in Paris, hoping that this might divert his mind. But Russell found no pleasure in Parisian attractions, and all he could remember in later years was copying out long dispatches dealing with fishing rights under the Treaty of Utrecht—British diplomacy being anxious to prove that a lobster was not a fish, and the French Government retorting that it counted as a fish when the Treaty was signed.

At the first opportunity he returned home: and on December 13, 1894, he married Alys at the Friends' Meeting House in London. He was twenty-two; his bride was five years older. It was a Quaker ceremony in which, as in all Quaker services, there was a period of silence when anyone who felt moved to speak could do so. Charles Trevelyan, sitting at the back, ran a book in penny bets on the chances of who would get up and talk.

C

CHAPTER III

Berlin and Marxism

❀

BERTRAND RUSSELL did not simplify the task of any future student or biographer by dividing his career neatly into distinct phases concerned with different subjects. He always had the confusing habit of being interested in any number of different things at once: the diversity of his interests was almost as great as the complexity of his character. He himself once summed up his career by the characteristic remark that when he became too stupid for mathematics he took to philosophy, and that when he became too stupid for philosophy he turned to history. It is true that, between the ages of eleven and thirty-eight, his greatest interest was in the foundations of mathematics; and that he abandoned any further work in this field when he was about sixty-five. But his overriding interest in mathematics and philosophy did not stop him working on economics in Berlin the year after his marriage, and his first published book was political.

He often described an occasion in March 1895, walking through melting snow in the Tiergarten in Berlin, when he resolved to write a series of books—one beginning with the most abstract subjects like mathematics, and becoming more and more concrete; the other beginning with politics and economics, and becoming more and more abstract. They were to meet in a complete synthesis, combining theory and practice. He wrote the books; but, since he had ceased to be a Hegelian, no final synthesis emerged.

Russell's family background ensured his interest in politics, and there were few important figures in British public life, from Gladstone to Churchill, with whom he was not familiar. He described in *Unpopular Essays* his most vivid recollection of

Gladstone—when he was visiting Pembroke Lodge, and young Russell was left to entertain the awe-inspiring guest after the ladies had left the table. Russell was far too shy to say anything; and Gladstone's only remark, to be followed by an even more unconquerable silence, was 'This is very good port they have given me, but why have they given it me in a claret glass?' Russell's first contact with Winston Churchill came when Russell was a Cambridge undergraduate, and Churchill was a Harrow schoolboy. Russell was having his hair cut one day in London when the barber told him: 'Lord Randolph's son's in 'ere next door, sir. 'E's a young cub, 'e is.'

As a member of 'The Society', with their belief in learning everything and being shocked at nothing, Russell did not confine his political contacts to the two ruling parties, the Conservatives and his own Liberal Party. Quite early, through the Pearsall Smith's, he became on friendly terms with the Fabians —the pioneer professional-class propagandists of Socialism whose efforts, though they failed to exterminate the capitalists of Britain, almost exterminated the class from which the Fabians came. Russell and his wife made two visits to Germany in 1895, and the second was largely with the object of studying the German Socialist* movement. This was a rather unconventional, if not shocking, interest for a young English aristocrat. Alys mentioned at the British Embassy that they had been to a Socialist meeting, and though the Ambassador passed it off diplomatically by saying 'We're all Socialists now', they were never asked to the Embassy again.

Russell was always a superb journalist. Unfortunately, in many countries nowadays, journalism is a profession which has been brought into disrepute by the newspapers. So I must make it plain that, here and afterwards, I do not describe some of Russell's work as 'journalistic' in any derogatory sense. The ideals of true journalism are identical with those inspiring the highest scholarship, and Russell's philosophy in particular—a determination to reject second-hand hearsay, question everything, and seek certain knowledge. Russell not only had gifts of acute observation and vivid description; he had the journalistic

* The words 'Socialist' and 'Social Democrat' were then used to include Marxists who would now be called 'Communists'.

instinct of sensing what developments are likely to prove important in future. Perhaps the most extraordinary example is that, as early as 1895, he should have gone to Berlin and investigated the two forces destined to shape the world's history for the next fifty years and more: German militarism and Marxist Communism.

He learnt about the Prussian state even in the process of attending Socialist meetings; he noticed the policemen who were always there, ready to bring proceedings to a close. He had first-hand experience of the arrogance of Prussian officers from their behaviour at his hotel. If they wanted anything they had to have it, even to the extent of hammering on and pushing in the locked door of a lavatory if they found it occupied.

Russell and Alys were earnest and persevering in their study of German Socialism, though they sometimes flagged. The story is told in three entries in their Diary. First: 'Went to a meeting of the Bookbinders' Trade Union, about 100 people present. Deadly dull, and exactly like every other meeting of the sort. Every word of the speeches was impregnated with Marx.' A few days later: 'A small dull meeting in a horrid stuffy beer hall. The speaker was as usual prosy and Marxian.' There is a final record of another meeting: 'Very dull, and we only stayed a short time.'

Russell's studies were thorough enough, however, for him to perform the rare feat of reading through all three volumes of *Das Capital*.

After returning to England he reported his conclusions in a lecture to the Fabian Society, and in a series of lectures to the newly-founded London School of Economics, the latter being published in 1896 as *German Social Democracy*, the first on the long list of Russell's books.

These different lectures still have a fascinating interest to-day. It is not only that they foreshadow, with uncanny foresight, Germany's future of dictatorship and war. They are a characteristic example of the attempt to discuss any political problem in a scientific, rational and dispassionate way.

Although Russell was a Liberal, his innate radicalism and fellow feeling for any rebel made him sympathize with the Socialists in their protest against poverty and suffering. He wrote in *German Social Democracy* that the *Communist Manifesto* was 'Almost unsurpassed in literary merit. . . . For terse eloquence, for biting wit, and for historical insight, it is, to my mind, one of the best pieces of political literature ever produced. . . . In this magnificent work we have already some of the epic force of the materialistic theory of history; its cruel, unsentimental fatality, its disdain of morals and religion, its reduction of all social relations to the blind action of impersonal productive forces.'

It is obvious that, for all his sympathy and understanding, Russell from the beginning had no illusions about Communism. In 1896, though he did not fully anticipate where Communist fanaticism would lead in practice—as I have already pointed out, no one in that optimistic age ever dreamed of the horrors which lay ahead in the twentieth century—nevertheless he was already making some sharp and penetrating criticisms of Marxism.

He pointed out fallacies in 'the dry and tedious details' of Marx's economics. The theory of surplus value, besides being false, was at variance with the theory of 'the concentration of capital', which Russell considered the most original and essential part of Marx's work. This latter theory, about the tendency of industries towards monopoly, was expressed by Marx in the words 'one capitalist kills many'. But Russell argued that the common-sense conclusion was that the state should take over different industries at different times as they reached the monopoly stage; and not simultaneously by a single decisive blow in the class war, instituting a 'dictatorship of the proletariat'.

The Marxist doctrine of the class war would only be true 'If all men were immortal, perfectly farsighted, and actuated exclusively by the economic motive'. Marx's picture of society splitting more and more into two hostile classes, bourgeoisie and proletariat, ignored the growth of a new middle class in between, created by the increasing importance of technicians in production.

In his Fabian lecture on Germany, Russell began by saying that he was not concerned with the merits or demerits of Socialism, but with the question of the best *tactics* to obtain it—whether German Socialists were right in preaching the class war, and refusing to have any truck with other progressives. He said he proposed to discuss this as 'a purely Machiavellian question'. He did not mean 'Machiavellian' in the common sense of the word: in fact he once pointed out that Machiavelli was a much misunderstood man, that his precepts were not categorical but hypothetical, and that he only shocked people by being honest in discussing political dishonesty. Nevertheless, some of the things which Russell said at this time have a curious ring today. Perhaps he may not have been entirely immune from the youthful practice of a pretended delight in dispassionate 'realism'; or perhaps it was simply that he had already acquired the habit of putting anything he wanted to say in the most provocative form possible. (Gilbert Murray once remarked to me that, if Russell was talking to a Bishop, he would invariably say straight out 'I am an atheist'; whereas he could easily have said 'I am not an adherent of any religious creed'.)

German Socialists had decided on their policy, said Russell, 'not from the exigencies of tactics, not from empirical observation of political human nature, but from Marx's *a priori* doctrine of class warfare'. Already Russell was showing his characteristic bent towards the empirical and dislike of the *a priori*, even though he was not at this time an empiricist in philosophy. He next asked whether, although the theory was wrong, class-war tactics were justified by practical results.

On the contrary, he decided, the tactics alone were making the class war doctrine come true, in the sense of uniting the German capitalists against the Socialists. 'Marx . . . has shown the bourgeoisie, from the first, the quarter from which its existence is really threatened. . . . Thus, even if the doctrine be true, it would seem unwise to proclaim it.' The Socialists had 'failed to perceive the importance of minimizing their opponents' alarm'.

Not only had the German capitalists been put on their guard. Liberals, as a result of the uncompromising hostility of the Socialists, had become less and less progressive, seeing that they could not hope to get Socialist votes by adopting more advanced views. As for the Socialists themselves, their extreme doctrinaire position had deprived them of 'all sense of what was practicable from moment to moment'. Moderates were driven

from the party, so that it came more and more into conflict, 'by
its opposition to religion, the family, and the Fatherland', with
the common sense of ordinary Germans.

If, instead, the Socialists had supported other progressives,
and secured universal suffrage as a condition of their support,
further reforms would have followed.

But Russell, continuing his rationalistic line of approach, then
set out with perfect fairness an argument on the other side. A
sweeping revolutionary programme could inspire far greater
enthusiasm, energy and self denial than small piecemeal reforms. Russell was so rationalistic that he could even make an
impartial admission of the uses of irrationalism: 'What
Marxian Socialism has done for the German workman, and
what a temporizing Socialism emphatically cannot do for the
English workman, is to produce this intense religious fervour . . .
With [it] has come, of course, the intolerance and sectarian
bigotry of all new religions, but also a compactness and fighting
strength such as religion and patriotism alone can give.
Whether the gain in strength is worth the loss in tolerance, . . .
whether unanimity is not too dearly bought at the price of uncritical dogmatism, it seems almost impossible to decide.'

Russell had no difficulty in deciding this point in the later days
of World Wars, Bolshevism and Fascism. But even in 1896, his
instinct and the burden of the argument was all for the more
moderate approach.

And he suggested a possible compromise. The German
Socialists should not make a formal renunciation of Marxism,
because of the fervour which it gave. Perhaps the best thing
to be hoped for was that 'they will lose something in logical
acumen, and adopt, in their political activity, maxims really
inconsistent with their fundamental principles, but necessitated
by practical exigencies, and reconciled by some more or less
fallacious line of reasoning.' Russell's spoken words can often
be misinterpreted in cold print, without the light in his eye
which made an ironic inflection obvious; but one cannot imagine
the later Russell ever suggesting, even as a joke, that fallacious
reasoning was ever to be tolerated.

What was the alternative to a more co-operative policy by
the German Socialists? Moderates among the progressives

would continue to throw in their lot with the Conservatives. 'The advanced Liberal, such as we know him at home, is almost non-existent in Germany: the force which produces him has been transferred to the Socialists, and instead of being urged forward, he has been pushed back by terror of the Red Spectre.' Meanwhile, 'all manner of oppression, tyranny and misgovernment are submi∴ed to because the bourgeoisie dreads socialism more than it dreads military dictatorship'—a striking forecast, some thirty years ahead, of the circumstances of Hitler's rise to power in Germany.

Russell not only called for tolerance and moderation on the part of the German Socialists. He appealed to the German rulers to cease political persecution and to allow complete democracy and freedom of speech, writing prophetically: 'If they do not, war and extinction of the national life are the almost inevitable doom of the German Empire.'

Russell's lecture to the Fabian Society was not well received by his audience. It was his first big public speech, and he was very nervous. ('I dreaded it, and wished I could break my leg before it.') He did not make much of a success of handling questions and criticisms, and Graham Wallas took him aside afterwards and gave him some hints on this. Above all, he was a Liberal aristocrat who was presuming to give advice on a controversial question for Socialists—whether they should work on their own through the Independent Labour Party, or by pressing for reforms in co-operation with the Liberal Party. The trend of Russell's argument was for the second course.

It must be said that his political foresight proved to be as great in connection with Britain as with Germany. The British Labour Party only succeeded in establishing itself, and eventually supplanting the Liberal Party, because it followed the kind of policy which Russell had urged on the German Socialists. For many years it had electoral understandings with the Liberals. By way of contrast, one of the most disastrous periods in British politics—the twenty years of Conservative supremacy between the two World Wars—can be largely attributed to the way in which the Labour Party had then become narrow and sectarian, with a class-war mentality. I believe that, had Labour leaders been willing to work with the Liberals during this period, the misery and waste of mass unemployment could have been ended earlier, and the Second World War might have been averted. Much suffering might have been spared the world in the twentieth century, if both German and British Socialists had paid more attention to what Russell said in the 1890's.

Since I draw attention later to cases where I think Russell's political judgment was wrong, it is fair to point out this early instance of his being right.

CHAPTER IV

The Work of Genius

IN 1896 the Russells went to America for some months. He visited Walt Whitman's house and gave lectures at the John Hopkins University and Bryn Mawr, based on his Dissertation on *The Foundations of Geometry*. After his travels in Germany and America he settled down in England, living mostly in a small cottage in Sussex, and continued the laborious and austere work on mathematical philosophy which was the foundation of his fame.

As mentioned earlier, he and his wife had close friends among the Fabians, especially Sidney and Beatrice Webb. Beatrice, with her intense love of order and method, recorded some characteristic comments on both Russell and Alys, writing in her diary on September 25, 1895:

'The Bertrand Russells spent some days with us. Russell is a *very young* man with considerable intellectual promise—subtle and contentious, but anarchic in his dislike of working in traces. He has married a pretty bright American Quakeress some years older than himself with anarchic views of life, also hating routine.'

The following year, after visiting their cottage in Sussex, Beatrice Webb wrote: 'The Bertrand Russells live idyllic lives—devotedly attached to each other—living with somewhat disorderly and extravagant simplicity—the simplest result extravagantly achieved—as might be expected with an anarchic American with means of her own. * Russell working some six or seven hours at his metaphysical book—Alys rushing up to town

* Russell said afterwards that he was puzzled by the reference to extravagance: 'Our income was small, and we lived within it.'

at short intervals to girls' clubs and temperance meetings'.

Occasionally Russell's wit would find itself provoked by the Quaker family into which he had married. His mother-in-law, for instance, had rather a fondness for quoting Biblical texts.

'Cast your bread upon the waters . . .' she once began.

'Nice mess it will be when you get it back again', said Russell.

In July 1901, Beatrice Webb recorded the fullest description of him available during these early years:

'In manner and dress and outward bearing, he is most carefully trimmed, conventionally correct and punctiliously polite: in speech, he has an almost affectedly clear enunciation of words and preciseness of expression. In morals, he is a puritan; in personal habits almost an ascetic, except that he lives for efficiency and, therefore, expects to be kept in the best physical condition. But, intellectually, he is audacious—an inconoclast, detesting religious or social convention, suspecting sentiment. . . . He indulges in the wildest paradox and in the broadest jokes, the latter always too abstrusely intellectual in their form to be vulgarly coarse. He is a delightful talker, especially in general conversation, when the intervention of other minds prevents him tearing his subjects to pieces with fine chopping logic. . . . He looks at the world from a pinnacle of detachment—dissects persons and demolishes causes. . . .

'The outlines of both his intellect and his feeling are sharp, hard and permanent. He is a good hater. . . . I have no sense of sin, and no desire to see it punished. Bertrand, on the other hand, is almost cruel in his desire to see cruelty revenged.'

At this time Russell was a strict teetotaller, and he once rebuked G. E. Moore for not showing the same restraint, to Moore's understandable annoyance. Russell had always trained consciously for intellectual achievements, with his days planned as carefully as any athlete in training. One account of his routine was given by Beatrice Webb after a visit. According to her, Russell and Alys breakfasted together in their study at 9. Then Russell worked on mathematics till 12.30. Next they read aloud to each other for three quarters of an hour, spent a quarter of an hour walking in the garden, and lunched at 1.30. After lunch Russell played croquet with Logan Pearsall Smith. Then would follow tea at 4.30, more mathematics till 6, reading aloud with Alys till 7.30, dinner at 8, general conversation with the Webbs till 9.30, and another hour's reading aloud, probably a history book or a novel, until Lights Out at 10.30.

When this account appeared in print, Russell's comment was that 'Mrs Webb always had a passion for tabulating things and collecting statistics.' His recollection was that there was more mathematics and less reading aloud—that he used to work at mathematics from 9 to 1 and from 5 to 8. But it is true that he kept to such a regular timetable that, however absorbed he was in his work, he would always break off for a meal: 'I enormously admire the people who can miss their meals, but it has never happened to me.' He would stop even if he was in the middle of a sentence, and then sit down again later to finish the sentence without a moment's thought, because the end of it was still in his head.

One point is worth mentioning: the kind of life led by Russell obviously depended on a small but sufficient independent income. In fact almost all the great philosophical advances of this epoch came from men who did not have to work for a living: this applied to Moore and Wittgenstein as well.

How philosophical advances are to continue in Britain, under changed economic circumstances, is a question which nobody can answer. It is certainly no answer to point to scholarships and research grants from wealthy foundations: for it is often the mark of new work in philosophy, and much creative work in science, that established orthodoxy regards it at first as rather foolish. It is hard, for example, to imagine Russell going to a local educational authority, explaining that 'I feel uneasy about the foundations of mathematics', and getting enough money to live on for fifteen years while he investigated them.

Russell's main approach to philosophy remained through mathematics. For instance, Kant and Hegel had made great play with difficulties about infinitesimals and infinity, from which they deduced the unreality of the world of common sense. But Russell, through his travels in Germany, learnt of Weierstrass, who showed that the calculus does not depend on infinitesimals; and of Cantor, whose theory of infinity seemed undoubtedly odd but not self-contradictory. When Russell first came on Cantor's work he did not understand it; but, with characteristic pertinacity, he laboriously copied it into a notebook almost word for word, and came to agree that Cantor was right.

Next there was a fortunate accident. McTaggart, who was going to lecture on Leibniz at Cambridge in 1899, wanted to visit his family in New Zealand: and Russell acted as deputy, his lectures being published as *The Philosophy of Leibniz*. By sheer intellectual analysis in his study, he offered a completely original interpretation of Leibniz's philosophy; and soon afterwards had the happy experience of having his views confirmed by the discovery of some of Leibniz's manuscripts which had never been published.

Even more important, however, was the fact that Russell's study of Leibniz helped him to a critical examination and rejection of the subject-predicate logic, and of Bradley's philosophy. Bradley, it may be remembered, had denied the ultimate reality of relations, using this as another idealist argument for saying that the common sense world with many different things in it was unreal, and that the only true Reality was an all-embracing whole. Russell found that Bradley's views made any philosophy of mathematics impossible. He revolted against Hegel and Bradley, and returned to realism; stimulated and encouraged by G. E. Moore, who led the way.

Russell put it afterwards: 'He found the Hegelian philosophy inapplicable to chairs and tables, and I found it inapplicable to mathematics; so with his help I climbed out of it, and back to common sense tempered by mathematical logic. . . .

'With a sense of escaping from prison, we allowed ourselves to think that grass is green, that the sun and stars' would exist if no one was aware of them. . . .'

Now although Cantor and Weierstrass, together with non-Euclidean geometry, had shown that Kant and Hegel had wrong theories about mathematical knowledge, Russell still had to find the right one. In the latter part of 1900 he decided that mathematics is a more highly developed form of logic. It was the answer which had already been given, although he did not know it at first, by Frege in Germany.

Earlier in 1900, visiting a philosophical congress in Paris, Russell had got to know the work of Peano and his Italian followers in Symbolic Logic, and studied and mastered Peano's symbolism. He extended it to the Logic of Relations, in an article reprinted many years later in *Logic and Knowledge;* and he planned his *Principles of Mathematics*, to establish his thesis that mathematics and logic are fundamentally the same. The book was to be in two volumes, the second consisting of a rigid argument worked out in symbols, the first a kind of commentary and introduction in ordinary language.

The first volume was published in 1903. By this time Russell and Whitehead, who had published the first volume of his *Universal Algebra* in 1898, had decided to collaborate in their future work. The result turned out to be, not simply a second volume of the *Principles of Mathematics*, but the three massive volumes of *Principia Mathematica*, the first of which was not published until 1910.

The collaboration was arranged in this way: Russell had mapped out the general scheme of the work in a course of lectures at Cambridge. Different parts were then divided between himself and Whitehead. Each produced a first draft, sent it to the other, and then revised it in the light of the other's comments, so that every part was worked over three times. Russell also spent some months of each year in Cambridge, where he could talk over points with Whitehead personally.

The actual writing out for the press was done by Russell. Each proposition had to be on a separate sheet of paper, to allow for the insertion of new ones; so the manuscript, kept in a long row of box files, became a marvel in sheer bulk.

Why did *Principia Mathematica* take so long? Russell explained afterwards that 'I got stuck for two years. When I got unstuck it took five years to write it down.' The agony of the two years in which he 'got stuck' (1903 and 1904) resulted from the fact that, after reducing mathematics to logic, he had found unresolved contradictions in logic itself.* He wrote about them

---

* The simplest of these contradictions is an ancient one, associated in classical times with Epimenides the Cretan, but only regarded then as an amusing puzzle. Suppose a man says 'I am lying'. Is he lying when he says this? If he is lying, he is speaking the truth; if he is speaking the truth, then he is lying. The contradiction Russell discovered, and which was the starting-point of his difficulties, was more complicated than this (being concerned with the class of all those classes which are not members of themselves); and he soon found many other contradictions as well.

to Frege, who replied '*die Arithmetik ist ins Schwanken geraten*'— as a very loose translation, 'Arithmetic is trembling on its foundations'. The solution which Russell finally reached in *Principia Mathematica* was a doctrine of Logical Types which is too technical, and also still too controversial, for discussion here.

Principia Mathematica is a book which very few people have read: in fact Schrödinger once told me that he did not believe Russell and Whitehead had read it themselves. Like most classics, it is now taken for granted rather than studied, even by those who should be professionally concerned with it; once, in later years in America, Hans Reichenbach told Russell that he had just thought of a new theory of mathematical induction, and was somewhat dashed when Russell gave him the reference to where it could be found set out in *Principia Mathematica*. There is little doubt about it being one of the supreme achievements of the human mind, into which Russell poured his most intense intellectual energy over a period of many years; but probably not more than twenty people have ever read it right through.

After it was finished Russell told G. H. Hardy, the Cambridge mathematician, that he had had a curious nightmare. He was in the Cambridge University Library about two hundred years later, watching an assistant going round with a bucket, in which he was putting books which he decided should be destroyed as not worth keeping. The assistant picked up the only copy still in existence of *Principia Mathematica*, and stood hesitating. . . . At this stage Russell woke up.

In the two following chapters I am going to embark on the heroic task—perhaps I should say the foolhardy task—of trying to explain in simple language some of the significance of Russell's work during these years. I want to end this chapter by saying a little more about how he did it.

No one has ever offered a worthwhile explanation of the occurrence of human genius. The only certain point is that heredity seems to count a great deal, and Russell is an obvious case in point. Beyond that all is guesswork, like Russell's own fanciful conjecture that exceptional intelligence might be due to some strange ingredient eaten with an infant's food, as a result of not being too scrupulous about cleaning pots and pans. White-head, who was the only outstanding child in his own family, used to joke that this was because his mother, before he was born, was involved in an accident with a coach which rolled over and over. But, while not embarking on such speculations, there is a certain interest in recording what might be called the tech-nicalities of genius; in collecting any available information about how a particular philosopher's mind worked.

In Russell's case there is one point of considerable interest. He worked through the ear rather then the eye: with auditory images rather than visual ones. He liked people to read aloud to him; he once remarked that, in order to follow something he was given to read, he had to read it aloud in his mind to himself; his memory would work through remembering the sound of spoken words rather than the look of printed words on a page. He made it a criticism of Bergson that he was 'a visualizer' (which Bergson denied); and he said that a man who could only think in terms of visual images would have difficulty in thinking about abstract things. For instance, you cannot form a visual image of the concepts used in logic, or of the fourth dimension.

Being myself an incorrigible visualizer, I was delighted to find so eminent a mathematician as Professor Littlewood deny-ing that there is any harm in visualizing; and I would be inclined to retort to Russell that the eye can at least allow us to perceive three dimensions, while a series of sounds is one-dimensional. Perhaps Russell, having a sensitive ear and a finely modulated speaking voice, could find in sounds some extra 'dimensions' of pitch or tone or volume. And perhaps the reason why he had no instinct for setting out something in visual form was simply because he was bad at it: he once re-marked that 'Whenever I try to draw a cow, it looks like a horse'. He had an intensely sensitive appreciation of poetry and music, but not so much of art. Perhaps what is involved is some-thing common to both auditory and visual images, something which will be reached through the ear or the eye according to individual proficiency. But this is vague speculation; the fact which is definite, to be noted for the benefit of future students of the psychology of the exceptional, is that Russell usually worked through the ear.

This was even reflected in his views on education and literary criticism. He said that it was more important to teach correct pronunciation than correct spelling, and that one secret of literary style was to aim at writing something which could be read aloud without difficulty in breathing. According to his own account, he at first wrote badly, but taught himself style by this method. (I have found little evidence myself of Russell writing badly, except for periods in after life when he was obviously tired and overworked; and I was interested to get T. S. Eliot's opinion that Russell's style was at his best in such austere work as the *Philosophy of Leibniz*.) In later years Russell said that the trouble with modern poetry was that it was written to appeal to the eye instead of the ear.

I do not, of course, want to exaggerate the point. Russell had exceptionally good eyesight (he was long-sighted); and he could do an extraordinary amount of reading without eye-strain or headache. He would not claim to be able to understand a complicated mathematical formula without seeing it; and *Principia Mathematica* is hardly a book which it is easy to read aloud. (Though Russell invented his own pet names for many symbols; in lecturing, for instance, he would refer to E! as 'E Shriek'.) But although his thought was not independent of visual *sensation*, he was independent of visual *imagination*. He had a vivid and detailed visual imagination in dreams, or when feverish in illness; but, he said, 'thought obscures it or gets in the way'.

There is another point about Russell's way of working which is of some interest. Dr Waismann once remarked that clear thinking can be the enemy of intellectual progress, because advances only come from some vague feeling of dissatisfaction. This, I believe, is certainly true of Einstein's discovery of the Theory of Relativity; he began with a kind of mystical or poetical insight into the truth, and the mathematics followed later. It might be thought that things would be different with so precise a thinker as Russell; but this is not so, certainly in his earlier work. Writing to Bradley in 1914, he said:

'I don't know how other people philosophize, but what happens with me is, first, a logical instinct that the truth must lie

D

in a certain region, and then an attempt to find its exact where-
abouts in that region. I trust the instinct absolutely, though it is
blind and dumb; but I know no words vague enough to express
it. If I do not hit the exact point in the region, contradictions
and difficulties still beset me, but though I know I must be more
or less wrong, I don't think I am in the wrong region.

'The only thing I should ever, in my inmost thoughts, claim
for any view of mine, would be that it is in a direction along
which one can reach truth—never that it is truth.'

He also wrote that reason is a harmonizing force rather than
a creative one: 'Even in the most purely logical realms, it is
insight that first arrives at what is new.'

A further example of Russell's technique was his conscious
use of the unconscious mind. He came to learn by experience
that, if he had to write on something difficult, he should think
about it as hard as possible for a few hours or days, and then
'give orders, so to speak, that the work is to proceed underground'. Months later he would return consciously to the
subject, and find that the work had been done. 'Before I had
discovered this technique, I used to spend the intervening
months worrying because I was making no progress; . . .
whereas now I can devote them to other pursuits.'

But however vague or subconscious his reasoning processes,
the final product of his thinking was always precise, and
apparently arrived in his mind completely formed. I had never
believed Ben Jonson's remark about Shakespeare, that 'he
never blotted a line', until I saw some of Russell's manuscripts.
I thought all good writing was the result of painful trial and
error and correcting and cutting, but Russell first convinced me
that an exception is possible; for his manuscripts and letters run
on page after page with an uncanny and almost inhuman neat-
ness, hardly a word being crossed out or altered. He explained
that, once his thinking was over and he sat down to write, it was
just as though he were copying out something already written.
He said he always wrote everything in his head first, because it
was easier to cross something out in his head than on paper. In
speaking, he never began a sentence without having the end of it
clear in his mind. Even in his dreams, any dialogue was

syntactically perfect.

When he was a very young man, Logan Pearsall Smith told him that after he had written anything he should always work over it again and rewrite it. Russell went home and rewrote something he had just written, and then decided that the original was far better. 'I have never,' he said, 'rewritten anything since.' And he gave this advice to authors: 'Never alter anything you write—especially if someone else asks you to.'

CHAPTER V

Mathematics and Philosophy

❦

IT is comparatively easy, given a few years and a capacity for reading about twenty million words without blinking, to write a full-length study of Russell's philosophy. In fact, I am doing so now. But it is fantastically difficult, in the course of two chapters for the general reader, to discuss his logical and philosophical discoveries during the early part of this century.

His greatest work was too technical for anyone to grasp thoroughly without specialized training; but to ignore it completely would give a grotesquely false picture of Russell's stature. I am therefore going to plunge ahead, on ground where any sensible person would fear to tread, and attempt to sketch a brief outline of its importance. I must warn the reader that I may do it extremely badly, and that a hundred years hence—or even today—most people may see Russell in some quite different perspective. But, in making my attempt, I am at least fortified by the fact that I could hardly do worse than Russell himself.

Having lived from childhood in the realms of mathematics and abstract thought, he had extraordinary difficulties in understanding why the ordinary man does not understand them; and few students today are brought up, like Russell, on Bradley's philosophy and the old logic. Russell could explain anything else to the man in the street with impeccable lucidity, while remaining incapable of explaining the importance of his own philosophy. When he made one such attempt, in the final chapter of his *History of Western Philosophy*, a critic commented that he had performed the remarkable achievement of being even more unfair to his own work than he was to Kant's.

There is one preliminary point. I am going to write throughout of 'Russell's philosophy', even though many of his views were shared with others, and some may have been derived from them. I have tried, in my longer and more technical study, to disentangle the derivations; it is an extraordinarily difficult task, because Russell was slow to claim credit for himself, while always meticulous and often over-generous in acknowledging what he owed to other people. I have mentioned his early conversion from Bradley under the stimulus of G. E. Moore; and there were some points in Bradley which he still accepted. The new Symbolic Logic had begun in the nineteenth century with Boole. A man almost forgotten today, Hugh MacColl, insisted on the vital point that the fundamental idea in logic was not inclusion among classes, but implication between propositions. Russell's interpretation of mathematics was anticipated by Frege; and Peano had shown how a system of logical symbolism could be invented less cumbrous than Frege's, providing the foundations on which Russell's work began. Finally, *Principia Mathematica* was itself written with Whitehead's close collaboration, and when someone once referred to it without mentioning Whitehead, Russell immediately protested that there was scarcely a page in it which did not incorporate the work of both of them.

And yet it is not only for the sake of brevity that I feel it is reasonable to refer to the new ideas simply as Russell's. Many of his most important points were reached quite independently of other people—for instance, he had never read Frege until he had reached much the same conclusions himself. There is something of an analogy here with the Darwinian theory of evolution. As everyone knows, this was formulated independently by Darwin and Wallace, and Wallace first prepared a paper for publication. But it is rightly referred to as Darwin's theory, because it was he who marshalled all the evidence to work out a fully-wrought conclusion which no one could ignore. Russell had the same sort of pre-eminence in logic. Few today would remember MacColl, but for a technical argument he had with Russell; and few would ever have heard of Frege, had not Russell drawn attention to his work. As for Whitehead, it seems that he was Russell's superior as an ordinary mathematician, and he was more adept at the art of inventing logical symbols. It is to Whitehead that we owe most of the system of flags and arrows and curious signs which cover the pages of *Principia Mathematica*. But, since Whitehead was only free from full-time University teaching during vacations, the bulk of the work inevitably fell on Russell: and I think it is fair to say that, but for Russell, *Principia Mathematica* would never have been completed. In fact a projected fourth volume on Geometry, which Whitehead was preparing on his own, was never brought to the stage of publication.

While inviting the reader, therefore, to keep in mind the work of others, especially Frege, I will simply talk about Russell. And I will begin by asking a simple question: what was the importance of Russell's reduction of mathematics to logic? What was the real significance of *Principia Mathematica*, that strange work which takes up 347 pages before reaching the definition of the number 1, and gets well into Volume II before reaching the proof that $m \times n = n \times m$?

Its main *philosophical** importance lies, I think, not in making the foundations of mathematics seem very difficult and complicated, but in making them simple and obvious. It took the mystery out of mathematical knowledge. The idea that there is something rather wonderful about mathematics is one of the most deep-rooted in human thought; even today there is a survival of superstitious feeling that certain numbers, like 3 and 7 and 13, have some special significance for good or evil. Numbers have always raised curious problems. Take such a simple thing as subtracting 7 from 3: it might be said that minus 4 does not exist, and so was nothing, and yet it is different from 0. And it was felt that there was something even more marvellous about an 'imaginary number', the square root of minus one. There is nothing which, multiplied by itself, gives minus one; and yet the square root of minus one plays an essential part in the kind of equations which any electrical engineer

---

* *Principia Mathematica* has also of course a very great importance for mathematicians—in fact Russell once said that nine-tenths of its interest was mathematical. To give some instances at random, we may mention the way that its symbolism is now written into Analysis, the clarification of the notion of a limit, the discussion of mathematical induction, the distinction between infinite and reflexive classes, and the examples of the immense care needed to establish an *inequality* between particular infinite numbers. As will be mentioned later, the Relation Arithmetic of Part IV, with the idea of structure, had enormous importance in turn for philosophy and science.

would use in planning a power station. The connection of mathematics with mysticism stretches right from Pythagoras to James Jeans, with his description of God as the supreme mathematician. All this was swept away by Russell's theories.

Empirical philosophers, who found the source of all knowledge in experience, had never been able to explain mathematics. Here was knowledge which seemed independent of experience, but which yet applied to the real world. It was never really plausible to argue, like J. S. Mill, that we know $2+2=4$ because of experiencing many instances where two things added to two things made four things. Philosophers like Kant could thus indulge in all sorts of high-flown philosophies to account for mathematical knowledge. Russell now produced the alternative theory that $2+2=4$ was akin to such simple logical principles as that a proposition cannot be both true and false. At one time he even came to believe—reluctantly, in view of his early delight and reverence for mathematics—that both mathematics and logic were merely conventions about the use of symbols and words. 'Two and two are four' was like saying that 'there are three feet to a yard'.

The removal of the idea that mathematics involves some strange intuition made it much easier to adopt a thorough-going empiricism: though Russell, unlike many of his successors, did not go the whole way in that direction.

This result, a step towards a positive conclusion because of a negative process of elimination, was very typical of Russell as a philosopher. One of the difficulties about understanding his importance is that so much of his work appears merely negative: in fact he stressed the negative side of it himself. When he used advances in mathematics to demolish much in Kant and Hegel, when he overthrew Bradley, it appears at first sight that he had merely earned the gratitude of future students by saving them from the study of nonsense. But, in fact, something much more positive and constructive was involved in each case.

We can take an analogy. Throughout history, a number of people tried to make perpetual motion machines, and they all failed; so one might imagine at the end that the story was nothing but failure. But when men grasped *why* they had failed, they had taken an essential step towards understanding the principles of mechanics. Much the same thing applies to the failure of every attempt to build a complete philosophical system. Understanding why they failed can mean taking a radically different view of the nature of reality.

Russell's controversies with Bradley and the Hegelians centred on difficult technical questions. But I think the most important point at issue, put in untechnical and loose language, was somewhat as follows:

If you wish to study a human eye, you can set about it in two different ways. The first would be advocated by philosophers who think like Bradley and Hegel. They would say, to begin with, that the eye was part of a human body, and that you cannot understand it unless you consider it as part of the body. Any good oculist, in fact, would say the same; and in examining a patient with weak eyesight would ask questions about his general health. Now the health of the body containing the eye will depend in turn on what food it has eaten; this will depend upon current agricultural technique and the transport facilities available for moving food from one place to another; these depend on the state of historical development of the world at the time in question; this in turn depends upon the whole history of the world, and when the solar system came into existence. Or you could say, to follow another line of argument, that an eye which has seen the stars at night is obviously different from an eye which has never focused on objects any further away than those on the earth: and that therefore the eye would be a different sort of eye if the stars were not there. In this kind of way, starting from a human eye or any other object, you can argue that it would not be the same if anything else was different, and that a method of analysis which considers anything in isolation must be misleading. You may say that the Universe, if you have the right view of it, is not a number of separate things but a complete unity, and you will probably call yourself a Monist. (A word derived from the Greek *Mónos*, 'Single'.)

But there is another way of studying a human eye, and that is Russell's way. You can consider it in isolation, and say that the only other things you need to know about it are the light rays entering it, the nerve messages which it transmits to the brain as a result of what it sees, and the motor impulses it receives back from the brain directing it where to look. You can say that anything else in the whole Universe, if it affects the eye, must affect it through these three things; and that if you know these three things you know everything you need. If you adopt this approach you will say you believe in the philosophy of analysis, you will deny that 'analysis means falsification', and you will eschew the attempt to build a grand all-embracing philosophical system. You will concentrate on isolating separate problems which can be solved piecemeal.

There is a sense in which both points of view are equally plausible, though both can be hard to defend if pushed to extremes. Consider, for instance, a man in England named Mr Jones, who has one nephew who lives in Australia. According to the first view, if the nephew dies, Mr Jones becomes a different man even before he hears of it, because he no longer has the attribute of being an uncle. This seems hard to believe, and common sense would say it makes no difference to Mr Jones until he is told: but if it is replied that Mr Jones becomes a different man in the eyes of God, I do not think a logical refutation is possible. The extreme analytical view also seems difficult to accept, though it again cannot be logically refuted. To put it very crudely—I will try to put it a little less crudely later—if you chop the Universe up into little bits you may find it extremely difficult to put it together again, and to explain why it works as it does.

I am inclined to think that the decision between the two approaches is usually a matter of the individual philosopher's temperament. You can have a mind which delights in contemplating the whole of reality as a mystic unity; or you can have a mind, like Russell's, which delights in dissecting things. (One hostile critic once said that he had a 'mincing' mind.) Granted that the choice is one of temperament, I think it is easy to see why Russell chose the method of analysis. If you believe, like the monists, that the only reality worth talking about is the whole Universe, then it is obvious that you can really say very little, even though most monists contrive to say a lot. You are reduced to uttering such grand sentiments as 'Reality is organic' or 'God is love', and your thinking may soon get in a grand muddle. In fact it is part of the monistic position that you can never say or think anything which is completely true, because you don't know everything (in the ordinary sense of 'know').

If, on the other hand, you dislike misty generalizations and vague appeals to the emotions, and have a craving for certain knowledge, then you will prefer the other approach. It was this craving which gave Russell a bias towards analysis, just as it gave him a bias towards empiricism. And his exposure of mistakes in the logical arguments used for monism gave him and his successors a powerful impetus along this direction.

Another point, even more important, was involved in Russell's work of destruction. He showed that his predecessors had over-estimated the capacity of logic to give us knowledge about the nature of the Universe.

When people ask why Russell has been described as the greatest logician since Aristotle, the conventional answer is that he showed that there were many more forms of inference than Aristotle had found. The Greek logicians tried to guard against fallacious reasoning by making a complete list—they might be called working rules—of all the forms of deduction which are valid. Aristotle decided that these were nearly all syllogistic: for example 'All men are mortal, Socrates is a man, therefore Socrates is mortal.' Russell showed how much more there was to logic, and that syllogisms should have no such pre-eminence. But this is not all. I think that if we ask why Russell was a great logician, there is another important answer which is a somewhat paradoxical one; it was because he showed how little logic can do.

'As logic improves,' he said, 'less and less can be proved.' He pointed out that it was often the mark of a man lacking in logical capacity to think that one proposition implies another when it does not: from this point of view, he once remarked that 'Logic is the art of *not* drawing conclusions'. For instance, some of Aristotle's syllogisms were not valid as they stood. Moreover, Russell insisted that the knowledge given by logic—and mathematics—is all hypothetical. It tells us that *if* something is true, *then* something else is true.

The above syllogism, for instance, should have been first stated in some such form as '*If* all men are mortal, and *if* Socrates is a man, *then* Socrates is mortal'. We must think of logic as rather like the modern electronic brains, which can solve a problem with the necessary data to work on, but which cannot produce any results unless some facts are fed into them first. Logic can only work on premisses supplied independently of logic; any proof must start with some premiss which is unproved. This point, once it has been put plainly, appears simple and obvious, and by no means original. But though recognized in theory as early as Aristotle, it has continually been blurred over in the history of human thought.

To begin with, there is the natural human craving for *certain* knowledge. We have recorded Russell's own disappointment, at the age of eleven, when he found that Euclid gave no proof of his axioms. His brother Frank did not tell him, as he might have done: 'You have got to start from something which you accept without proof, and you might as well start here as anywhere.' As it happened, if Frank had said this, he would have been wrong; for not all Euclid's axioms are beyond question, and the beginning of the deductive system can be pushed much farther back. Russell was naturally inspired to see if, by pushing it back far enough, he could arrive at something absolutely certain; and it took all the labours of *Principia Mathematica*, and the continuation of the same work by Gödel, to show exactly what could not be proved in the foundations of mathematics, and why not.

Russell's philosophical predecessors, like Kant, had assumed that Euclid's theorems gave us knowledge about the actual world. It was not realized that, like any other deductive system, Euclidean geometry could not go further than saying that *if* certain premisses were true, *then* certain conclusions followed. Russell's insistence on this point had much more originality than may appear in retrospect, because when he first worked on geometry it was assumed that actual space was in fact Euclidean; the Theory of Relativity had not yet made scientists think of it as non-Euclidean.

One common reason for not seeing that any argument in logic or pure mathematics must be hypothetical could be a strong desire to prove some emotionally satisfying belief. Thus, again and again, philosophers thought they had succeeded in using logic to prove the existence of something they wanted to believe in, in spite of the impossibility of logic proving the existence of anything; just as countless inventors kept on imagining they had solved the secret of perpetual motion, in spite of it being a scientific impossibility.

Descartes thought he had proved his own existence by saying 'I think, therefore I am'; and he then proceeded to deduce a philosophic system from this foundation. Many philosophers thought they could prove the existence of God by the 'ontological' argument. As late as Russell's own time, McTaggart believed that he had arrived at a logical demonstration of personal immortality. Even philosophers who realized that logic could not prove the existence of anything *directly* thought it could do so *indirectly*, by proving that all philosophies were logically impossible except their own. An example was the way in which Bradley, like Kant and Hegel, claimed to have found contradictions in the ordinary world of Appearance.

Some of these attempted proofs by logic depended on technical errors, some on mistakes about the use of words. Others depended on assuming that something which we cannot help believing must be true; one of Russell's most important services was to disentangle logic from psychology, and to say that logic does *not* mean 'the laws of thought'.

The implications of realizing the limitations of logic have only become obvious gradually, and Russell himself took some time to realize them all.

For instance, no logical argument can establish that something is good or bad, unless you start from some such proposition in your premises. In Russell's *Problems of Philosophy*, published in 1912, he still wrote that we have *a priori* ethical knowledge. But on this he was immediately challenged by Santayana, who denied that we have any objective premises on which an ethical theory can be built. Santayana said that 'good' and 'bad' were like 'right' and 'left', depending on the individual point of view.

He argued by way of analogy that, for human beings, whisky was more intoxicating than coffee, but that this did not mean that whisky was 'pervaded, as it were by an inherent intoxication, and stands dead drunk in its bottle! Yet just in this way Mr

Russell and Mr Moore conceive things to be dead good and dead bad.' Russell had accepted G. E. Moore's arguments in *Principia Ethica* for saying that there is such a thing as objective ethical knowledge. But now that Santayana challenged him, Russell decided that Santayana was right: and that the premiss for an ethical argument could not be 'such and such a thing is good' but 'I think such and such is good'. Moral judgments became purely subjective.

Once again, there was nothing original in this conclusion: the originality lay in the fact that Russell was willing to face it. Other agnostics, after rejecting God and the Bible as a measure of ethical values, had still assumed in a vague sort of way that they could give a rational defence of the ethical code they advocated. Nor would a failure to do so have seemed important when traditional moral rules still had much of their force. Even the advanced advocates of new moralities, like the 'Bloomsbury' group who thought they based their way of life on the teachings of G. E. Moore, had few disagreements among themselves on what constituted the 'Good'. But within Russell's own lifetime men came to power in great nations who openly challenged both old and new moralities. They said Christian ideas were mistaken, that it was right for the strong to kill off the weak, for a Nordic race to exterminate non-Aryans, and for Bolsheviks to enslave non-Bolsheviks. They defended cruelty and falsehood, and Russell could not prove that they were wrong. On his principles he could only say 'I dislike your views very much, but I have to admit this is purely a matter of personal opinion'. Only a man of supreme intellectual integrity could have admitted a conclusion so completely at variance with everything he wanted to believe, and everything he did believe.

Once he was expounding to Lowes Dickinson his theory that 'good' and 'bad' had no objective validity. A few minutes afterwards Lowes Dickinson was laughing because the name of somebody Russell disliked had come up in conversation, and Russell had declared in the fiercest tone of conviction: 'He is a *scoundrel!*'

This is the great paradox of Russell. All his instincts were on the side of the 'rationalists'; his greatest hatred was for those who exalted emotion, or any sort of mystic intuition, at the expense of reason. But because Russell was the greatest rationalist of all, he had to admit that reason cannot prove the mystics wrong. In fact, in some private moods he was a mystic himself. (Though one of a most unusual kind: a mystic who hated mysteries, and devoted his life to dispelling them.) This side of his nature was often unsuspected, although he wrote in *Mysticism and Logic* that 'The greatest men who have been philosophers have felt the need both of science and of mysticism'.

CHAPTER VI

The Theory of Descriptions

❧

I MUST now come, with many misgivings, to Russell's Theory of Descriptions. Here again, there are appalling difficulties in explaining it in any book for the general reader, mainly because it is so easy. Russell's first formulation of it, and the results derived from it, were technical and very difficult; but any simple explanation of it may make it seem too obvious to be worth bothering about. Yet the attempt to say something about the Theory of Descriptions must not be shirked. There is general agreement that it was Russell's most important single contribution to philosophy. This was not only his own opinion, but that of such good judges as G. E. Moore and Wittgenstein. 'The Theory of Descriptions,' said Moore, 'was something quite new. It was Russell's greatest philosophical discovery, more important than anything he said later. It was his own work, and not influenced by anyone whatever.'

When the expectant reader, with his interest aroused in this way, asks what this remarkable discovery was, he is bound to find the reply a little disappointing at first. He will have to be told that the theory arose partly as a reply to the Austrian philosopher Meinong, who had been much exercised by the status of certain things which do not exist. Suppose you say 'The golden mountain does not exist', or 'The round square does not exist'. These are not only true statements, but useful ones. The first might well be used to give some romantic explorer, misled by myths and legends, a realistic fact about the world. The second might be used by a teacher to correct a pupil who had mistaken views about geometry—or, at any rate, about the definitions used in geometry. Now can you have true and meaningful statements about nothing? It might be argued that both sentences were equivalent to saying ' "Something which is nothing" does not exist'. A golden mountain certainly seems 'something which is nothing'; so does a round square. But, according to this view, the sentences are simply identical; which they are certainly not. One of them tells us something about golden mountains, and the other tells us something about round squares. And it seemed that there must be *some* sense in which both golden mountains and round squares exist, or else we could not talk about them.

This was the problem considered by Meinong, and he decided that things like golden mountains and round squares, if they did not actually exist, must still have some kind of being, though in a different way from ordinary objects like tables and chairs. And if such things were there, he had to find somewhere to put them; so he created a whole realm of these shadows.

Against this doctrine Russell rebelled. He pointed out that instead of saying 'The golden mountain does not exist', you could say 'There is no entity which is both golden and a mountain'. Any 'analysis' of this kind removes the phrase 'the golden mountain' from the sentence, and removes any cause for believing that it has some kind of being. This, of course, is only the beginning of Russell's Theory of Descriptions, put in an over-simplified form; but I think it is the basic beginning.

At this stage, I think, the intelligent layman is quite entitled to lose his temper. He has been told to expect something special. Now it merely seems that one philosopher has shown another philosopher that he need not talk nonsense about things which do not exist. Russell had solved a puzzle; but he may well have left the ordinary man quite unable to understand why anyone should have bothered about the puzzle in the first place. All Russell had done, apparently, was a kind of rather obvious playing with words. The intelligent layman may well feel that his misgivings about the uselessness of philosophy have been confirmed to the hilt.

The first thing we can point out to him is that all great intellectual advances usually have the same quality of obviousness, once they are made. When Galileo dropped his different weights from the leaning tower of Pisa, he did something which any child could have done, yet Galileo had all the wise men of the time against him. To take a more transient modern example: the basic idea of Keynes on the theory of employment—the denial of Say's Law—is now so generally accepted that it is hard to imagine how anyone could ever have disputed it: yet millions went hungry, less than twenty-five years ago, because almost all academic economists and Treasury experts failed to see the point.

So far as Russell's Theory of Descriptions is concerned, we must note the historical fact that it evoked, if not hostility, at least complete bewilderment as to what Russell was talking about, and why he thought it important. The theory was put forward in an article called *On Denoting*, first published in 1905 in *Mind*, the leading British philosophical journal. The editor of *Mind*, Professor Stout, thought poorly of the article; and would undoubtedly have rejected it if it had come from some unknown young philosopher. Russell's international standing was now such that anything he wrote had to be accepted automatically. But according to G. E. Moore, when the article was finally published 'Nobody could make head or tail of it'. Moore told me that he himself never understood the Theory of Descriptions until Russell gave a clearer statement of it in the Introduction to *Principia Mathematica*.

Now it is easy and tempting to assume that the philosophers who failed to understand Russell, like the economists before Keynes, were simply fools. But this is obviously wrong, and it is well to look for some more fundamental explanation, beyond the difficulty and obscurity which often attends the first formulation of a new idea.

The reason why great intellectual advances often arouse violent opposition, but later seem obvious, is that they do *NOT* challenge what everybody is *thinking* at the time. They challenge ideas which are assumed so *unthinkingly* that people do not even realize that they are assuming them. The supremely difficult task is bringing this subconscious assumption into consciousness; once that is done, the immediate reaction may be bewildered annoyance that anyone should challenge it, but the rest is comparatively easy. For instance, it was much easier to believe that the world was round than that it was flat, once people started thinking about it at all. Belief in a flat earth involves a host of

E

insoluble questions—How is the earth supported? Is it infinite, or do you fall off when you get to the end of it? How is it that the sun and moon, after disappearing in the West, go underground and reappear in the East? The vital step forward was taken by the man who first doubted the seemingly obvious fact that the earth is flat; the idea of it being round then followed almost as a matter of course. A great thinker is a man who questions something which seems so obvious that everybody takes it for granted. Russell was a great philosopher because he had this capacity.

The Theory of Descriptions was a fundamental advance, in which something subconsciously assumed to be obviously right was shown to be obviously wrong. The false assumption, exposed by Russell, was that one word must stand for one object, and that words mean something like what they say. It had been natural to suppose that the grammatical structure of a sentence was the same as its logical structure. It has been assumed, to take Meinong's example, that a sentence about golden mountains was saying something about golden mountains, and that therefore such things must have being, or they could not be talked about. Russell's analysis proved this assumption wrong: and it also suggested that there may be many other ways in which we can be misled by words and the form of sentences.

Suppose we say something about Winston Churchill. Now Churchill was at different times in his life a squealing baby, a Harrow schoolboy, a bumptious subaltern, an artist, a bricklayer, a party politician, and a great world statesman. All these different individuals were described by the same word 'Churchill'; yet the baby named Churchill was somebody very different from the octogenarian statesman named Churchill, the two individuals probably not having a single molecule of their bodies in common. There was *something* in common or *some* connection between the baby and the elder statesman: I do not want now to go into the abstruse metaphysical question as to what the connection was. At the moment, remaining still in the realms of common sense, it is obvious that anyone who thinks the unchanging word 'Churchill' stands for an unchanging person is obviously wrong.

Now Russell believed that we frequently make analogous mistakes, which are less obvious, about other words—thinking that, because a word is fixed and definite, it must refer to something changeless and substantial.

The most celebrated instance is the ancient doctrine of 'substance'. We may say of a table that it is made of wood, that it is heavy, that it is dark and shiny, and so on. It was assumed that there was something of substance which had these different attributes. Russell later came to question this view. When we want to explain what it is that is made of wood, and is heavy and dark and shiny, we use the word 'table' each time; and this deceives us into thinking there is some permanent substance behind the attributes, even though there is not. This, as we shall see, was the conclusion which Russell reached in 1914 in his *Our Knowledge of the External World*. Some years later he used the same approach to question Descartes' 'I think, therefore I am', and to question the popular conception of what is meant by 'I'. Russell wrote that 'to suppose that thoughts need a thinker is to be misled by grammar (or rather syntax)'.

These points will be developed in later chapters: but enough has been said to show how the Theory of Descriptions, which at first sight merely appeared to be a trick for saying the same things in different words, can be the starting point of a complete revolution in our view of the nature of the universe. Russell perhaps summarized his view best when he said 'Don't let grammar dictate to ontology'—that is, don't let it govern our views about what exists. The Theory of Descriptions was associated with a precise explanation of what is meant by existence, and a refutation of the 'ontological' argument for the existence of God. It reinforced Russell's objection to the 'subject-predicate' logic. It was also important in connection with epistemology, or the branch of philosophy which deals with how we acquire our knowledge. Russell made a distinction between what we know directly by 'Acquaintance', and what we know at second hand by 'Description'.

It may still seem strange, at first, that so much should follow from the discovery of a faulty use of words: but it is not so surprising when it is remembered that nearly all our thinking, and nearly all our communication of ideas, is done by words;

so if they are used wrongly there is no hope of our ideas being right.

It is true that the first results of the Theory of Descriptions were negative: it showed how some previous philosophers had gone wrong by drawing false inferences from words to reality. But once again Russell could use these negative means to reach a positive conclusion; for he still kept the same assumption that language, *if the false inferences were avoided*, gave some sort of a picture of the real world. Consider such a sentence as 'The cat/ is on/the mat'. It has two nouns, and a verb and a preposition which together express a certain relation: and it gives a correct description of two objects, a cat and a mat, having a certain relation to each other. There is only one respect in which the phrase 'the cat is on the mat' is a little misleading; the words 'is on' appear just as substantial as the words 'the cat' and 'the mat'. But 'is on' stands for a relation, whereas the others stand for physical objects. Language would give a better picture of reality if we simply wrote

<blockquote>
'the cat
the mat'
</blockquote>

Now Russell for some time believed that, if we first carefully note all these ways to which words can be misleading, and suggest false assumptions, we can then learn a great deal about the nature of reality from the words we use to describe it. He even talked about the idea of a perfect language, which would mirror reality perfectly. But this is a point to be mentioned again later.

CHAPTER VII

Reviews and Politics

IN the later stages of writing *Principia Mathematica*, Russell broke his rule that he would 'Never indulge in any excess, including any excess of work'. He abandoned his regular and restricted time-table, and overworked to such an extent that afterwards he told Professor Littlewood, the Cambridge mathematician, that *Principia Mathematica* had taken so much out of him that he sometimes doubted whether he would ever be the same man again.

The intellectual labours which went into it were so monumental that one tends to assume that Russell could have done very little else between 1900 and 1910. But the fact is that, throughout this period, he continued his usual scatteration of philosophical articles and book reviews, to be found in *Mind* and similar technical publications. It seems that whenever a philosophical work arrived in German or French or Italian which nobody else understood, the editor of *Mind* would send it along to Russell as a matter of course, and Russell always obliged promptly with a swift but thorough appraisal.

It must be said that Russell was often an unkind and merciless critic, particularly in his earliest reviews. His manner was something like a surgeon at an operating table, and his precise and dispassionate dissection could be devastating for various authors who would be forgotten for ever but for the fact that he wrote about them.

For instance the unfortunate Edmond Goblot, author of an *Essai sur la Classification des Sciences*, would probably have endured columns of abuse and criticism rather than face Russell's cruel and matter-of-fact summing up that 'The work appears to have few merits'.* Dr Julius Schultz, author of *Psychologie der Axiome*, received from Russell such cold condemnations as that 'His remarks on Geometry are a farrago of logical fallacies, historical blunders, and mathematical errors' . . . 'The subject invites to confusion between logic and psychology; and the author does not refuse the invitation'.

It is hard to reconcile such strictures with Russell's tremendous capacity for human kindness, which he would even extend to foolish philosophers; and with the immense help which he was always ready to give generously to students. As Santayana said of him: 'He was benevolence itself to the most humble and hopeless intellectual waifs.'

If asked to justify his harshness, he would probably have said that the essential thing was to tell the truth about a book uncompromisingly, and that everything else had to come second. Perhaps Beatrice Webb gave the best account of this side of Russell's character when she wrote that 'Compromise, mitigation, mixed motives, phases of health of body and mind, qualifying statements, uncertain feelings, all seem unknown to him. A proposition must be true or false; a character good or bad; a person loving or unloving, truth-speaking or lying.'

Yet, in these years and for the rest of his life, his wit could sometimes be unnecessarily wounding. I believe that Russell, like many others of exceptional sensitiveness and sensibility, developed at times, as a condition of survival, a superficially hard skin to protect himself against the bruises and uglinesses and tragedies of human life. (The same thing happened with Shaw, who in early life was almost as shy and nervous as Russell; but Russell never went as far as Shaw's verbal cruelties.)

Another explanation is that Russell's wit was so effervescent that he was often carried away by it without thinking. One

* This review provides a rather striking example of Russell's powers of memory. It appeared in 1898, when he was 26. I chose it for mention here because it is very little known, and was unlikely to have been referred to since it was published. On the above passage in my draft being read aloud to Russell in 1955, when he was 83, he promptly protested that the quotation was incomplete, and gave the full paragraph almost verbatim: 'The work appears to have few merits, except an unusually scrupulous acknowledgment of sources. On p. 43, for example, it is asserted that knowledge is power, and M. Egger is cited as having anticipated M. Goblot in this novel and weighty aphorism.'

could almost put it that he never said an unkind word except in jest. Like the character in Oscar Wilde who could resist anything but temptation, Russell could resist anything but a joke. Slower-witted philosophers had some justification for complaining that, whenever they thought they had got Russell pinned down in argument, he would divert their attack by some devastating flash of humour; just as Winston Churchill, when caught in an impossible position in the House of Commons, had a knack of bludgeoning his way out with some boisterous piece of repartee.

During the years spent on *Principia Mathematica*, Russell even found some time for politics; he joined a discussion group known as the 'Co-efficients', so called because of the hope that the members would prove jointly efficient, and with H. G. Wells as another member. He was roused by agitation for Protection to write and speak whole-heartedly for Free Trade. And in 1907 he even stood for Parliament.

There was a by-election at Wimbledon which looked like being a Conservative walk-over; the Liberal candidate, having become Mayor, felt that he should abstain from party politics. Russell agreed to stand as a candidate of the 'National Union of Women's Suffrage Societies'. At this time there were two bodies agitating for women's suffrage; Russell stressed that he represented the one which believed in only using constitutional means.

In this, as in most political matters, he came to dislike extremism. When a violent Feminist told him that 'The half of every man is a lunatic', he replied: 'The better half.'

Russell explained at Wimbledon that he stood for 'democracy, liberty and justice', all of which meant the granting of votes to women. According to a newspaper report of one speech, he supported the Liberal Government on all questions except its attitude to women's suffrage. 'He was a Liberal, and had been a Liberal all his life'; and the most important part of Liberal policy was Free Trade.

Though not an official Liberal Party candidate, Russell received the 'personal sympathy and good will' of the Liberal Chief Whip. His opponent was Henry Chaplin, a leading Conservative politician of the day.

It is some indication of the serenity of those pre-war years that Russell could have said that 'the question of Votes for Women, if not the most important, is almost the most important question at present before the country'. But though the issues at stake in politics might seem less serious than today, the public were much more interested in political contests.

Electioneering still meant oratory from public platforms, instead of smooth television performances. When Russell held his first meeting, a gang of hecklers often shouted him down; and his opponents tried to ridicule Feminism by letting two rats loose in the audience when one of his lady supporters was speaking, with the object of making the ladies squeal. 'There was,' said *The Times*, 'great commotion until the rats were killed.' But according to the local paper, the *Wimbledon Borough News*, the plan misfired: 'The terrified animals, instead of creating a panic among the suffragists, showed more dis-crimination, and made for a little group of men in front of the platform, who appeared somewhat disturbed at the unwelcome apparitions. After a little chase, however, the rats were disposed of, and the gentlemen resumed their normal calm again.'

It must be admitted that the *Wimbledon Borough News* was hardly unbiased. Strongly pro-Russell, it supported him with all the gusto and scandalized invective which marked politics at the time. Some of its headlines speak for themselves: 'Cowardly cads turn rats loose in Worple Hall,' 'Larrikins and hooligans yell themselves hoarse', 'The ladies' brilliant oratory wins the hearts of their hearers', 'Ruffianly assault on Mrs Russell at Raynes Park'. This latter incident was described by the paper as follows:

'Another dastardly outrage was committed on Tuesday eve-ning, when an egg was thrown at Mrs Russell—the charming lady who is taking such an active part in her husband's cam-paign—as she was driving away from a meeting at Raynes Park, the unpleasant missile hitting her full between the eyes and putting her to considerable pain. . . . Soon a large bump had swollen up. . . . Great disgust has been expressed at the brutality of these savages, who seem hardly fit subjects for the wilds of South Africa.'

At the end, Chaplin beat Russell by 10,263 votes to 3,297.

In May 1910, with *Principia Mathematica* almost finished, Russell made a more serious attempt to get into Parliament, seeking selection as an official Liberal candidate. It was characteristic of how little anybody was expecting or thinking about a war that, addressing his adoption meeting, he did not mention foreign policy. He attacked the Lords' Veto on legislation, and supported the taxation of land values, Free Trade, and women's suffrage. Though his adoption seemed certain, a committee of the local constituency association discovered that he was an agnostic. When he said he would not go to church occasionally to keep up appearances, another candidate was adopted, who was duly elected to Parliament.

It is interesting to speculate about the possible historical consequences if Russell had gone into public life at this stage, joining a Liberal Parliamentary Party led by Asquith as Prime Minister, and including Winston Churchill, Lloyd George, Haldane, Herbert Samuel and John Morley. Personally I agree with Charles Trevelyan that 'Russell was far too uncompromising to be a success as a politician'.

A less serious episode occurred during the Constitutional Crisis of 1911, when the House of Lords was blocking the reforms of the Liberal Government. There was a proposal to create enough new Liberal peers to ensure a Liberal majority in both Houses. When somebody suggested Russell might be considered for a peerage, he said that he would choose the title of 'Lord Snooks'; and, when this caused surprise, protested: 'But I thought the Government wanted to make the House of Lords look as ridiculous as possible.'

Russell sometimes maintained, partly I think out of perverseness, that there was no connection between his philosophical and political opinions. He was fond of pointing out that in philosophy he came nearest to Hume, who was a Conservative. But in fact I think there are perfectly obvious connections between Russell's philosophical and other views. One effect of his philosophy was to show that many philosophical questions, previously thought capable of solution by logic, could only be decided according to individual temperament; and it was natural that a temperament which led to certain conclusions in philosophy should lead to parallel conclusions in politics.

To begin with, it is natural enough to find an analytic anti-monist philosopher like Russell upholding the individual against the state, whereas Hegel did the reverse. (In view of the way Hegelianism contributed to both Fascism and Communism, its overthrow in Britain and America perhaps had more than academic importance.)

The whole bent of Russell's mind in philosophy was an attempt to eliminate the *a priori* and to accentuate the empirical; and there was exactly the same trend in his political thinking, in spite of his sometimes using abstract words like 'justice'.*
Unless it is realized that Russell's approach to political questions was usually empirical and practical, based on the evidence of the moment and not on *a priori* principles and preconceptions, it is quite impossible to understand why his views appeared to vary so much. This was perfectly legitimate, and even praise-worthy, in a world which never stays the same, and where changing circumstances continually change the balance of argu-ments on different sides.

Failure to grasp this point can also lead to an unjustifiable feeling of disappointment with some of Russell's political writings; there may be a false presumption that his job was to solve every problem by some Ism or Ideology or highflown theory of which he could proclaim the eternal truth. The be-ginning of political wisdom is to realise that no such theories exist.

Yet I must note here an apparent oddity about Russell. While cheerfully describing all his changes of mind in philosophy, he would tend to regard references to his political changes as criticisms of himself, although here they are even more ob-viously justifiable. I think the reason is as follows. He had expressly excluded any moral or practical considerations from his intellectually austere discussions of philosophical problems. He said rightly that anybody who objected to change and de-velopment was still confusing philosophy with its origins in

---

* This, again, is easily understandable; for justice and impartial freedom from prejudice are the social and political counterparts of that search for *generality* which marks the great mathematician, and which is exemplified in the pages of the *Principles of Mathematics* and *Principia Mathematica*.

theology, and was assuming that a philosophical theory should be as rigid as a theological creed. The passionate side of his nature, with no outlet in his technical work, was poured into political and social issues. He never championed a political cause unless he was moved by a deeply-felt horror of unnecessary human suffering and a determination to fight the folly which produced it. In philosophy his overriding consistency throughout was one of method and purpose, like a superb technician with the utmost pride in his craft. In politics his fundamental consistency was one of fierce human compassion, and he went into action in the mood of a man raising a standard which he meant to defend against all attacks.

But Russell, whatever conclusions he reached on a particular political issue, was always capable of first considering and stating fairly the two conflicting points of view. This habit of seeing both sides applies just as much to him as a philosopher: Whitehead once called him a Socratic dialogue in himself.

Anyone who tries to trace the development of Russell's political views is likely to come across a few puzzles: although, for the reasons just given, I do not think the puzzles are important. He had been brought up as a Liberal. Then, coming under the influence of the Webbs, he joined the Fabian Society (which, in those days, did not mean leaving the Liberal Party). For a time he was an Imperialist and supported the Boer War. But early in 1901, according to one of his broadcasts, 'I had an experience not unlike what religious people call conversion. . . . In the course of a few minutes I changed my mind about the Boer War, about harshness in education and in the Criminal Law, and about combativeness in private relations.' Thereafter his attitude to politics never attempted the same aloofness as in his youthful lectures on German Socialism.

Russell's 'conversion' in 1901 followed from his becoming 'suddenly and vividly aware of the loneliness in which most people live, and passionately desirous of finding ways of diminishing this tragic isolation'. The result of this feeling, on the personal side, was reflected in what is probably the best known of all Russell's essays, his *Free Man's Worship*. All that I will say about it is that the reader should buy *Mysticism and Logic*, where it is reprinted, and read it; when he will discover, among other things, that some of Russell's precepts read like paraphrases of texts from the New Testament.

Russell left the Fabians because of his fervour for Free Trade. In foreign policy, he was opposed to an Entente with France and Russia against Germany, which he first heard advocated by Sir Edward Grey at a meeting of the 'Co-efficients' in 1902. At the Wimbledon by-election in 1907, however, he described himself as a supporter of all the policies of the Liberal Government; and there is other evidence of him apparently supporting Grey's foreign policy. In November 1911 Leonard Woolf had just returned from Ceylon, and went down to stay with G. E. Moore at Cambridge. One vivid recollection Woolf had of this visit was of an occasion when Russell and Sanger had both called on Moore, and had an argument over Grey's foreign policy. Sanger was bitterly opposing him, and Russell was championing him.

Russell's explanation of this incident, given to me in 1956, was that he had only supported Grey's foreign policy because he did not know what it was at the time. Grey had 'lied like a trooper' in concealing the way in which Britain had been committed to France. The mistake had been in the estimate of Grey's character—'I had thought him a comparatively honest man, and that when he made a statement in Parliament he was speaking the truth'.

CHAPTER VIII

'A Quiet Life'

WE can I think presume that the year 1901, when Russell became 'suddenly and vividly aware of the loneliness in which people live', also heralded the beginning of a change in his views about marriage. He was to pass gradually, over a period of many years, to a belief in free love, only restricted where children were involved.

By the end of his life Russell had married four times: and he had other friendships which were not Platonic. This book will contain no revelations in this regard. I do not believe that intimate relations between any man and woman are the concern of anybody but themselves; and it must be left to Russell to give his own account of this aspect of his life. It is an important aspect, and it is important to fill in the bare facts and discount malicious gossip and rumour. But I propose to confine myself to a brief summary of the facts which can be found by anybody today, or by future historians, in the newspaper reports of the various divorce proceedings, in books of reminiscence and biography, and in Russell's own writings. He produced numerous articles from time to time on marriage and sex morality, and later I will discuss the views in his fullest work on the subject, *Marriage and Morals*, which was published in 1929.

As early as May 1902 Beatrice Webb noted 'a consciousness that something is wrong' between Russell and his first wife, and the following year her diary recorded 'a tragic austerity and effort' in their relations. It seems that Russell's quickness of mind and spirit was incompatible with the earnest Quaker outlook of Alys. (She used the Quaker 'thee' in speech, and was much occupied with good works; she had the reputation, on entering a room, of often seeking out and talking to whoever was the most boring person present, and whom everyone else would be avoiding.)

As outsiders, we need only note the subsequent effect on Russell of his typically uncompromising decision, in the end, that it was better to make a clean break than to pretend to conventional married happiness which did not exist. He was always an aristocrat in his tastes and his fastidiousness, but he began to be cut off from people of his own class and outlook, in the first place by the breaking up of his marriage, and later by his Pacifist propaganda against the First World War. The result was his turning for friendship to unconventional men and women with what were called modern ideas.

The reputation of his brother can also have hardly been helpful. Frank Russell became a Buddhist at Oxford, was sent down from Balliol, was married three times, was imprisoned for bigamy (on a technicality concerning the validity of an American divorce), and was referred to by gossips as 'the wicked Earl'. According to his friend Santayana, he was nearly ruined by law suits and business losses, and 'kept going precariously by being director of various precarious companies'. There naturally grew up a disposition to regard both Russells as rather odd and not very respectable people.

But all this is looking ahead. The parting from Alys did not come till 1911, and it was 1921 before there was a divorce. It must be recorded, as posterity's debt to Russell's first wife, that it was during the period they were still living together that he did the work usually considered his best; he was provided with the external essentials for creative thinking, such as a study in a well-run household where he could work without interruption.

Russell once wrote that 'A quiet life is characteristic of great men, and . . . their pleasures have not been of the sort that look exciting to the outward eye. No great achievement is possible without persistent work, so absorbing and so difficult that little energy is left over for the more strenuous kinds of amusement.' This, to some extent, is true of Russell himself. For instance, he was fond of dancing, but gave it up when he went to the country to work on mathematics. He was bad at games; and, though he played a little tennis, 'the only person I could beat was McTaggart'.

In June 1902, just after finishing the *Principles of Mathematics*, he wrote to Beatrice Webb from Cambridge, where he had gone to stay with the Whiteheads:

'The May term here's a perpetual round of social functions . . . but I have been in no mood for garden parties and balls and such nonsenses . . .
'I often go into College and sit late in the Fellows' Garden, watching the fading twilight through the willows. Since I finished my book, I have devoted myself to what you would call mental hygiene, with good results so far. Beyond reading a mathematical MS of Whitehead's, I have done no work for the last fortnight, but have spent my whole days out of doors basking in the return of summer.'

Yet it must be borne in mind that Russell's usual idea of a non-strenuous holiday was to walk from Austria into Italy, or to join a reading party in the Lake District where he could intersperse work with climbing and swimming.

Robert Trevelyan had married a charming Dutch girl, who many years later could still remember a few days when she joined a walking tour which her husband and Russell were making together in the West Country. Mrs Elizabeth Trevelyan, unaccustomed to the strange customs of young Englishmen at the time, found to her horror that she was expected to walk at least fifteen or twenty miles a day. What was worse, instead of taking things leisurely and admiring the scenery, Russell talked philosophy the whole time. As Mrs Trevelyan reasonably explained afterwards: 'I cannot walk and philosophize at the same time. To think about philosophy I must sit down.' In the evenings, by way of relaxation, she read aloud George Eliot's *Middlemarch* to Russell and Trevelyan. She walked valiantly for three days; on the last day she gave up and took a carriage.

Russell was always impeccably neat in his dress. He wore glossy white starched collars which were the highest ever seen, so high that his chin seemed to disappear in them. On this walking tour he consented to wear soft collars during the day; but he still carefully changed into the high collars at night, even in the most remote little inns.

(Mrs Trevelyan, a very good amateur violinist, also had a disconcerting experience when she first met G. E. Moore, who was very fond of playing the piano, and asked her to play sonatas with him. Moore's style was, as she put it, 'very enterprising'; he had a strong sense of rhythm and an invincible keenness which made him regard nothing as too difficult for him to tackle, and he would set upon the piano with such gusto that he sometimes seemed to forget the violin part altogether.)

Russell was fond of cycling as well as walking, and in 1902 he had a bicycle accident in London which might have ended his life. Caught between a light horse-drawn van and a heavy dray, he thought quickly enough to crash into the dray, rebound from it, and thus fall under the van, which passed over him without serious injury.

These were the days before passports, when a man of culture would move freely and feel equally at home in England or Europe. Russell's travels included visits to Florence to stay with Bernard Berenson, who took him round the art galleries, and took him on bicycle trips through the surrounding countryside. Berenson said afterwards that sometimes Russell 'would rhapsodize about mathematics in a way so poetical, so mystical, that I used to listen with rapture—*bouche bée*.' Berenson was less successful in awakening any reciprocal interest in works of art. He could only remember one occasion when Russell showed appreciation of visual beauty. They were walking up from Berenson's villa, 'I Tatti', to the hills; and Berenson pointed out the beauty of some chance arrangements of pebbles and chips of wood by the wayside. For a moment Russell was deeply moved. 'But this is out and out mysticism,' he said.

There is other evidence that Russell was more sensitive in visual appreciation than Berenson believed. But the auditory arts still had more appeal for him, especially the lyric poets. He could recite whole passages from Shelley, or from Shakespeare's sonnets, or from many other poets; and he had a passion for Blake.

It was not only as regards foreign travel that this was a golden age for English intellectuals. It was also an age of sufficient incomes and ample leisure. As Beatrice Webb wrote of herself and Sidney in her diary, when going off for a week at Beachy Head with a party which included Graham Wallas, Bernard Shaw, Charles Trevelyan and Herbert Samuel:

'What fortunate people we are: Love, Work, Friends and Health, given holidays whenever we need it! An ideal life!'

Succeeding generations could only obtain brief glimpses of this life in fragmentary memories of long stays in pleasant country houses, with the Russells and the Webbs and the Shaws all busy with their respective work in the mornings, but devoting their afternoons to walk and talk. There were recollections of Russell watching fascinated while Shaw, working on a play, would write the names of his characters on square pieces of paper, and manoeuvre them on a chessboard to remind himself who was supposed to be on the stage at the time. There was the occasion when Shaw was learning to ride a bicycle, and smashed up Russell's bicycle by colliding into him. There were the occasional visits from H. G. Wells, who shocked Russell by saying that though he believed in free love, he did not mean to admit this in public until he had saved enough money from royalties to be able to live on the interest. And there were the standing jokes about Beatrice Webb's vegetarianism, and whether or not it had improved her temper.

She carried out careful systems of dieting, beginning with one which kept her to exactly 1 lb of food a day—4 oz for breakfast, 6 oz for lunch, 6 oz for dinner; the system became more and more exact and exacting, with precisely 2 oz of bread to eat with one egg for breakfast, and so on. Once she told Russell that her fasting made her more spiritual, and gave her exquisite visions. 'Yes,' said Russell, 'if you eat too little you see visions; and if you drink too much you see snakes.'

Sometimes the serious-minded Sidney Webb also found Russell's wit annoying. Once Russell said that democracy had at least one merit; an MP could not be stupider than his constituents, because the more stupid he was, the more stupid they were to elect him. Webb took this typically Russellian remark quite seriously and angrily.

One might describe a Russellian remark as something

F

analogous to a 'Shavianism'; but Russell's wit was much more subtle than Shaw's and, except when he indulged in delicate irony, was founded on a logical deduction from the facts. Jean Nicod, the French mathematical philosopher, said that Russell's remarks had 'that slightly ludicrous quality which comes from being true'. Whereas Shaw liked to stand on his head, Russell liked to turn head over heels and land the right way up again—in fact Russell once recalled that he used to delight in literally turning head over heels as a boy.

Another member of the group was Gilbert Murray, who could remember Russell drinking up to four cups of tea at a time, holding the cup with both hands to warm them. This latter habit became so well known among his friends that, on one occasion when G. M. Trevelyan had brought his future wife to tea for the first time, he suddenly exclaimed: 'Look, Janet! He's doing it!'

Gilbert Murray could also remember being in the middle of a game of tennis when a telegram came announcing that Frank Russell had got into one of his scrapes, and needed someone to go bail for him. 'Hang it,' said Russell, 'let's wait till after the set.'

In later years Murray compared their group to Shelley and Godwin and their circle; they had the same scepticism and rationalism, and the same presumption that previous customs and conventions were always wrong.

Murray, who had married one of Russell's cousins, first got to know Russell well when he went to Cambridge to read aloud his translation of the *Hippolitus*. Russell was delighted with it, and went up afterwards to ask Murray if he could borrow a copy. They became close friends, and it was partly because of this friendship that the Russells moved in 1905 to Bagley Wood, just outside Oxford, where they could see more of the Murrays.

Perhaps another reason which attracted Russell to Oxford was the prospect of enjoying arguments with the 'idealist' philosophers there. Sometimes it is hard to remember how slowly the new ideas of Russell and Moore were accepted. The recollection of Professor Brand Blanshard of Yale, who went to Oxford as a student in 1913, is that idealism was then 'so much in the ascendant, and blazing so brightly at the zenith, as to

obscure everything else in the sky . . .'. The great figure of
Bradley, 'magnified now to legendary proportions, hovered
everywhere over the scene' in Oxford: and Oxford was 'undoubtedly' the philosophical capital of Britain. This seems a
staggering statement from the point of view of later retrospect,
but it is probably no exaggeration of how most people felt at the
time. For Russell, Oxford was a hostile citadel to be stormed
with relish.

In particular, he formed a virulent dislike of J. A. Smith of
Balliol, a kind of Hegelian idealist. Once, after Smith had said
that truth consisted of ideas in the mind of the Absolute,
Russell asked: 'Does that mean that, if the Absolute stops
thinking about the hairs of my head, I will go bald?' Smith
replied in a shocked voice: 'I feel that this observation by Mr
Russell is designed to cast ridicule upon a statement made
by the Founder of our religion, a religion which to some of us is
very sacred, and in which all of us have been brought up.'

As for Russell, he decided that Smith was a 'humbug and a
hypocrite'. One remark he made about him afterwards was
characteristic: 'On the pretext of moral improvement of the
young, he depraved them by teaching them to believe things
which are not true. I hope he roasts.'

Once Gilbert Murray and Russell were having an argument
over a certain tutor in Oxford. Murray was praising him;
Russell was uncompromising, and would not hear a word in his
favour. Murray said how the tutor had a gift for entering into
his pupils' minds, making them feel that it was important what
they thought. Russell said immediately: 'You mean that he tells
them lies to make them like him.'

Russell also used to have arguments with Schiller of Corpus,
the leading British philosopher of pragmatism. While both
agreed in criticizing Oxford idealism, Russell was also critical of
pragmatism, which he once described as the philosophy which
believes that truth is on the side of the big battalions. One
young student who heard Russell and Schiller arguing carried
away a recollection of a vivid contrast. Schiller's philosophy was
supposed to be humanistic, but in argument he was dogmatic
and dry. Russell had a philosophy which was cold and logical;
but in argument he was warm and human.

Russell ended up with the cheerful disrespect for Oxford which sometimes characterizes Cambridge men: in his case, he emphasized the way in which Oxford used to neglect the study of science. He would recall gleefully how, the first time he visited Oxford, he was told proudly that Oxford now had a Science Department, consisting of one lecturer with a magic lantern and slides showing portraits of famous scientists. And he would remark that 'Roger Bacon once did an experiment and was put in prison for fourteen years. Since then no one has ever done an experiment at Oxford'.

According to Russell, the only man he found in Oxford who understood mathematical logic was G. G. Berry (mentioned in *Principia Mathematica*), a humble clerk in the Bodleian who had no academic recognition in the University. Berry took Russell's fancy by introducing himself with a neat logical conundrum. He went to Russell's door, and handed him a sheet of paper on which was written 'The statement on the other side of this page is false'. Russell then turned the page over and found written on the other side 'The statement on the other side of this page is false'.

At this time one of the gasometers which disfigure the view of Oxford from the south was already causing complaints: but Russell defended it on the ground that 'it's the only thing in Oxford designed to give light'.

His wit in argument also enlivened meetings of the Aristotelian Society in London. Once, when Russell had been criticizing Kant with his usual vehemence, some well-meaning person said in extenuation: 'Kant was kind to his mother, and that will be remembered when his system is forgotten.' Russell immediately replied: 'I cannot accept the cynical assumption that being kind to one's mother is more rare than the possession of philosophical ability as great as Kant's.'

It was during his Presidency of the Aristotelian Society that Russell shaved off the mustard-coloured moustache which is a feature of earlier photographs of him. The change in his appearance was so great that, at the next meeting of the Society, nobody recognized him at first. Russell himself said that, when he demolished his moustache with scissors and razor, he found for the first time that he had a satiric mouth, and that this discovery changed his whole character. I have the feeling that this should perhaps be classified as a Russellian remark.

According to report, the removal of his moustache was due to the wishes of Lady Ottoline Morrell, whose country house at Garsington, only a few miles out of Oxford, was later to become celebrated. She will probably be remembered chiefly for her close friendship with Russell: but she was a remarkable woman in her own right, who must be mentioned in any chronicle of these times. Like Russell, she was an aristocrat, being a half sister of the Duke of Portland. She was over six feet tall, with vivid auburn hair; she delighted in flamboyant dresses, and she attracted attention wherever she went. Santayana, after meeting her, described her as 'A marvellous creature, very tall, very thin, in blue silk flounces'.

Her reputation for unconventional dress and behaviour grew to legendary proportions, built up by a prolification of published stories which are mostly untrue. But she was also a woman of wide reading and artistic appreciation. Her greatest genius lay in recognizing and encouraging talent, bringing together the most diverse and stimulating people as a hostess; a role at which, as will be described later, she excelled at Garsington during the First World War.

There was one incident during the period when Russell was living near Oxford which is so characteristic of him that it cannot be omitted. A labourer, a little the worse for drink, had passed by the home of a certain unpopular man in the neighbourhood, and scribbled an uncomplimentary remark about him on the fence. The labourer was prosecuted, and sentenced to prison with the option of a fine. He did not have the money to pay. If he went to prison he would lose his job; and his wife, who was expecting a baby, would have to go to a workhouse. Russell found out the position, championed the labourer when nobody else would do so, and went to see the man whose fence had been scribbled on. He found him just coming out of church on a Sunday, and appealed to him to let the labourer off. The man refused, virtuously saying that wrong-doing must be punished. Russell came away in a furious rage at this example of Christian charity, and paid the labourer's fine himself.

CHAPTER IX

Cambridge and Harvard

IN October 1910 Russell returned to Trinity as Lecturer in Logic and the Principles of Mathematics (at a stipend of £210 a year). His classes were small but distinguished: one course of lectures on mathematical logic was heard by only three men— C. D. Broad the philosopher, E. H. Neville the mathematician, and H. T. J. Norton, whose work anticipated J. B. S. Haldane's application of mathematics to the problem of heredity. They made it possible for Russell to claim that 'One hundred per cent of my pupils get Fellowships'.

J. M. Keynes was also teaching at Cambridge at this time. Whitehead left Cambridge the year Russell returned, but G. E. Moore came back as Lecturer the year afterwards. The arrival of Ludwig Wittgenstein completed the group of Cambridge philosophers who were destined to dominate philosophical thinking for many years to come.

Wittgenstein was a rich young Austrian who had gone to Manchester University as a research student in engineering, having become fascinated by the new and adventurous science of aviation. He experimented with kites, then decided it was no use designing an aeroplane without first designing an engine for it, and was then led on to design a propeller. This involved working out the right mathematical formulae; and in doing this he grew so interested in the mathematics that he forgot all about the propeller. He asked if there was anyone who knew anything about the principles of mathematics, and was told about Russell. So Wittgenstein went to Cambridge to attend Russell's lectures, and to study under him.

In later years, C. D. Broad described Wittgenstein as 'a genius with all the *prima facie* appearances of a charlatan'.

Russell himself was uncertain at first whether Wittgenstein was anything more than a crank. For instance, Wittgenstein once put forward the strange theory that all propositions asserting or denying existence are meaningless. Russell then cited the proposition that 'There is no hippopotamus in this room at present', and proceeded to look under all the desks in the lecture room without finding one: but Wittgenstein was still not satisfied.

Wittgenstein also attended Moore's lectures, and Russell asked Moore what he thought of him. Moore replied that he had a high opinion of Wittgenstein. When Russell asked why, Moore made the classic response: 'Because he's the only one who looks puzzled during my lectures.' Wittgenstein had a way of 'knitting his brows', which showed that he was thinking hard and often disagreeing.

At the end of his first term at Cambridge, Wittgenstein asked Russell to tell him if he was a complete idiot, because if so he would abandon philosophy and go back to aviation. Russell asked him to write an essay on a philosophical subject, and after reading the first sentence said that Wittgenstein must keep to philosophy.

Wittgenstein's letters leave no doubt of how much he owed to Russell's encouragement. Moore, who had rooms in Trinity on the other side of Nevile's Court, used to look across and see one solitary light burning long after midnight in Russell's room, and knew that Wittgenstein would be there talking about logic with Russell.

Sometimes, however, Wittgenstein would simply pace up and down the room in silence. According to Russell's subsequent account, Wittgenstein would preface his remarks on arrival by saying that, when he left Russell's room, he proposed to commit suicide. Russell therefore had some diffidence about trying to get rid of his guest and go to bed. Making due allowances for Russellian exaggeration, I think we can take it that this happened at least once.

Wittgenstein, with his intense Teutonic seriousness, sometimes found Russell and Moore hard to understand. Once they were all having coffee and talking together when Russell suddenly turned to Moore and said: 'You don't like me, Moore, do you?'

Moore thought carefully and replied: 'No'.

They went on chatting about other things, and Wittgenstein was left puzzled and upset as to how Moore and Russell could still seek and enjoy each other's company. It was a little incident very typical of all three men.

At this time there was a strong clerical party among the Fellows of Trinity, and Russell seemed to take an impish delight in going out of his way to irritate and annoy them. On one occasion in the Combination Room he picked up an examination paper which had ten questions, and had the usual kind of note at the bottom that candidates need not answer more than six of them. 'Ah yes,' said Russell, 'Just like the Ten Commandments —you're not expected to attempt more than six.'

The impression of pre-war Cambridge given by Keynes' *Two Memoirs* is that the one outstanding figure was G. E. Moore, while Russell is barely mentioned except by way of criticism. There is no doubt of Moore's enormous influence, extending from early days down to and beyond the period when he came back as a teacher. But Keynes may give a misleading impression about Russell, reflecting the views of a group in King's of whom Keynes was the leader, who were referred to disparagingly by other Cambridge men as 'the Aesthetes', some of whom were disliked for one particular reason.

There is other testimony, however, that Moore was the only man who could cope with Russell in argument, with his persistent 'Do you *really mean* that?' and his unanswerable way of wagging his head sorrowfully to express incredulous reproach. Some of those who heard them arguing during this period thought that Moore was solely concerned with searching for the truth, whereas Russell liked to score debating points. Once again, I think the blame lies with Russell's incorrigible wit, which was always making him say things which were meant to amuse and startle and provoke argument, but which he never meant to be taken literally. As an example, I need only give one remark which has actually been quoted to me as evidence of insincerity. 'My own beliefs,' said Russell, 'are really very simple; but I don't put them forward, because they would not give me a chance of exercising my wits.'

This, of course, was on a par with his remark that, if there was a written examination on the Day of Judgment, he was not sure of his chances; but he would do all right on a Viva.

Dr Johnson said that 'there is in human nature a general inclination to make people stare; and every wise man has himself to cure of it, and does cure himself'. I do not think Russell ever cured himself; but nobody ever regretted this who had a chance of enjoying his conversation.

So far as Keynes and Russell were concerned, there seems to have been a certain latent hostility on both sides. Keynes said that Russell made the mistake (which he certainly made himself) of thinking ordinary people were too rational. Russell, on the other hand, found in Keynes 'a touch of Machiavellism', which he ascribed to Keynes' cleverness giving him something of a contempt for ordinary people. According to Russell, Keynes had the 'sharpest and clearest' intellect he ever came across: 'Annihilating arguments darted out of him with the swiftness of an adder's tongue. When I argued with him, I felt that I took my life in my hands, and I seldom emerged without feeling something of a fool.' This recollection, however, does not tally with that of Leonard Woolf, who had the impression when they were together that it was Russell who was even quicker than Keynes to score a point.

One event worth mentioning here is Russell's celebrated lecture on Bergson, to the Cambridge society called 'The Heretics'. Bergson's mystical philosophy of evolution was then enjoying a tremendous vogue, which Russell set out to demolish; there was an eager audience to hear him, and everyone had a sense of a great occasion, The lecture can be found reprinted in Russell's *History of Western Philosophy*; to enjoy its savour, the reader must imagine it delivered in Russell's dry, precise and ironic voice, and punctuated by the laughter and applause which greeted his sallies. It was an event of some importance in Russell's life, helping to re-establish him as one of the leading figures in Cambridge; and especially because it was his first big success as a public speaker.

Russell's own philosophical views at this period were explained with marvellous lucidity in his *Problems of Philosophy*, written for the Home University Library at Gilbert Murray's suggestion. It was an important book in its own right, which also remains by far and away the best introduction to the subject. It is somewhat disappointing to the beginner, however, when he has read it and been delighted to discover that he can understand it all, to find that Russell completely changed his mind afterwards about many points in it. There is no similar short statement of his later ideas available, because the further his thoughts advanced, the more was found of increasing subtle distinction and complex changes of viewpoint. One cannot sum up his philosophy by attaching his name to one single specific doctrine; in the way that is sometimes done, for instance, with Descartes or Berkeley.

We usually find a great philosopher taking up some striking and challenging position—often in comparative youth—which thereafter becomes associated with his name, his title to fame; and ordinary human vanity will suffice to make him cling to this position, with reluctant modifications, for the rest of his life. Russell was not so inhuman as to be devoid of human weaknesses; and he once put forward the speculation that all unusual energy is inspired by an unusual degree of vanity. But he was exceptionally free from the vanity with which most philosophers cherish their own philosophies. He would give birth to a theory which he was proud to call his own, and then commit infanticide a year or so later. He would chop and change his own doctrines as ruthlessly as most philosophers chop up those of their rivals.

This procedure had its origin in his overriding passion for truth; and there may be a subsidiary explanation, once again, in human and easily understandable terms. Less than halfway through his career he had already achieved immortality; his place was secure as a thinker who had made the greatest advances in logic since Greek times. When he turned again to general philosophy he was therefore under no incentive, conscious or unconscious, to create some distinctive Russellian doctrine to be made secure against all attacks. His love of pungent and provocative epigrams gives a superficial impression of polemic dogmatism. But closer study shows careful reservations and continual qualifications, with Russell at any time seeing the arguments against his views as clearly as his critics, and always ready to consider new ideas from any source.

Despite all the shifting of position, however, there was

always a consistency of method, the method known as Occam's Razor, based on the principle that entities should not be multiplied unnecessarily. (Occam's own words were: 'It is vain to do with more what can be done with fewer.') Russell's use of Occam's Razor was derived from his work on mathematical philosophy, and the Theory of Descriptions. For instance, is there such a thing as the number 2? Russell at first thought there was, as a kind of Platonic idea laid up in Heaven. But he then came down to earth, after his celebrated definition of numbers as classes of classes, and declared that the number 2 *was* simply the class of all couples, and that there was no mystic '2' associated with every couple. Similarly, a length of two feet was simply the class of all things two feet long; we need not imagine some heavenly foot rule applied to them all.

This point is of some importance with regard to religion, owing to the way in which Platonism is interwoven with Christian theology. There is a connection between believing in eternal numbers, believing in a heavenly foot rule, and believing in heaven.

In the Theory of Descriptions, Russell had shown that a sentence containing a phrase like 'the golden mountain' could have a meaning without the phrase itself standing for anything. He called such phrases 'incomplete symbols'; having defined numbers as classes of classes, he decided that symbols for both numbers and classes were 'incomplete symbols' in the same way. Then, following a lead given by Whitehead, he eliminated points and instants of time; and so on.

Associated with Occam's Razor was the method of analysis. To put it crudely, Russell's technique as a philosopher considering the Universe was to cut out anything he could do without, and then chop up what remained in as small pieces as possible to see exactly what he had got left. What he came down to were 'sense-data'; our perceptions of patches of different colours in different directions, and so on. These he called 'hard data', the most certain empirical knowledge we have. The problem is how, starting from such empirical sense-data, we can arrive at the existence of the physical world.

To get a definite illustration, let us consider a table. Philosophers, for some reason, always enjoy talking about tables, and Russell talked about them in both the *Problems of Philosophy* and his next book, *Our Knowledge of the External World*. The contrast between what he said about tables in them will show exactly the change in his ideas.

In the *Problems of Philosophy* he had no doubt, after a long discussion, that the 'idealists' were wrong and that the table at which he was writing was really there. In *Our Knowledge of the External World* he made one of his most startling uses of Occam's Razor. What, asked Russell, do we really know about the table? It presents certain appearances when we look at it, certain sounds when we knock on it, and a certain feel when we touch it. Why assume a metaphysical table, with 'substance', behind these appearances? And so Russell arrived at the seemingly paradoxical suggestion that 'All the aspects of a thing are real, whereas the thing is a mere logical construction'.

Russell soon found difficulties in arriving at a table as a 'logical construction' from 'hard' sense data alone, and had to add more uncertain knowledge—what he called 'soft' data. And as well as sense data he had to admit *sensibilia*, which might be called 'unsensed sense data', or the appearances of a table from places where no one is looking at it. I am not writing any more here about his logical construction programme, because it was highly technical; and I think it only becomes interesting to the general reader when, as described later on, it led to 'neutral monism', or the belief that there is no fundamental difference between mind and matter.

In the meanwhile I will only mention two points about it. First, as to its main motive. Russell wanted to cut out any need for the uncertain inference from appearances to physical objects by *defining* physical objects in terms of their appearances, in the same way that he had defined the number 2 as the class of couples. He could thus describe physics in terms of things we know, instead of talking about things we don't know. But there is one obvious difficulty about defining a table, for instance, as the class of its appearances. A class means a collection; and we naturally ask why we should find sense data collected to form a table in this way. I shall say more about this later.

The reader may at first think of Russell's use of Occam's Razor, and his 'logical construction' programme, as a typical example of technical philosophy which is of no interest to anyone but professional philosophers. Russell himself once admitted that one of his subsidiary motives was his sheer delight in the technical skill needed to see how much could be made of how little; as he described it, the pleasure of 'making philosophical mud pies'. But in fact the use of Occam's Razor brings us into what is perhaps the most fascinating of all realms of thought; the realm where philosophy interpenetrates with science, and where each can prompt advances in the other. Modern science has followed the Russellian procedure of elimination. The Theory of Relativity, for instance, got rid of the nineteenth century 'ether', and of the ideas of absolute time and space. Atomic theory, later on, divested itself of the imaginative picture of the atom as a miniature solar system, and admitted that we know nothing about the atom except when it emits observable energy.

Russell's *Our Knowledge of the External World* was written for the Lowell Lectures at Harvard for 1914; but he gave the lectures first in Cambridge, at the beginning of the year, as a kind of preliminary try-out. At that time C. K. Ogden, later famous as the inventor of 'Basic English', was the editor of the *Cambridge Magazine*. He saw that people knew about Russell's lectures in advance, with the result that sixty or seventy people came to hear them, and the double doors connecting the lecture room with an adjoining room had to be opened to accommodate the crowd. Russell, only used to tiny classes for his ordinary University lectures, was still so shy and diffident as a speaker that, when he arrived and saw the size of his audience, he was seen to hesitate and nearly retreat. One recollection is that Ogden happened to be just behind him, and it almost looked as though he pushed him into the room.

When Russell got going, the reception which greeted some early touches of wit gradually put him at his ease; and the lectures had the same success later at Harvard.

It is pleasant to pause here and say something about this visit to America, coming just before the tragic years of the First World War. It is also pleasant to record that Russell praised Americans (at that time at any rate) for their willingness to consider new ideas. 'Anyone,' he said, 'who has attempted to present a new philosophy to Oxford and the Sorbonne and the Universities of America, will have been struck by the greater readiness of the Americans to think along unfamiliar lines.'

As well as his Lowell Lectures, Russell gave a course on Symbolic Logic, and invited his students to tea for informal discussions. In a letter written from Harvard at the time, he remarked that his students there were not very interesting or able, but that there were two exceptions. One was a Greek, Raphael Demos, later Professor of Philosophy at Harvard. T. S. Eliot was the second.

Eliot wrote his own description of Russell in his poem *Mr Apollinax*. In later life he remarked that he had found it 'great fun' to study Symbolic Logic under Russell's guidance. He said that 'It did not seem to have anything to do with reality. But it gave me a sense of pleasure and power manipulating those curious little figures.' And his recollection of Russell himself was that he was 'very delightful' as a teacher of philosophy, 'because he had no pomposity and was so approachable'. At that time most Professors of Philosophy in American took their tone from their German counterparts, who usually tried to be as aloof as possible in order to look profound.

After Russell had returned to England, T. S. Eliot himself came to Europe; and one day they met by chance in a street near the British Museum, Russell having gone out to buy some milk for his tea. They went back together to Russell's flat in Bury Street. When Eliot married, Russell suggested that he and his wife should come to live in the flat, since at this time the Eliots had very little money. Russell also gave Eliot an introduction to Sydney Waterlow, the representative in Britain of the *Monist* and another American philosophical journal, resulting in Eliot getting work reviewing philosophical books; and later Russell took a cottage at Marlow largely so that the Eliots could live in it.

Sometimes Eliot read his poems aloud to Russell, and it is fair to say that Russell was one of the first to see their merits. Some ideas in them may possibly have been suggested by the talks Russell and Eliot had together. They certainly have points of affinity with Russell's writings; and when Russell's *Mysticism and Logic* was published towards the end of the First World War, he declared that the only review of it which showed any understanding was that by Eliot in the *Nation*.

CHAPTER X

First World War

KEYNES, in his *Memoir* describing Cambridge thought before the First World War, wrote that 'Bertie in particular sustained simultaneously a pair of opinions ludicrously incompatible. He held that in fact human affairs were carried on after a most irrational fashion, but that the remedy was quite simple and easy, since all we had to do was to carry them on rationally.'

I do not know whether this was a fair representation of Russell's way of talking: probably it was. But it was certainly a surprising criticism to be made of Russell by Keynes. For Russell at least recognized, the moment the war broke out in August 1914, that a lot of his previous ideas were wrong, and that men were not so rational as he had believed. He radically altered his way of thinking and his way of life accordingly. But for Keynes and some of his friends in the 'Bloomsbury' group, the war meant no such crises of thinking or feeling. For Keynes himself it meant an interesting position at the Treasury, with exemption from military service. He obviously enjoyed the way the war had brought him up in the world, and had given him friends among important people, including Asquith when he was Prime Minister. Russell once asked Keynes how he could sympathize with conscientious objectors, and yet continue his work at the Treasury—which, according to Russell, consisted in showing how to kill Germans as cheaply as possible: 'the maximum slaughter at the minimum expense.' Keynes did not reply.

Though many of Keynes's Bloomsbury friends were conscientious objectors, they did not carry conscience so far as to go to prison for it; they secured exemption by such means as working on the land. They disliked the war, but did not bear the drudgery and opprobrium of direct anti-war agitation; they tried to ignore it, and continued to devote themselves to writing or painting or talking.

Their attitude can be not unfairly summed up by the story of the elegant young man who was accosted by an angry old lady in the street, and asked: 'Aren't you ashamed to be seen out of uniform, when other young men are fighting for civilization?'

'Madam,' he replied, '*I* am the civilization they are fighting for.'

This, most emphatically, was not Russell's attitude; though he would have had more justification than most men for adopting it.

It is true that the first effect of the war was to plunge him into a shock of despair and horror. A few nights after it began, he dined with Charles Sanger's wife at the Ship Restaurant, where everyone they met—including Eddie Marsh, Churchill's private secretary—was full of the joy of battle and predictions of early victory. Walking on the Embankment afterwards with Mrs Sanger, Russell said that he could not bear it; he talked of retiring and becoming a recluse. And the outbreak of the war always remained something of a dividing line for him. 'It is utter hell to be alive these days,' he said once, 'I wish I had died before 1914.'

Soon, however, his mood passed from passive despair to active agitation against the war, which first made him a well-known public figure.

One of the commonest charges of inconsistency against Russell is that he opposed the First World War but supported the Second. There is no doubt whatever that, in this case, his critics are wrong. Russell was quite entitled to say that a war was worse than being conquered by the Kaiser, but that being conquered by Hitler was worse than a war, because Russell never said that war was morally wrong under all circumstances. His opposition was not a matter of principle.

This is the main point of interconnection between his philosophy and his writings on human problems, and an essential key to understanding the latter. It must be remembered that, shortly before 1914, Russell had been convinced by Santayana that there are no such things as objective ethical

G

values. 'Good' and 'bad' merely expressed subjective likes and dislikes. It must also be remembered that Russell had stressed the limitations of what logic could do. All rational argument could only be hypothetical, of the form '*If* you want such and such a result, *then* you must do so-and-so'.

Russell therefore could not condemn war either on purely moral or on purely rational grounds. His discussion of this and every other political or social subject had to depend on a mixture of emotional propaganda (about ends) and logical or scientific argument (about means).

This curious combination of passion and dispassion explains why Russell was so easily misunderstood or misrepresented; and misunderstandings were increased because he himself did not always keep the above distinction clear, and he did not always keep strictly to his professional opinions as a philosopher. He constantly wrote as though 'good' and 'bad' had some objective meaning: faulty education, he said, could lead to 'a complete inversion of values', so that 'what is good is thought bad'. And he constantly used words which encouraged the mistaken belief that he was an old-fashioned rationalist who exaggerated the importance of reason. He wrote, for instance: 'I cannot doubt that, sooner or later, reason will conquer the blind impulses which now lead nations into war.'

By 'reason' here he must have meant something like 'self-control' or 'enlightened self-interest'; for his main position was that a bad impulse could only be overcome by encouraging a good impulse.

Of course it is a little unfair to confront a philosopher with a few sentences from his popular writings, and point out that they contradict the considered opinions in his professional work. Russell would doubtless say that, in the former, he used 'good' and 'bad' as convenient short descriptions easily understood by his readers; just as an astronomer off duty can talk about the 'sunrise' and the 'sunset', without being accused of not understanding Copernicus. But I think there is more than this kind of verbal inconsistency involved. I have always felt certain that Russell, at heart, never believed his official moral philosophy; and the result was an internal contradiction which he himself sometimes recognized but never solved. When he protested against the wholesale killing of young men, he did not merely mean that he had a subjective dislike of it; his real opinions came out clearly enough in the way he spoke and wrote and acted.

There is a tendency to assume that when Russell was writing books about things which ordinary people could understand, his work was on a lower level than in his mathematical philosophy. Russell did not think so himself: his political and social crusades involved the passionate effort of his whole being. The intellectual difficulties might not be the same, but there were the added difficulties of imaginative feeling and persuasion. From 1914 onwards he always felt that a purely academic life would not satisfy him.

He said afterwards: 'I have never been so wholehearted or so little troubled with hesitation in any work as in the pacifist work that I did during the war. For the first time I found something to do which involved my whole nature.' And so he flung himself into defiant propaganda against the full tide of war-time public opinion.

Thou shalt not follow a multitude to do evil . . .

A strong will is above all to be desired. . . .
To contend against every ill will that
pleaseth a company, to oppose the
cry of the multitude;
To drive the goodwill of princes before us
like chaff . . .

Russell was not pro-German. His dislike of the Kaiser and Prussian militarism dated back to his visit to Berlin in 1895. And he wrote that 'so far from hating England, I care for England more than for anything else except truth'. He said that Germany was more to blame for the war than the Allies, and that he wanted the Allies to win. But war was so great an evil that an inconclusive peace would be better than prolonging the struggle indefinitely.

Even so, in an article on the *Ethics of War*, he carefully distinguished different kinds of wars, and said some could be justified. A justifiable 'War of Colonization' was the defeat of the Red Indians by the American colonists, where the new settlers represented a superior civilization. 'If we are to judge by results,' said Russell, 'we cannot regret that such wars have taken place.' No argument could be more annoying to most pacifists and anti-imperialists: Russell's candour in stating it was a good example not only of the utilitarianism of his approach, but also of his gift for carrying intellectual integrity into a political discussion.

Among justifiable 'Wars of Principle', Russell instanced the Dutch at the time of Charles II. Discussing 'Wars of Self-Defence', seldom justified, he wrote:

'We cannot destroy Germany even by a complete military victory, nor conversely, could German destroy England, even if our Navy were sunk and London occupied by the Prussians. English civilization, the English language, English manufactures would still exist, and as a matter of practical politics it would be totally impossible for the Germans to establish a tyranny in this country.'

Amongst 'Wars of Prestige', always unjustified, Russell included the First World War. He said: 'When two dogs fight in the street, no one supposes that anything but instinct prompts them, or that they are inspired by high and noble ends. They fight merely because something angers them in each other's smells. What is true of dogs in the street is equally true of nations in the present war.'

All this must not be read with unconscious reference to the kind of Germany which emerged under Hitler. It is a sharp reminder of a past civilization to recall that, for Russell and others, it was simply unthinkable that any nation would exterminate or enslave a defeated enemy: and Russell afterwards justified his pacifism by saying that it was the First World War which led to the horrors of totalitarianism and the Second World War.

He prophesied in 1915 that, after a German defeat, 'The ordinary German . . . would resolve to be found better prepared next time, and would follow the advice of his militarists more faithfully'.

Russell naturally soon found himself working with other

pacifists, in spite of the difference between his views and orthodox pacifism. One of them was D. H. Lawrence, who went to stay with him at Cambridge. Long afterwards Keynes recalled how Russell had asked him to breakfast with Lawrence, and how most of the talking was done by himself and Russell. According to Keynes, Lawrence 'was morose from the outset and said very little, apart from indefinite expressions of irritable dissent. . . . Cambridge rationalism and cynicism, then at their height, were, of course, repulsive to him.'

Lawrence entered into a considerable correspondence with Russell, and it is characteristic of both that he did not bother to keep Russell's letters, while Russell kept Lawrence's. These reflected a growing and irreconcilable antagonism between Russell's intellectual precision, and Lawrence's emotionalism and distrust of democracy. (According to Russell, 'Lawrence was a Fascist before Fascism was invented'.) Lawrence appealed to Russell in vain to support a social revolution which would nationalize all industries 'in one fell blow', after which man could begin 'the adventure into the unexplored, the woman'. So Lawrence wrote to Russell 'Let us become strangers again'; and told him, rather oddly, that:

'You are simply full of repressed desires. . . . As a woman said to me, who had been to one of your meetings: "It seemed so strange, with his face looking so evil, to be talking about peace and love." '

Russell kept up his association, however, with other pacifists; and he joined the committee of the No Conscription Fellowship, or NCF, the main organization for pacifist propaganda.

Russell was the inspiration of the conscientious objectors on the intellectual side, writing and speaking and taking on humdrum jobs of journalism for the *Labour Leader*. He was also the main link between the NCF conscientious objectors, who incurred the odium of active anti-war propaganda, and the before-mentioned 'Bloomsbury' conscientious objectors, who found a haven during the war in the gatherings arranged by Lady Ottoline Morell—whose husband, Philip Morrell, championed the pacifists in Parliament as a Liberal MP.

Every Thursday she would invite these social outcasts to her home at 44 Bedford Square, where they would gather in the great double room on the first floor, with its soft lights and modernistic pictures and banks of flowers. Here they would talk over coffee and cigarettes, listen to chamber music, or dance in their pullovers and corduroy trousers. Russell did not dance. He sat and talked, the centre of an eager circle of listeners.

Still more remarkable were the house parties at Garsington Manor near Oxford, where some conscientious objectors secured exemption by doing some work on Philip Morrell's farm. The guests would spend most of their time in endless talks; occasionally they would vary the routine by going for walks.

While the others were talking, Ottoline Morrell used to delight in crocheting bedspreads in vividly contrasting colours— she gave a particularly garish one to D. H. Lawrence. Her own contributions to the discussions were few, but always direct and outspoken. Once she was sitting working on a bedspread, while Clive Bell and others were talking in their usual clever way, when Bell turned to her and said reproachfully: 'You're not listening, Ottoline'.

'It's not worth listening to,' she replied, going on with her crocheting.

Some people at Garsington also found Russell an uncomfortable conversationalist at times, with the quickness and relentlessness of his arguments. There is a reference in one of Lytton Strachey's letters to how 'Bertie worked his circular saw as usual. I've never been able to feel at ease with him, and I can only suppose that he dislikes me—*pourquoi?*'

Russell was a constant visitor to Garsington, together with most of the other pacifist intellectuals. Lytton Strachey lived there for a time, and so did Aldous Huxley. Garsington was a refuge for many young writers of talent whom Lady Ottoline helped and encouraged, and some of whom later wrote books criticising or lampooning her. There is a caricature of herself and a Garsington house party, for instance, in Aldous Huxley's *Crome Yellow*.*

* *Crome Yellow* also has a Professor to whom Huxley attributes, as serious sayings, some jokes made by Russell.

Russell's subsequent explanation of the way some writers attacked Lady Ottoline was that she had to be punished because she had been so good to them: 'People cannot bear to be under an obligation to anybody. They always malign them in order to reduce their obligation. It is a law of human nature.'

Another visitor to Garsington was Keynes. While Russell was the centre of attraction, Keynes would sit back quietly and contribute some occasional remarks in a soft voice. As an incongruous addition, Ottoline Morrell would also invite Mr Asquith, the Prime Minister, who delighted both in the witty conversation and the attractive feminine company always to be found at Garsington, and who was always treated informally. There was surely nowhere else in England where a new maid could have been heard ushering in two visitors with the announcement 'Mr Keynes and another gentleman'—the other gentleman being the Prime Minister.

There were other distinguished visitors as well. On one historic occasion, Lady Ottoline was having her living room painted a pillar box red, and then decided that it would look better with the panels picked out in gold. At the time she had with her Russell and Bishop Gore, the Bishop of Oxford. She insisted on them both helping with the painting, turning to Gore and saying 'Come on, Bishop, you've got your apron on'. So the two men painted side by side; and it is reported that Russell proved much better at it than the Bishop.

While Russell was acquiring new friends and admirers through his pacifist activities, he was also incurring the growing hostility of the Government and of his Cambridge colleagues.

Supporters of the war in Trinity often found themselves prickled and annoyed by his wit. Russell noticed that, when he dined in college, the other dons would avoid the table at which he sat; and A. E. Housman once remarked to E. H. Neville, the mathematician, that 'If I were the Prince of Peace, I would choose a less provocative Ambassador'. The gentle Lowes Dickinson, though as convinced a pacifist as Russell, never roused the same hostility among the Fellows of Kings.

The younger Fellows of Trinity believed in Russell's right to freedom of expression; but, as they were away fighting, they could not say so till afterwards. The older stay-at-home dons, as often so happened, were much more belligerent and intolerant; and, unhappily, the most intolerant among them was McTaggart.* They had their chance with the 'Everett Case'.

A conscientious objector, Ernest Everett, had been conscripted into the Army and then sentenced to two years' hard labour for disobeying orders. The NCF issued a leaflet protesting, and six men were arrested for distributing it. Whereupon Russell wrote a letter to *The Times*, saying that 'I wish to make it known that I am the author of this leaflet, and that, if anyone is to be prosecuted, I am the person primarily responsible'.

Russell was tried before the Lord Mayor at the Mansion House, on June 15, 1916, for 'statements likely to prejudice the recruiting and discipline of His Majesty's Forces'. The proceedings were brightened by the appearance of Lady Ottoline Morrell in a cashmere coat of many colours, and wearing a brilliant hat; she was most indignant, after she had found some steps to sit on, at being ordered to stand up because people must not 'lie about'.

Russell conducted his own defence, arguing—for instance—that 'The purpose of the leaflet is to make it known that a man is liable to two years' hard labour for refusing to obey discipline. Does this encourage a man to resist discipline?' His logic was so devastating that a report of his speech and of the court proceedings, published by the NCF, was suppressed by the Government. But Russell was found guilty and fined £100.

Thereupon the Trinity College Council unanimously decided, on July 11, 1916, that Russell should be dismissed from his Lectureship. In those days, as always, he was much more sensitive than he appeared on the surface; and he was sufficiently hurt by his dismissal to take his name 'off the books' of the college; that is, to sever his connection with it completely. The strain of bearing continual public hostility and unpopularity had probably put Russell himself into a rather prickly state, as well as prickling others. He remarked many years afterwards that 'All the dons in Trinity hated me': a statement for which I was

---

* An exception was G. E. Moore, who contributed the ironic proposal that chapel services should be banned in Trinity, since the precept 'Love your enemies' was obviously subversive.

unable to obtain complete confirmation from such dons as survived. (It was certainly not true of Hardy and James Ward, who had been one of Russell's philosophy tutors as an undergraduate.) In fact the general opinion, at least after the war, was that it was McTaggart who had forfeited respect by his behaviour towards Russell.

Russell continued with his pacifist propaganda: preparing for publication, under the title *Principles of Social Reconstruction*, a series of lectures delivered earlier in the year. In these he had put forward radical ideas not only about the war, but also about education, marriage, and other subjects on which I will discuss his views later.

One thing which had struck Russell particularly, at the beginning of the war, was that people in the streets seemed to be enjoying it. He commented on this to Robert Trevelyan, who suggested that he should read Bernard Hart on *The Psychology of Insanity*. Hart's theory was on Freudian lines, with a stress on unconscious impulses; and Russell realized that he himself had arrived at something like a Freudian theory independently of Freud. As noted earlier, he had already discovered the unconscious by finding that he could work on a problem, set it aside, and then find later that it had been solved in his mind. He decided that peace was impossible so long as such things as repressive systems of education gave people an unconscious impulse towards fighting and killing, and that everything in the social order had to be reconsidered and revised accordingly.

Lytton Strachey wrote one characteristic account of Russell's lectures: 'I dragged myself to that ghastly Caxton Hall yesterday, though I was rather nearer the grave than usual, and it was well worth it. It is splendid the way he sticks at nothing— Governments, religions, laws, property, even good form itself— down they go like ninepins—it is a charming sight! And then his constructive ideas are very grand. He puts it all together and builds it up, and plants it down solid and shining before one's mind. I don't believe there's anyone quite so formidable to be found just now upon this earth . . .'

So far as the war was concerned, Russell said that the wisest course for each side was to conclude peace at once on the best terms obtainable.

It was one thing to lecture and write a book on these lines; it was another to get it published in 1916. But at this stage Russell came into contact with Stanley Unwin, a publisher who was also a pacifist.

Unwin, later Sir Stanley Unwin and the doyen of British publishers, had acquired the firm of George Allen and Unwin early in July 1914. He took it over in conjunction with debenture holders, and at the beginning was only one of four directors.

He was so impressed by some of Russell's war-time articles that he wrote asking Russell if he had enough material for a book; and the *Principles of Social Reconstruction* arrived in reply. Unwin was delighted; the other three directors were all upset by the book, leaving Unwin in a minority of one. But he produced a wily piece of strategy, suggesting that the manuscript should go to Professor Muirhead, the editor of the 'Library of Philosophy', for a decision. Unwin's fellow directors were certain that Muirhead would turn the book down, and agreed. But Unwin had been certain that Muirhead would accept it, and he proved right. For Muirhead's report said in effect that he disagreed with almost everything in the book, but that it was of such outstanding importance that it ought to be published.

It is still of outstanding importance today.

The publication of the book was something of a landmark in Russell's career, because it was the first to show he could have a wide sale among ordinary readers. For the rest of his life he was not only a philosopher writing books for dons, but a prophet appealing to the people and pleading for human happiness. 'The war,' he wrote, 'has made me feel the terrific importance of being constructive, building up positive things . . . I do not want to remain a voice crying in the wilderness; I want to be a voice that is heard and answered, saying things men care to hear . . .'

The *Principles of Social Reconstruction* also began an association with Stanley Unwin which was important for Russell as well as for Unwin; and which continued, with occasional deviations to other publishers, for the rest of his career.

Unwin was a business man of a type more common in the nineteenth century, combining the highest moral principles with the hardest business sense. He was particularly known for his thoroughness in finding foreign markets for his books. He had served his publishing apprenticeship in Germany, and he made personal visits all over the world. The information gained from these journeys, a catalogue of meticulous detail about remote booksellers, was entered in a card index system by Unwin himself.

Russell already had a high professional reputation in Europe and America. But it was Unwin who had most to do with building up Russell's fame among ordinary readers abroad, making him by far the most widely read British philosopher in Germany, and turning him into a best-seller in such countries as India and Japan. There were times when, with the continual changes of fashion which characterize academic circles, other philosophers were admired more in Britain itself; but Russell's international reputation was always supreme.

It cannot be said, of course, that Russell's lasting philosophical achievements owed anything to any particular publisher. But, without Unwin, his popular writings would certainly not have found as widespread a public; and they in turn, by arousing interest in him as a man, encouraged the study of his technical work. Few ordinary people will take an interest in metaphysics except under the inspiration of a great teacher; and it was the fascination of Russell's personality that brought thousands of people all over the world, from Wang in China to Quine in America, to the study of philosophy. Thus Russell's intellectual progeny spread and multiplied everywhere, while those of Whitehead and Wittgenstein were more confined to select bands of disciples.

CHAPTER XI

The Prisoner of Brixton

IN the year 1916, however, international fame and the praise of posterity were of less practical importance for Russell than the problem of finding work after his dismissal from Trinity. He had been invited to lecture at Harvard, but the Foreign Office refused him a passport to go to America. He decided to fall back on public lecturing in Britain as a profession. But after preparing a course on 'The Philosophical Principles of Politics', he came up against a farcically stupid War Office order. He was told that he could lecture in inland towns like Manchester, but not in 'prohibited areas', which included practically all coastal towns. Theoretically the idea was that he or his hearers might be encouraged to send signals to German U-boats.

This was so obviously silly that Lloyd George was questioned on the subject in Parliament by Charles Trevelyan. He replied that Russell's speeches 'undoubtedly interfere with the prosecution of the war. . . . We had information from very reliable sources that Mr Bertrand Russell was about to engage in the delivery of a series of lectures which would interfere very seriously with the manning of the Army.'

To this Russell retorted: 'I can only earnestly hope that the Secret Service is less inaccurate as regards the Germans than it has proved to be where I am concerned.' And he asked why, if his lectures on Political Principles were really so pernicious, they should be permitted in Manchester.

It is really easy enough to understand how the Government should have seemed to lose their heads over Russell. They feared especially that his speeches might bring about strikes among armament workers. He was the one man in the pacifist movement whose name already carried prestige; and the fact that he himself was above military age proved that his attitude was disinterested. His support was thus invaluable for such young men, completely unknown at the time, as Fenner Brockway and Clifford Allen. He acted as their champion, their counsellor, and their comrade.

Clifford Allen, who for a time became Russell's intimate friend, was the man who really turned the conscientious objectors into a coherent body. He was an admirable chairman, with a grasp of all the problems facing different young pacifists, and a very good public speaker. His political ambitions were partly thwarted by his tuberculosis, made worse by long periods of imprisonment as a conscientious objector—he refused alternative service, like working on the land. Nobody understood his talents and his difficulties, nor did more to encourage him as a young man, than Russell.

Something of the warmth of human affection in Russell's nature, hidden behind the dry precision of his wit in public, is reflected in a letter he wrote to Allen, just after he had been released from a prison sentence:

My dear Allen,
The news of your release is an unspeakable joy. I cannot tell you how profoundly glad I am. I will come to see you the first moment the doctor permits . . .
My dear Allen, your time in prison has been terrible for all who care for you. . . . There is much to follow before very long—rest happily and get well—things are ripening, and you will have wonderful things to do later on.

B.R.

In moments of depression, Russell would cheer up his young friends by remarking 'This is history, and we are helping to make it'. When the Treasurer of the NCF argued that 'We must not manufacture consciences', Russell brushed aside all hesitations by exclaiming 'Good heavens, I've been doing that for years!'

Once he went with Clifford Allen to an unsuccessful lunch with Lloyd George—they wanted to talk to him about treating conscientious objectors better, and Lloyd George said that during lunch was the only time he could spare. Russell reluctantly accepted Lloyd George's hospitality, but refused to smoke or drink. (He was no longer a total abstainer. When George V announced that he was giving up drink for the duration of the war, Russell characteristically decided to do the opposite and give up teetotalism.)

Fenner Brockway, subsequently a leading Socialist MP, summed up his recollections of Russell in the NCF days by saying that 'he had not the conceit and showmanship of Shaw, but he had the same love of tearing down false idols'. According to Brockway, 'Russell was delightful. . . . Full of the spirit of fun, like some irrepressible but clever Puck. . . . He was very hard up during this period, and arrived late for committees more than once because he hadn't any coppers to pay for a bus—but perhaps this was sometimes due to his forgetfulness of mundane things.' Once it turned out that Russell had met a beggar with a hard-luck story when leaving for a meeting, had turned out his pockets, and then had to walk.

Russell was sometimes known to the committee of the NCF as Mephistopheles or 'Mephisto', because of his high cheek bones, narrow face, and the way he enjoyed all their different plots and plans to hoodwink the police.

As they feared that the NCF might be suppressed, they had a duplicate underground organization, complete with an elaborate system of code names. Once Fenner Brockway left a brief case containing all their secret plans in a taxi, and it was handed in to a police station. When he broke the news to a committee meeting, Russell said 'I move that we adjourn to Scotland Yard —we may as well save the police the trouble of arresting us.' But the bag containing the papers was recovered intact, one of the committee having a brother who was a high police official.

The NCF had an extra office, and one day they were meeting there when they got word that their main office was being raided by the police. Six detectives were outside in the street. Russell was delighted at the excitement. 'They'll be looking for us,' he said, 'let's get arrested in the house of a Lord.' So he crowded the committee into three taxis and took them to his brother Frank's home in Gordon Square, gleefully speculating about what Earl Russell would say if the police came to arrest his young brother there. Russell could scarcely conceal his disappointment when they found the Earl was not at home, and when the police never arrived.

The trouble which eventually landed Russell in prison was the result of an article in *The Tribunal*, the NCF weekly. Russell was always ready to write anything for the NCF, signed or unsigned. He had decided towards the end of 1917 to withdraw from active pacifist agitation, believing that by then it was more important to wait and work for a constructive peace after the war was over. But, when *The Tribunal* needed a front page article in a hurry, Russell was willing to oblige as usual. He wrote:

'Unless peace comes soon there will be starvation throughout Europe. . . . Men will fight each other for possession of the bare necessities of life. . . .

'The American garrison, which will by that time be occupying England and France, whether or not they will prove efficient against the Germans, will no doubt be capable of intimidating strikers, an occupation to which the American Army is accustomed when at home.

'I do not say that these thoughts are in the mind of the Government. All the evidence tends to show that there are no thoughts whatever in their minds, and that they live from hand to mouth consoling themselves with ignorance and sentimental twaddle . . .'

The comment on the American Army certainly seems mild in comparison with some things which have been said freely about Americans since. The reference to strike-breaking was in fact based on an official Congressional Report. It is hard to say whether Whitehall was more displeased by Russell's disparagement of the Americans or by his disparagement of Whitehall. But the former gave an excuse for action to work off any irritation caused by the latter.

The article appeared on January 3, 1918. About a month afterwards, two detectives visited Russell one morning and found him in his bath. They asked if he had written the article, and Russell confirmed that he had.

Russell was summoned for trial at Bow Street, where the court was crowded with a distinguished gathering of his friends. The prosecuting counsel read out extracts from Russell's article in *The Tribunal*, but did not quite get the effect he intended. He came to the passage ' . . . I do not say that these thoughts are in the mind of the Government. All the evidence tends to show that there are no thoughts whatever in their minds. . . .' Russell's friends in the Court proceeded to roar with laughter. The Prosecutor, frowning severely, read out the passage a second time in an even more reproving voice: and everyone laughed again. But the laughter in court could not save Russell; and the Magistrate, Sir John Dickinson, sentenced him to six months' imprisonment in the Second Division.

Dickinson's comment on Russell, in passing sentence, was: 'Mr Russell seems to have lost all sense of decency and fairness, and has gone out of his way to insult by a deliberate and designed sneer the army of a great nation which is closely allied to us. . . . The offence is a very despicable one.'

Russell's comment on Dickinson, in a letter written the next day, was: 'The magistrate was incredibly fierce; I have never encountered such a blast of vitriolic hatred. He would have had me hanged, drawn and quartered if he could.'

Another description of the proceedings is also preserved, in a letter written by Lytton Strachey: 'It is really infamous . . . and generally wicked and disgusting. The spectacle of a louse like Sir John Dickinson rating Bertie for immorality and sending him to prison! . . . James [Strachey] and I came away with our teeth chattering with fury. It makes one abandon hope that such monstrosities should occur.' But Russell himself, in later retrospect about the war years, said that 'I cannot complain about the way the authorities treated me: I did not make any effort at all to be conciliatory. I made them do something about me.'

An Appeal was heard, but the sentence of six months' imprisonment was upheld. And so, in May 1918, Russell was taken by taxi to Brixton Prison—he regretted afterwards that he had missed the experience of riding in a Black Maria—and he went down on the Brixton Register as *Prisoner* No. 2917, *Name:* Russell, B.

Thanks to the representations of Gilbert Murray and others, Russell was transferred on his Appeal to the First Division, where his time was his own for reading and writing: and Frank Russell bullied the authorities into letting his brother have everything he wanted. His cell was furnished comfortably with a desk, chair, bed and carpet by Frank's wife Elizabeth—author of *Elizabeth and her German Garden*—and he was always well supplied with books and flowers.

Russell had a cell larger than usual, for which he had to pay a rent of 2*s* 6*d* a week. One of his first acts was to go to the Governor of the prison, a worthy retired soldier named Captain Haynes, and ask solemnly what the penalty was for falling behind with the rent, remarking that if it was eviction he would not pay a penny.

A fellow convict was assigned to keeping the cell cleaned out. He delighted Russell by telling him that he had tried all the prisons, and 'Brixton's the best in London'. Of his fellow prisoners, Russell said that 'Life here is just like life on an ocean liner; one is cooped up with a number of average human beings, unable to escape except into one's own stateroom. I see no sign that they are worse than the average, except that they probably have less willpower, if one can judge by their faces. . . .'

One of the warders told Russell proudly that he was a member of the ILP, and that his branch had passed a resolution calling for Russell's release.

Russell was allowed to keep his light on till ten at night, instead of eight. Typically methodical, he arranged his daily routine in prison so that he did four hours' philosophical writing, four hours' philosophical reading, and four hours' general reading—the latter ranging from Voltaire to Tchekov, from the history of the French Revolution to travel books about the Amazon and Tibet, and with some thrillers thrown in.

The main deprivations which Russell felt were lack of tobacco—almost the only break, apart from illness, in over sixty years continuous smoking—and missing his friends. He ate chocolate instead of smoking; and, being allowed three visitors together every week, carefully arranged his friends in trios who would mix well together.

Going to see Russell in prison provided some memorable ex-

H

periences for those who had this rare privilege. On one occasion Frank Russell, Lady Ottoline Morrell, and Gladys Rinder, an official of the NCF, had agreed to meet on the Embankment to take a tram down to Brixton. The first to join Miss Rinder at the rendezvous was Lady Ottoline, wearing a superb dress in three tiers of colourful taffeta, decked on top with silver trimming, and wearing her Marie Antoinette pearl necklace. Next came Frank in a top hat and frock coat. They mounted to the top of the tram amid the fascinated gaze of all the other passengers, who listened enthralled while Frank talked at the top of his voice about his own experiences when he had gone to prison for bigamy.

Another recollection was that of T. S. Eliot, who remembered going to see Russell with Frank Russell and Desmond McCarthy. They sat talking in an arbour in the prison yard, 'rather like in a Pullman car', with the guard watching them from a carefully calculated distance.

Russell would prepare for these visits by making long lists of things he wanted to ask and talk about, but when his friends actually arrived he was so excited that he usually forgot what he was going to say. He wrote to Gladys Rinder: 'Remember what one wants is news of one's friends. I get politics from the papers and can manufacture sentiments and jokes on the premises, but news I can only get through visits and letters.' Miss Rinder responded with a letter so full of personal gossip, about people referred to by initials, that the Governor held it up, suspecting that the initials might represent some complicated code.

Russell's philosophical work in prison consisted of his *Introduction to Mathematical Philosophy*, a long review of Dewey's *Essays in Experimental Logic*, and his first preliminary reading along the line of inquiry which led to his *Analysis of Mind*. The prison Governor had to censor any manuscript sent out; and Captain Haynes was sorely tried by the *Introduction to Mathematical Philosophy*, a book which is by no means such easy reading as the word 'Introduction' might suggest. The Governor, floundering hopelessly from the start, said he would be satisfied if Russell would give a personal assurance that the work contained nothing subversive. It was understood among pacifists that they would always do everything they could to make things difficult for those in authority. But Russell decided that compulsory mathematical philosophy would be carrying this principle too far, and he gave the assurance.

It is hard not to have some sympathy for Captain Haynes, who never knew quite what to make of his distinguished guest. Once Desmond McCarthy sent him a message that Russell was longing to have a canary in a cage; and the Governor summoned Russell and asked if this was the case. 'No,' said Russell, 'what I would really like is an orang-outang'. (Because, as he explained in a letter to Gladys Rinder, he hoped it 'would throw light on Mind in its origin and in the Cabinet'.) Whenever Russell saw the Governor he would make jokes to try and make him laugh, so that he could amuse himself watching the Governor's struggles to keep a straight face.

One suspects that, for all his levity, Russell felt his imprisonment deeply; just as he had felt his dismissal from Trinity. Early on he had written 'Days have succeeded each other monotonously but not very disagreeably. I believe I missed my vocation by not being a monk in a contemplative order.' But something of his real feelings were revealed in one of the letters which he smuggled out of prison:

'Oh, won't it be glorious to be able to walk across fields and see the horizon and talk freely and be with friends . . . I am settled into this existence, and fairly placid, but only because it will end soon. All kinds of delights float before my mind—above all Talk, *Talk*, TALK. I never knew how one could hunger for it—the time here has done me good, I have read a lot and thought a lot and grown *collected*, I am bursting with energy—but I do long for civilization and civilized talk—and I long for the SEA and wildness and wind—I hate being all tidy like a book in a library where no one reads—prison is horribly like that—imagine if you knew you were a delicious book, and some . . . millionaire bought you and bound you uniform with a lot of others and stuck you up in a shelf behind glass, where you merely illustrated the completeness of his system—and no anarchist was allowed to read you—that is what one feels like—but soon now one will be able to insist on being read.'

After Russell's release, in September 1918, he wrote to Clifford Allen that 'I came out from prison with a curious over-sensitiveness which made me think everyone disliked me'. But he added that it was wearing off fast, and that he would soon be normal and robust. This prediction was happily fulfilled, and I cannot end this chapter better than by quoting something which Russell wrote shortly before he left prison, and which remains one of the finest testaments to the freedom of the human spirit:

'There never was such a place as prison for crowding images —one after another they come upon me—early morning in the Alps, with the snow of aromatic pines and high pastures glistening with dew—the lake of Garda as one first sees it coming down out of the mountains, just a glimpse, far, far below, dancing and gleaming in the sunlight like the eyes of a laughing, mad, Spanish gypsy—thunderstorm in the Mediterranean, with a dark violet sea, and the mountains of Corsica in sunshine far beyond—the Scilly Isles in the setting sun, enchanted and unreal, so that you think they must have vanished before you can reach them, looking like the islands of the Blest, not to be achieved during this mortal life—the smell of the bog myrtle in Skye—memories of sunsets long ago, all the way back into childhood—I can hear now as if it were yesterday the street cry of a man in Paris selling *"artichaux verts et beaux"*, twenty-four years ago almost to a day. Quite apart from childhood I remember a certain row of larches after rain, with a raindrop at the end of every twig—and I can hear the wind in the treetops in midnight woods on summer nights—everything free or beautiful comes into my thoughts sooner or later.

'What is the use of shutting up the body, seeing that the mind remains free? And outside my own life, I have lived, while I have been here, in Brazil and China and Tibet, in the French Revolution. . . . In such adventures I have forgotten the prison in which the world is keeping itself at the moment: I am free, and the world shall be.'

CHAPTER XII

The Analysis of Mind

AFTER he came out of prison Russell occupied himself, as he put it, in 'crawling back into the atmosphere of philosophy'. His first task was a series of lectures in London, eventually repeated in Peking and published as *The Analysis of Mind*, which he had begun to work on in Brixton.

These lectures had a curious origin. Though Russell had inherited enough money to have a small independent income, he had gradually over the years given almost all his money away. He had, for instance, paid for a studentship at the London School of Economics, once held by Tom Jones, later famous as the secretary to four Prime Ministers.

Russell had shown by his *Principles of Social Reconstruction* that he could earn his living as a popular writer; but, since the 'military age' for conscription had now been raised, he could be called up and put in prison again unless he qualified for exemption as a 'teacher'. Towards the end of 1918, some of his friends therefore started a private fund to give Russell enough to live on for three years, devoting himself to philosophical research and lecturing; the first result being the fee paid for his lectures on *The Analysis of Mind*.* But as soon as the war was over Russell asked for the fund to be closed, saying he would prefer to earn his living again by writing. In fact by the end of 1919 he was lending £40 to Clifford Allen, with whom he shared a flat in Battersea for some time. The £40 was more than Allen had asked for, but Russell explained 'I know one always under-estimates one's needs under such circumstances, at least I do';

---

* There is a certain curiosity value about the original list of subscribers: Charles Sanger, Wildon Carr, Lucy Silcox, Siegfried Sassoon, Charles Trevelyan, Lady Ottoline Morrell, Prince Antonio Bibesco, J. M. Keynes, Rendel Harris, Miss J. E. Norton, James Ward.

and he said that 'I always have money to spare except in the month of December, when I pay insurance premiums'.

We have seen how, in prison, Russell had proclaimed the freedom of the human spirit, and the power of mind to move unfettered even though the body was confined: 'I am free, and the world shall be.' Simultaneously he was working towards a philosophy whereby not only were the thoughts of his mind hardly free, but his mind did not even exist in the commonly accepted sense, and any difference in kind between mind and matter was declared illusory.

He told Clifford Allen in April 1919 that 'the gods, seeing I was engaged in proving there is no such thing as mind, have sent me such a cold as to give me, for the present, personal proof of the truth of my thesis'.

Put more precisely, his thesis in *The Analysis of Mind* was that 'Matter is not so material and mind not so mental as is generally supposed'. . . . 'Both mind and matter seem to be composite, and the stuff of which they are compounded lies in a sense between the two, in a sense above them both, like a common ancestor.'

This kind of philosophy, developed in America as 'neutral monism', owed a great deal to William James. Russell's affirmation of it at this time might be cited as an example of something he often insisted on: a complete distinction between his technical views as a philosopher and his political and every-day writings. There was no question of any logical contradiction. It is quite permissible to use the word 'free' differently in a philosophical and a rhetorical sense, since nobody knows exactly what the word means anyhow. And even a neutral monist can hardly avoid using the words 'mind' and 'body' in ordinary speech, with the result that ordinary readers interpret them in the ordinary way.

Ordinary speech, according to Russell, was the root of misunderstanding. When we say 'the table is brown' we assume there must be a table of substance, but all we really know is that there is a sense datum—a brown patch of colour. When we say 'I think', we assume there must be an 'I' which thinks, whereas all we know is that there is an experience of thinking. Russell wrote that 'the subject . . . '—that is, in his case, Russell himself—'appears to be a logical fiction, like mathematical points and instants. It is introduced, not because observation reveals it, but because it is linguistically convenient and apparently demanded by grammar.' As he put it in his lectures on 'Logical Atomism', delivered early in 1918, 'a person is a certain series of experiences'.

Russell's object in *The Analysis of Mind*, was, he said, 'to subject Mind to the same kind of analysis as I applied to Matter in *Our Knowledge of the External World*'. In this he had treated a piece of 'matter' as a logical construction based on 'sense data'. He now decided that mind was a logical construction based on 'sensations', and decided that sensations and sense data were the same.

This latter step was the most difficult one for him in reaching neutral monism.

Russell had insisted in *Our Knowledge of the External World* on a distinction between '(1) our sensation, which is a mental event consisting of our being aware of a sensible object and (2) the sensible object of which we are aware in sensation'. Abandoning this distinction meant abandoning part of his fighting faith in refuting Berkeley and ridiculing Bergson. His case against them was that they had muddled up subject and object in various ways. Some idealists had argued in effect that, since all we know about a table can only be the idea of it in our minds, the table itself is somehow mental. And Russell had written that 'Only one who has never clearly distinguished subject and object can accept Bergson's "intuitionism" '.

To abandon the distinction was characteristic of the way Russell, once he gave all his thought to a line of inquiry, would carry it through however repugnant the conclusion was to his original preconceptions.

It seems that he was brought to reconsider the whole question, arriving at neutral monism and the identification of sensation and sense datum, by contemporary tendencies in psychology and physics. Russell was well versed in Dr Watson and the Behaviourists, with their view that human beings are all body and no mind; for instance, that thoughts are merely slight incipient motor reactions in the larynx. Meanwhile Einstein was altering the traditional view of mass and matter. Thus, according to the psychology and physics of the time, mind was becoming more dependent on matter, while matter was becoming less material; and neutral monism appeared as a natural meeting point of these trends.

Having 'constructed' physical objects from sense data, and having decided that a brown sense datum and the sensation of seeing brown were the same, Russell was on the way to showing that minds were constructions using the same ingredients as physical objects. He said that 'physics, in so far as it is an empirical science, not a logical fantasy, is concerned with particulars of just the same sort as those which psychology considers under the name of sensations'. *

There followed a typical piece of patient painstaking philosophizing, of the kind which often passed notice behind the glitter of Russell's wit. If the only function of mind was to have sensations, if consciousness simply consisted of seeing things and hearing things and touching things, then out and out neutral monism could be established. Both mind and matter could be represented as constructions from sensations (or sense data), grouped in different ways. But minds also have beliefs, desires, memories and so on. If all these were also constructions from sensations, then exact neutral monism could be triumphantly established. Some philosophers might have assumed that this must be possible, simply because of an instinct that such a strikingly neat and symmetrical philosophy must be true.

Wittgenstein as a young man, for instance, would at times be carried away by a theory in this way, not stopping to examine in detail whether it would work. In *The Analysis of Mind*, however, Russell proceeded to consider in turn these additional functions of mind, to see if neutral monism could account for them. He had a great deal of success, but he did not let his preconceived wishes delude him into thinking he had succeeded completely: so instead of a sweeping and satisfying generalization he was left with an untidy theory which had loose ends sticking out, a lack of symmetry, and a confession that he himself was not always satisfied with his conclusions.

* As he explained in a lecture room, the class of all the appearances of one chair, as seen by all the different people in the room, gave something belonging to physics; the class of the appearances of all the different chairs, from a given perspective, gave something belonging to psychology.

Some of the additional functions of mind he explained on Behaviourist lines. He decided, for instance, that desire was a behaviour cycle stimulated by discomfort. 'The primitive non-cognitive element in desire seems to be a push, not a pull, an impulsion away from the actual, rather than an attraction towards the ideal.'

When Russell came to belief, memory and imagination, however, he had more difficulty: and though he reduced them to 'complexes of sensations', he revolted from the Behaviourists by admitting introspection and mental images. 'The Behaviourists,' he wrote in a letter, 'say images are small movements of the tongue and throat silently pronouncing words. This is obviously ROT.'

Russell was thus left with two irreducible elements of mind: sensations and images. But images did not differ intrinsically from sensations; just as *sensibilia* (if any) were 'analogous in their nature' to sensations. Mind was a construction from images and sensations, matter a construction from sensations and perhaps *sensibilia*; with sensations as the 'intersection of mind and matter'.

To this extent, therefore, Russell had succeeded in eliminating intrinsic differences between mind and matter; but another kind of dualism had now crept in. Desire might be a behaviour cycle; but it was necessary to explain why the behaviour of living beings should be distinguished by a capacity for learning from experience. Russell had to explain why a burnt child should dread the fire, and behave accordingly, while a burnt piece of toast did not. His answer was that psychical causal laws were different from physical causal laws. The essential difference was that in psychology 'the causal unit is not a single event, but two or more events'—one of the events (in the above instance, the previous burning of the child) having ceased to exist.

Russell would obviously have liked to show that psychical laws could be reduced, with greater knowledge, to physical ones; but with characteristic candour he admitted that he did not know yet whether this could be done. And so a fundamental dualism remained, perhaps even more uncomfortable to philosophical common sense than the original dualism between mind and matter.

Russell's philosophy of 'neutral monism' was continually developed during the following years; I will put forward here three doubts and suggestions, all on a common sense basis, concerning his position in *The Analysis of Mind*.

In the first place, since he did not succeed in arriving at an out-and-out neutral monism, I think he might have reconsidered some of the steps he made in the attempt to get there. In particular, there is his analysis of desire. I do not think what he says can be refuted. But I have a strong prejudice that, in explaining why Sir Edmund Hillary climbed Mount Everest, it is better to say that he wanted to get to the top, rather than that he felt discomfort at the bottom.

(Later Russell was inclined to agree that his theory of desire in *The Analysis of Mind* might be inadequate; but he would not agree that an adequate theory demanded the reinstatement of the Ego.)

Secondly, Russell's main reason for denying the self was that he could find no empirical evidence for it. Thoughts involved an experience of thinking, but not of an 'I' which thinks. This argument lost some of its force in itself when he became more and more ready to recognize and even emphasize the limits of empiricism.

Thirdly, it must be admitted that Russell's very failure to establish symmetry between mind and matter had one great virtue. It led him to reject psycho-psychical parallelism; and thus to believe that mind can interact with matter, and *vice versa*. Neutral monism made it much easier to accept this commonsense view of the 'mind-body' problem, which I think is obviously right, and obviously nearer the truth than most philosophies.

I must also make some further mention here of Russell's lectures on 'Logical Atomism', referred to earlier. They were based on ideas originating from his discussions on logic with Wittgenstein. During the war Wittgenstein completed his own *Tractatus Logico-Philosophicus* while serving in the Austrian Army; and towards the end of 1919 Russell and Wittgenstein met at the Hague to discuss this book, first published in German and then in an English translation in 1922. *

Russell wrote an Introduction to it which infuriated Wittgenstein, who said it misrepresented him; so far as I know, Wittgenstein always repudiated any explanation of his views put forward by anyone else. In fact, there is some doubt about the extent to which he could explain them himself.

The most brilliant disciple of Russell and Wittgenstein, whose own original work was cut short by a tragically early death, was Frank Ramsey. On one occasion he grew impatient with the endless arguments in Cambridge about the interpretation of the *Tractatus*, and decided to go to Austria, where Wittgenstein had retired for some years, and ask him directly what he meant by certain of the more obscure passages. He was somewhat disconcerted when Wittgenstein replied that he could not remember.

In the circumstances, I will not attempt to write anything here about the *Tractatus*, in spite of its very great importance. I will simply mention what I think was the most important idea which Wittgenstein shared with Russell at this time, and which I think must undoubtedly be attributed to Russell, since its origin can be found in *Principia Mathematica* and earlier.

This is the emphasis on *structure*. One example, previously mentioned, is the theory about a sentence having the same structure as the reality which it describes. But the idea is of wider importance than this. To quote from Russell's *Introduction to Mathematical Philosophy*:

'It is often said . . . that phenomena [or "appearances"] are subjective, but are caused by things in themselves. . . . Where such hypotheses are made, it is generally supposed that we can know very little about the objective counterparts. In actual fact, however, if the hypotheses as stated were correct, the objective counterparts would form a world having the same structure as the phenomenal world, and allowing us to infer from phenomena the truth of all propositions that can be stated in abstract terms, and are known to be true of phenomena.'

* Since it has been stated by one writer that Russell was responsible for the translation, it is worth putting on record that he had nothing to do with it. But it is undeniable that the mistakes made in it, which materially increased the book's unintelligibility for English readers, helped to increase Wittgenstein's reputation for profundity.

This idea was not so important from the point of view of Russell's philosophy at the time; but it became of great importance on reverting to the ordinary view of an external world which causes our perceptions. Such knowledge as we have from our perceptions is knowledge of its structure, only expressible in abstract mathematical formulae. Here again we are in the fascinating realm where philosophy and science meet. For modern science, after agreeing with Russell in trying to eliminate the kind of unobservable entities cut out by Occam's Razor, also agreed with him that knowledge of structure is what remains.

The ordinary reader, to satisfy himself on this point, need only notice how often Eddington quoted the passage from Russell given above. For another easily accessible example of the importance of structure for scientists, the reader may also refer to Schrödinger's *Science and Humanism*. In this Schrödinger argues that individuality is determined by structure, not by identity of matter. To revert, for instance, to my own previous illustration, we might say that Churchill as a young man and Churchill as an elder statesman were distinguished by a certain similarity of structure.

CHAPTER XIII

A Visit to Bolshevism

LEFT-WING thought in Britain, between the First and Second World Wars, was marked by two major aberrations. The first was the conviction that a Second World War would mean the end of Western civilization, and that any attempt at defence was useless. The second was a benign belief that anybody who thought the leaders of Soviet Russia were ruthless totalitarians must be a Tory reactionary. The prevalence of the first error nearly led to the victory of Hitler in 1940. The second nearly lost the peace in the years after 1945.

Russell cannot be acquitted of the first mistake, as we shall discover later. But he was remarkably free from the second, and was almost unique among British radicals in facing the truth about Russia.

The First World War helped to change Russell from a Liberal to a Socialist—mainly because of the argument that capitalism leads to wars. He declared, like the Marxists, that 'the existing capitalist system is doomed'. But when Russell advocated Socialism at this time he meant Guild Socialism, or Syndicalism; he wanted industries to be run by the men working in them, not by the Government. Today a Socialist is somebody who rejoices in increasing the sphere of operations of the state. Russell thought that some of the state's powers had to be increased, but looked on this as a necessary evil. He confessed to a 'temperamental leaning to anarchism'; and described 'the excessive power of the state' as 'one of the chief causes of misery in the modern world'. (After all, the main activity of the state in these years was making war.) He predicted correctly that nationalization, or substituting the state for the private employer, would leave the individual workman with 'almost as little control over his work as he has at present'.

In a lecture in Manchester in 1916, on 'Pitfalls in Socialism', Russell showed again his gift for accurate prophecy. The fundamental defect in State Socialism was that it believed reform possible by merely altering the machinery; but nationalization would not remove evils in industry without some corresponding change in outlook.

The power of the official, said Russell, 'is a great and growing danger in the modern state. . . . Love of power . . . is an extremely dangerous motive, because the only sure proof of power consists in preventing others from doing what they wish to do'.

Nowadays, unhappily, one only associates such criticisms of state bureaucracy with the opponents of Socialism; but forty years ago there were many other Guild Socialists who thought the same as Russell. Even Marxists had, as an ultimate ideal, the 'withering away' of the state. It was uncritical admiration for Soviet Russia which convinced left-wing intellectuals that State Socialism was the only kind of Socialism which counted. The state in Russia certainly showed no signs of withering away, and British Socialists assumed that Russia must be right. Thus nationalization, which even according to Marxist theory was only a means to an end, was exalted into an end in itself.

It is true that Russell, like other Socialists, began by greeting the Russian Revolution with enthusiasm. In January 1918, he wrote to Clifford Allen that 'The world is damnable. Lenin and Trotsky are the only bright spots.' And soon afterwards he was writing: 'The world grows more full of hope every day. The Bolsheviks delight me; I easily pardon their sacking the Constituent Assembly, if it at all resembled our House of Commons. . . . How they succeed! . . . They have stirred revolt in Austria and Germany; they have even made some English people think—but they will never make America think.'

Where Russell differed from other progressives was that he did not go on admiring Soviet Russia after he had seen it.

His visit came in the summer of 1920, when he was invited to go as an unofficial member of a Labour Delegation which included Clifford Allen, Dr Haden-Guest (later Lord Haden-

Guest), and Mrs Philip Snowden. They were in Russia from May 19 to June 16, and arrived in such a state of enthusiasm that, when they first saw a Soviet flag on reaching the frontier, the delegates spontaneously burst into song with the *Internationale* and *The Red Flag*.

Russell recalled afterwards that 'I was prepared for physical hardship, discomfort, dirt and hunger, to be made bearable by a splendid hope for mankind. Our communist comrades, no doubt rightly, did not judge us worthy of such treatment. After crossing the frontier we had two feasts and a good breakfast, several first-class cigars, and a night in a sumptuous bedroom of a palace where all the luxury of the *ancien régime* has been preserved.'

Sometimes, however, conditions were not so luxurious. Russell was amused to find that the trade unionists with him were much more upset than himself when they found bugs in hotel beds. He ascribed his immunity from being bitten to the fact that his blood was so full of nicotine.

The delegation travelled in special trains decorated with red bunting, green branches of trees, and copious mottoes about the Social Revolution and the proletarians of the world. At their first public reception the *Internationale* was played no less than seventeen times, to greet each important new arrival and to round off every speech. There was some lighter relief when Mrs Snowden, relaxing her temperance principles in honour of her hosts, drank enough vodka to show some amorous leanings towards the surprised Haden-Guest.

One night they were joined at the Opera by Trotsky, as a victorious Army leader on a visit from the Polish front. When introduced to a conscientious objector from the delegation, he remarked 'We can have nobody *here* who preaches peace and wants to stop the war'. But later Trotsky relaxed and, during the playing of a tender love scene on the stage, leant across to Mrs Snowden and remarked '*There* is the great international language'.

Russell recorded this account of Trotsky at the time: 'Very Napoleonic impression. Bright eyes, military bearing, lightning intelligence, magnetic personality. Exceedingly good looking, which surprised me. Would be irresistible to women, and an

agreeable lover while his passion lasted. I felt a vein of gay good
humour so long as he was not crossed in any way. Ruthless, not
cruel. Admirable wavy hair. Vanity even greater than love of
power; the vanity of an artist or actor.'

The delegation's journeys included a trip down the Volga
from Nijni-Novgorod. The nights were bitterly cold, and
Clifford Allen nearly died from pneumonia and pleurisy.
Russell wrote a description of the voyage—published in part in
The Problem of China—which he considered his best piece of
prose writing.

Not being an official delegate, Russell could miss some of the
functions and meet ordinary people in the streets and villages.
(He found some Russians who had been prisoners of war in
Germany, and to whom he could talk in German.) He tried to
learn such things as the procedure for buying an umbrella at the
Soviet Stores in Moscow, 'which proved as difficult as fathoming
the ultimate mysteries'. He saw the long queues of tired women
waiting patiently outside the Government bread shops for their
ration of black bread. Like the rest of the delegation, he was
appalled at the poverty and misery: Mrs Snowden recalled afterwards that, though they had all deliberately gone in their oldest
clothes, the Russians thought they were 'attired like princes',
turning the delegates round to admire them, and patting and
stroking their coats and dresses.

But Russell noticed that there was no drunkenness, 'or at any
rate so little that none of us ever saw a sign of it', and also
'infinitely less' prostitution in Moscow than in any other
capital city. Women were safer from molestation than anywhere
else in the world. 'The whole impression,' he said, 'is one of
virtuous, well-ordered activity.'

Russell came to the conclusion, in fact, that the Bolsheviks
were rather like the Puritans. The comparison was perhaps a
little unfair to the latter: but it must be remembered that Russell
had all the hatred of the Puritans which is only possible for a
man who was a Puritan himself. 'The Soviet form of Government,' he said, 'is almost exactly the same, down to the
minutest particular, as the form of Government established in
England by Cromwell in the seventeenth century.' Both
belonged to a somewhat similar stage in economic development,

with a feudal system in decay, a middle class gradually rising, and a population which was mostly illiterate. And the Red Army was the equivalent of Cromwell's Army of Saints, led by men chosen for the strength of their conviction in a creed.

Russell had an interview in the Kremlin with Lenin, who said that he wanted to see a Labour Government in London, and wanted British Communists to work for it, but simply so that the futility of Parliamentarianism might be exposed. When Russell said it might be possible to achieve Socialism in England without bloodshed, Lenin 'waved aside the suggestion as fantastic'. Lenin obviously had no idea that it was the attitude of British workers which had stopped an outright war against Soviet Russia.

Russell found Lenin a great contrast to Trotsky: 'Nothing in his manner or bearing suggests the man who has power. He looks at his visitor very close, and screws up one eye.'

Many of the delegates left Russia in a mood of bitter disappointment and disillusionment. Mrs Snowden reported one of them as saying that 'There is practically no Socialism in Russia worthy of the name, and the people are utterly wretched'. She herself wrote frankly of 'the misery the unhappy people of Russia endure'. But other delegates, when they came home to receive rapturous welcomes from mass meetings eager to hear praise of Russia, made their reports glow brighter as their memories grew fainter. As for Russell, he proceeded to write a considered critical analysis, the *Practice and Theory of Bolshevism*.

Russell was able to reprint this book, virtually without alteration, in 1949—an astonishing example of political observation and prediction standing up to the passage of time. But Russell was not, in fact, so completely anti-Bolshevik as some people have gathered from later statements, like his summing up in 1943 of his visit to Russia: 'When I went there in 1920 I found nothing I could like or admire.' His book, in some passages, was less hostile to Soviet Russia and Lenin than the book Mrs Snowden wrote, and gives at first the impression of a strange alternation between damnation and praise for the Bolsheviks, owing to his determination to present both the bad and good sides fairly.

I

Something of the division in his mind about Russia at the time was shown in a letter:

'I reproached myself for not liking it. It has all the characteristics of vigorous beginnings. It was ugly and brutal, but full of constructive energy and faith in the value of what it was creating. . . .

'I was infinitely unhappy in that atmosphere—stifled by its utilitarianism, its indifference to love and beauty and the life of impulse. I cannot give that importance to man's merely animal needs that was given there by those in power. No doubt that is because I have not spent half my life in hunger and want, as many of them have. But do hunger and want necessarily bring wisdom? Do they make men more or less capable of conceiving the ideal society that should be the inspiration of every reformer?

'I cannot avoid the belief that they narrow the horizon more than they enlarge it. But an uneasy doubt remains, and I am torn in two.'

Russell's fundamental point in the *Practice and Theory of Bolshevism* was to make clear that British Socialists were wrong in thinking 'the dictatorship of the proletariat' was merely a new form of representative government. He insisted that 'dictatorship' meant 'dictatorship', whereas the word 'proletariat' was used 'in a Pickwickian sense', and meant the Communist Party.

Under the Bolshevik dictators, said Russell, 'Opposition is crushed without mercy, and without shrinking from the methods of the Czarist police, many of whom are still employed at their old work.' After what he had seen in the War, he would no longer admit the possibility—as he had when he lectured about Germany in 1896—that there might be compensating advantages in the fervour which accompanies intolerance and dogmatism. 'Contact with those who have no doubts has intensified a thousandfold my own doubts, not as to Socialism itself, but as to the wisdom of holding a creed so firmly that for its sake men are willing to inflict widespread misery.'

His conclusion was that 'One who believes, as I do, that the free intellect is the chief engine of human progress, cannot but be fundamentally opposed to Bolshevism as much as to the

Church of Rome. . . . The hopes which inspire Communism are, in the main, as admirable as those instilled by the Sermon on the Mount; but they are held as fanatically and are as likely to do as much harm'.

Russell was, I think, the first observer to point out that Communism was a form of religion; and a religion which, like Christianity, could be used to justify persecution. (It may be remembered that he had described Marxism as a religion as early as in *German Social Democracy*.) So far as the theory of Bolshevism was concerned, Russell elaborated the criticisms he had made in 1896. He said that Marxists placed too much stress on economic motives, and not enough on the strength of nationalism, religion, pride, and love of power. And he re-iterated that the right kind of socialism for Britain was not Communism, but Guild Socialism or self-government in industry.

That was one side of the picture, the summing up against the Soviet system. On the other side, Russell wrote that 'Russia is not ready for any form of democracy, and needs a strong Government. . . . In Russia the methods of the Bolsheviks are probably more or less unavoidable.'

Throughout he alternated in this fashion between condemnation and extenuation, giving both the case for the Prosecution and the case for the Defence. On one page he would write: 'I cannot share the hopes of the Bolsheviks. . . . I regard [them] as tragic delusions, destined to bring upon the world centuries of darkness and futile violence.' On another page he would write: 'I believe that Socialism is necessary to the world, and believe that the heroism of Russia has fired men's hopes in a way which was essential to the realization of Socialism in the future.'

In spite of his attempts to be fair to the Communists, the *Practice and Theory of Bolshevism* was violently disliked by British Socialists. There was a feeling that, even if his criticisms were just, he should not have made them, because they would help any Tory who wanted to attack Soviet Russia for reactionary reasons.

It was a criticism which raised the whole problem of the intellectual in politics—how to combine love of truth with corporate political activity.

With Russell the difficulty was particularly acute, and he see-sawed between two conflicting feelings. He believed in the individual intellect, not mob emotion. He wrote that 'Russia confirmed me in the belief that whatever is good is to be found in individuals, not in Societies'; he once remarked that 'the one thing I am frightened of is the herd'. Yet he had a craving for friendship and affection; with him love of truth and love of his fellow human beings went together, it being natural enough for a man exceptional in the one way to be exceptional in the other. He wrote during the war that 'I feel mankind in these days like a pitiful dumb animal with an open wound out of which blood drops and life is oozing away—and one's own life must go with it, or else one must grow callous for the time. I find selfishness a rest from the unendurable pity. But only temporarily: one's life is not life unless it is linked on to that of the world.' In human relations, as in philosophy, he found strict atomism impossible. The result was he was always seeking to associate himself in political movements with friends who he thought shared his views, and trying to think that his differences from them were relatively unimportant.

'Throughout my life,' he said once, 'I have longed to feel that oneness with large bodies of human beings that is experienced by the members of enthusiastic crowds. The longing has often been strong enough to lead me into self-deception. I have imagined myself in turn a Liberal, or a Socialist, or a pacifist, but I never have been any of these things in a profound sense. Always the sceptical intellect, when I have most wished it silent, has whispered doubts to me. . . . I would tell Quakers that I thought many wars in history had been justified, and Socialists that I dreaded the tyranny of the state.'

The only solution to the problem of the intellectual in politics seems to lie in part-time and non-party activity. Just as war is too serious to be left to the generals, so political problems are too serious to be left to professional politicians, because they are the very people who are debarred by their occupation from discussing them truthfully. It is noticeable that Russell was usually right in his political views when he was disagreeing with everybody; he was at his worst when he was closest to some standard political standpoint.

Another point to recognize is that, when a philosopher or scientist writes about politics, his writings should be judged by different criteria from his professional work. Russell himself emphasized this again and again. At one time during the war, for instance, he had suggested a theory that in politics there was only a duty to preach what was practicable: 'For instance, I believe in scientific breeding, but I see no point in preaching it at present.' He insisted that a book like his *Principles of Social Reconstruction* 'was not intended as a contribution to learning, but had an entirely practical purpose'. He did not write it as a philosopher, but 'as a human being who suffered from the state of the world'. Unfortunately, in spite of such disclaimers, people were sometimes so mesmerized by Russell's reputation, and his work about subjects they did not understand, that they were frightened to criticize him even when they understood him.

The reception of Russell's report on Soviet Russia emphasized the difficulties in telling the truth and trying to keep political associations at the same time. Having lost many friendships because of his opposition to the war, Russell now lost many of his new pacifist friends through his opposition to Russia. It was the beginning, for instance, of his break with Clifford Allen, who wrote to Elizabeth Russell soon after the delegation returned that 'You will find Bertie and myself particularly interesting at the present moment, as for the first time in our lives we are like two cats, fighting bitterly over Russia'.

It also meant a disagreement with Charles Trevelyan, who had championed his cause against Lloyd George in the House of Commons during the war.

Doubtless the criticism of Russell among British Socialists was not so strong as he himself believed; his sensitiveness was such that he always tended to think that people were more critical of him than they really were. But it was enough to give him a feeling of political isolation in a hostile world.

CHAPTER XIV

'China is Delightful'

WHEN he was in prison, Russell had thought of going back and giving unofficial lectures in Cambridge after the war. He said that 'I want still to teach and have to do with young men, but not ever again to be officially part of a University—I foresee a rather delightful career as a freelance philosopher like Abelard': and he talked of advertising a course of metaphysics 'intelligible to all except those who have studied philosophy'. At the end of 1919, however, he accepted an offer for reinstatement at Trinity. He applied for a year's leave of absence, having been asked to lecture at the Peking Government University. Then he resigned from Trinity again, as he did not want a fresh controversy over his forthcoming divorce from his first wife. He thought this would confuse the issue for those who had championed him when he was dismissed in 1916, and who had secured the invitation for him to return.

During these years Russell had two particular friends among women: and Clifford Allen once had the task, when staying with Russell and others on a farm, of seeing that one of them went off on a train before the imminent arrival of the other. One of these friends was Dora Black, who was to become Russell's second wife. She was a girl of considerable ability, vigour and vitality, and with views which in those days were strikingly unconventional. There was one occasion when Russell, hearing her steps coming up the stairs outside, turned to a companion and said 'Don't leave me alone with her'. But Dora went with Russell to see Wittgenstein at the Hague in 1919, and went to China with him in 1920.

The result of Russell's visit to the Far East was *The Problem of China*, as shrewd in its observation and analysis as *The Prac-*

tice and Theory of Bolshevism, and which has stood up equally well to the test of time. One of the leading present-day authorities on China, Professor C. P. FitzGerald, has described it to me as 'a remarkable book by any standard', a book of 'shrewd and astute foresight'. The only important point on which Russell has been proved wrong, so far, was his prediction of a form of federal government for China.

He stressed the future importance of China in world affairs at a time when most people in Whitehall, the Foreign Office included, could hardly be induced to take any interest in it. He pointed out that the pressure of population was driving Japan towards chauvinism and aggression; and he said that without birth control 'disaster is sooner or later inevitable'. He saw quite clearly the danger that China, if it was to avoid foreign conquest, would have to abandon its traditional ways of life and develop patriotism and militarism; and he saw that this might go too far. He warned that, in spite of their usual calm, the Chinese could be capable of 'wild excitement', and said that 'one can imagine a section of them becoming fanatically Bolshevist'.

His summing up was that 'All the Great Powers, without exception, have interests which are incompatible, in the long run, with China's welfare. . . . The Chinese must seek salvation in their own energy, not in the benevolence of any outside Power. . . . It is much to be feared that, in the process of becoming strong enough to preserve their independence, the Chinese may become strong enough to embark upon a career of Imperialism.'

Needless to say, Russell regarded this probable change in China with abhorrence. According to him, in most battles being fought at the time between Chinese war lords, 'both sides run away, and the victory rests with the side that first discovers the flight of the other. But this proves only that the Chinese soldier is a rational man.' In fact Russell approved of nearly everything he found in China, his only criticisms being confined to such things as avarice and corruption, and a certain callousness. His general conclusion was overwhelmingly on the side of Chinese civilization: he thought that 'China and the Chinese are most delightful'. He regarded China as 'an artist nation, with the virtues and vices to be expected of the artist', and declared that

'We have quite as much to learn from them as they have from us, but there is far less chance of our learning it.'

In China Russell shook himself for a time out of the remains of his subconscious Victorian belief in progress, and the assumption that a new idea must be better than an old one. He found himself, for the first time in his life, a conservative. That is to say, he found himself admiring a civilization which was passing away, and whose disappearance he regretted. He complained that his Chinese friends were too ready to have shoddy Western furniture in their homes, and copy Western ideas. He himself was delighted to buy some antique Chinese furniture, but his Chinese interpreter saw his purchase with disgust, and said 'It smells Buddhist'.

According to a later writer on China, Professor Schwartz of Harvard,* 'many of the advance guard intelligentsia were exasperated by what they regarded as his perverse tendency to find values in traditional Chinese civilization'. Russell himself gloomily predicted a time when 'the only difference between East and West will be that the former is more Western'.

For those who say that Russell was always at heart an eighteenth century Whig aristocrat—which is not necessarily a criticism—it is interesting to note some of the traditional virtues for which he praised the Chinese. He praised them for their tolerance, their imperturbability and dignity, their apparent absence of passion, and their preference for understatement—all of which are English virtues, and the last of which are particularly associated with the English aristocracy. He noted that the Chinese had an English love of compromise; that 'disputes can always be softened by a joke'; and that, like English aristocrats, the Chinese believed in etiquette rather than ethics. They had no dogmatic religious doctrines, but they had firmly fixed codes of conduct. And Russell made a defence of *laissez-faire* which might well have come from an eighteenth century English Whig: 'Nine-tenths of the activities of a modern Government are harmful; therefore the worse they are performed, the better. In China, where the Government is lazy, corrupt, and stupid, there is a degree of individual liberty which has been wholly lost in the rest of the world.'

* Benjamin Schwartz, *Chinese Communism and the Rise of Mao.*

And yet, as in Russia, Russell saw two sides to the situation. In spite of praising *laissez-faire*, he said in *The Problem of China* that 'There are many arguments for State Socialism, or rather what Lenin calls State Capitalism, in any country which is economically but not culturally backward'. He advocated the state ownership of railways and mines in China. (But he suggested that the latter should be deferred for the time being, 'in view of the need of rapid development of mining'.) It appears that his views had moved more in the direction of orthodox Socialism, by the time he returned to England and wrote *The Problem of China*, than when he was still in Peking. According to Professor Schwartz's account:

'During the latter part of 1920, Bertrand Russell and a young Chinese journalist, Chang Tung-sun, roused a violent controversy by contending that the root of all China's misery lay in its poverty and low productivity, and that this could be alleviated only through industrialization and not through empty discussions about this or that 'ism', and that however much one might object to capitalism on ethical grounds, it appeared that only capitalism could achieve such an industrialization.'

But the point between Socialism and Capitalism was not so important, perhaps, as the belief that industrialism was essential one way or the other. Russell therefore saw China's problem as twofold. On the one hand, it had to make itself strong enough to resist aggression, without becoming militaristic. On the other hand, it had to apply scientific methods to conquer poverty, without acquiring the vices of Western industrialism. He doubted whether either would be possible; but he gave his own suggestions for solving the second problem—that of combining scientific techniques with a respect for human values—in *The Prospects of Industrial Civilization*, written in collaboration with Dora Black. This book was inspired by their separate visits to Russia (where Dora was an enthusiastic admirer of Bolshevism), and by their mutual journey to China.

So far as China was concerned, Russell pinned his hopes to Sun Yat Sen, describing him as the one exception, and the only one, 'to the rule that the Chinese war lords are merely ambitious brigands'. He compared his outlook to that of old-fashioned English liberals, saying that he aimed at diminishing poverty, but not at an economic revolution. This was at a time when the British Foreign Office, with the incredible folly which characterized its policy towards China then and during the rise of Mao, was busily backing one of Sun Yat Sen's rivals and doing its best to discredit him.

Having recorded what Russell thought about China and the Chinese, it is interesting to ask what the Chinese thought about Russell. His impact was tremendous. For the first time they heard an English aristocrat who was ready to criticize British Imperialism; for the first time they found a foreigner ready to consider China's problems from the point of view of the Chinese. Sun Yat Sen is reported to have said that Russell was the only Englishman who had ever understood China; and the enthusiastic students of Peking University started a special 'Russell Magazine' (*Lo-ssu Chi-k'an*) to propagate his views. It must be remembered that the Chinese have as high a veneration for distinguished scholars as other nations have for sportsmen and film stars; and there may still be people in China today who hold Britain in higher regard because of Russell's understanding of their problems.

John Dewey was in China at the same time as Russell; and, according to Professor Schwartz, 'While Russell's influence was to prove restricted and evanescent . . . Dewey was to leave a lasting mark on Chinese thought'. This view of Russell's influence is not entirely supported by Professor FitzGerald, who first went to Peking as early as 1923, and was thus in a good position to judge. It seems that Dewey's influence was in fact mainly confined to the Kuomintang.

There were others who complained that Russell's influence was not too little, but too great. His strongest critics were the missionaries. When the Young China Association arranged a series of lectures on religion in Peking, Russell informed his audience that it was possible for a man of the highest moral principles to be an atheist, and that morality often became hypocrisy when it was too closely related to religion. The missionaries also thought it regrettable that, just at a time when Chinese women were learning Western ways of life, they should have before them Russell's journey in company with Dora Black as an example. This criticism, again, is not accepted by Professor FitzGerald, who says that emancipated young Chinese women of the time did not need much encouragement. Russell himself, visiting a school in Peking which was training girls as teachers, noted that 'the spirit of free inquiry among the girls would horrify most British headmistresses'.

His visit to China was almost more than a passing chapter in his life; it nearly meant the end of it. He exhausted himself giving lecture after lecture in the cold and draughty halls of Peking; then, one day after he had driven out to the Western Hills and had a swim in a hot sulphur bath, he was seized by a violent fit of trembling. When he arrived back in Peking it was discovered that he had acute pneumonia. Complications set in, both lungs were attacked, and for several weeks he was critically ill in the German hospital.

The Russian community in Peking sent gifts of champagne and whipped cream to the hospital, saying that Russell must not be allowed to die, because 'He will be needed for the Revolution'—thus showing themselves sadly mistaken about the trend of his views. A delegation of Chinese sages, more pessimistically, arrived to say that he would be accorded the supreme honour of burial in a specially built shrine by the Western Lake, the haunt of ancient poets and scholars, and to ask if they might hear the last words of the dying philosopher.

There are many stories of sceptics who retreat towards orthodox faith towards the end of their lives. Russell faced death with unrepentant courage and gay irony. He would emerge for a moment from the delirium of a high fever to tell his doctors defiantly: 'Nothing the matter with me. Never felt better in my life.' He asked Dora Black when her birthday was, and remarked 'You'd better buy yourself a present from me now, in case I snuff out by then'. And he said that, if she ran short of funds, all she need do was to put a notice in the paper saying: 'Russell dead. Money needed to bury the old dog.'

One doctor said reproachfully afterwards that so long as Russell was too weak to speak he behaved 'like a true philosopher': but 'every time you came to yourself you made a joke'.

Reports of his death were actually circulated by Japanese

journalists. When they reached England Frank Russell refused to believe them, declaring robustly that 'the whole thing's nonsense—Bertie wouldn't die in China without telling me'. But others were not so sceptical; and after the German doctors at Peking had finally saved his life, Russell had the privilege of reading some of his own obituary notices.

Russell was nursed devotedly by Dora Black throughout his illness, and when she was not actually in the room with him she waited and had her meals on a chair in the corridor outside. To her surprise, she found her appetite increasing, and then she realised that Russell was going to have an heir.

One incident on their journey home to Britain is worth recalling, as showing that he had none of the tameness which might be expected of an abstract philosopher of pacifist views. He and Dora were going down some steps in Japan when press photographers suddenly let off a flash light in their faces, the shock almost causing Dora to stumble and fall. Russell was so furious that he charged the photographers with his stick and dispersed them.

CHAPTER XV

Chelsea Candidate and American Lecturer

RETURNING from China, Russell married and settled down with Dora at 31 Sydney Street, Chelsea, where their two children were born. During the period of his second marriage, or roughly for the next ten years, he came much closer than before to orthodox Labour Party opinion, and Socialists took his criticisms of British Imperialism in China as atoning for his previous criticisms of Soviet Russia.

Russell stood for Parliament as Labour candidate for Chelsea in the General Elections of 1922 and 1923. Chelsea was a Conservative stronghold where the sitting member was Sir Samuel Hoare, later Lord Templewood.

The house at 31 Sydney Street was used as the Labour Party Committee Rooms. In the words of a visiting *Times* reporter, 'a select body of workers toil zealously in the basement'; while 'the surroundings are pleasantly marked by the owner's good taste'—a reference to Chinese furniture and rugs which Russell had brought back from Peking. Russell, announcing that he supported the Labour Party's policy on all points, opened his campaign with a triumphant meeting in the Chelsea Town Hall. He urged a capital levy and the nationalization of mines and railways, he opposed cuts in expenditure of education, and he criticized the Treaty of Versailles. There was tremendous applause when he addressed the meeting as 'my future constituents'. When he told them 'You will very probably be told by other people that I am unpatriotic', a voice shouted back 'You are a gentleman'. The cheers held up proceedings for some minutes.

Russell criticized the policy of financing 'reactionary adventures' in Russia, and said that the recognition of Soviet Russia would be one of the first acts of a Labour Government.

In both elections Russell was defeated—by 13,437 votes to 4,513 in 1922, and by 10,461 votes to 5,047 in 1923. Nevertheless, all the enthusiasm was on his side: he was cheered and chaired after the declarations of the polls, while Samuel Hoare went away through a back door to avoid the crowd. Hoare had been made particularly unpopular by the discovery that, while opposing an increase in the tax on sparkling wines, he had supported higher taxation on beer. Once one of his supporting speakers, a young man with a very refined Oxford accent, was replying to questions. He said 'And as for the beah . . .'. There was an immediate shout from the back: 'Heah! Heah!' Thereafter Hoare's speeches were always liable to be interrupted by ironic cries of 'Heah, heah—beah, beah'.

Russell's defeats were only to be expected: and, like his failure to get into Parliament in 1910, can hardly be regretted. One incident in Chelsea suffices to confirm that he would not have got far in politics. A Labour canvasser had suffered some slight injury falling down a flight of steps. It was pointed out to Russell that it would make a nice impression if he visited the patient's sick bed, perhaps taking him some flowers, and perhaps having a press photographer present to record the gesture. Russell uncompromisingly refused to indulge in any pretence: 'I don't like him, and I won't go to see him.'

Another incident worth mention in this connection goes back to the time when he was sharing a flat with Clifford Allen. Russell once pointed out to Allen that, since in politics they were champions of the People, they should take some interest in what interested the People. It was therefore disgraceful, said Russell, that neither of them had even been to the Derby. They decided that it was their duty to go to Epsom next Derby Day: but when the time came they had both forgotten all about it.

Though Russell did not stand again in the General Election of 1924, his wife took his place; and 31 Sydney Street remained a kind of Socialist strongpoint in the heart of Conservative Chelsea, with Russell upstairs writing at his desk, and Dora downstairs energetically running Committee meetings or conducting propaganda campaigns for organizations like the Workers' Birth Control Association. Once a tomato was hurled through Russell's window by an angry Tory.

One source of confusion during these years was that Alys Russell was living at the same time in St Leonard's Terrace. Chelsea thus had two Mrs Russells, both of them members of the Chelsea Labour Party, and both of them with many friends in common. Elaborate arrangements were made to see that the two did not meet, for instance at the austere evening parties given by the Sangers in Oakley Street.

During one of Russell's election campaigns, Leonard Woolf met him and Dora at a dinner party. Russell remarked that he had been canvassing that afternoon; and Woolf said, in the kind of unthinking way in which a joke can suddenly come straight out, 'I hope you didn't forget to canvass St Leonard's Terrace'. Woolf stopped short, horrified at what he had said, and at the expression on Dora's face. There was a dead silence. Then Russell saw the humour of the situation, looked at Woolf and suddenly began to laugh.

The position with the two Mrs Russells in Chelsea was only made possible by the continued absence of any bitterness, on either side, about the ending of Russell's first marriage. The feelings of Alys towards him never altered, and she was always eager for news of him. In fact when Lady Constance Malleson published a book with references to her friendship with Russell, Alys took a copy to Mrs Sanger, who was in hospital at the time, and gave it to her to read with the remark 'I think this may interest thee'.

One description of Russell after his return from China was written by Beatrice Webb, who saw him a few months before his fiftieth birthday, when he was still not recovered from his illness in Peking. She described him as 'prematurely aged', playing the role of 'a fallen angel with Mephistophelian wit', and 'not at peace with himself or the world'. But she said that, in spite of 'impaired vitality', he was 'more brilliantly intellectual than he has ever been. He is cynical and witty. His paradoxes are more impatiently perverse than those of GBS [Shaw]. He never seems serious; and his economic and political views follow on his temperamental likes and dislikes. . . .

'He thinks he believes, with an almost fervent faith, in libertarian pacifism. But I doubt it. If, for instance, there arose a creed war he would be on the side of a secularist rebellion. Religious faith with puritan morality is to him *L'Infame.*'

It is characteristic of both that whereas Russell admired China, Beatrice Webb admired Japan. They had a strenuous argument about it, and apparently Russell deliberately set out to provoke her by praising China as highly as possible, even praising the Chinese indifference to science. Beatrice Webb wrote, rather surprisingly, that 'He has no interest in the scientific method: he would even object to applying science to society, seeing that it might mean constraint on the will of some who desired to do anything they pleased without considering like liberty in others'.

After his return from China, Russell was almost entirely dependent on his pen for a living, and in addition to his work on philosophy he had to pour forth a profusion of articles and books to keep going. (When E. H. Neville sent him the draft Preface to his *Prolegomena to Analytical Geometry*, Russell told him cheerfully 'I shall certainly buy your book, unless I am in the workhouse'.) His 'popular' work was often of far more importance than might be judged by Russell's own jokes about it: he would make such remarks, for instance, as that 'I'm paid by the word, so I always choose the shortest words possible'.

Many of his articles were written for the Independent Labour Party's *New Leader*, on subjects ranging from popular science to criticisms of British policy in China. At this time the *New Leader*, under the editorship of H. N. Brailsford, reached a standard never since approached in left-wing journalism; its contributors, in addition to Russell, included Wells, Shaw, Keynes, and Julian Huxley. Star contributors are often temperamental and difficult to handle; so it is interesting to note that Russell was a model of what any editor could wish. His articles would always arrive punctually on time; they were always clearly legible, with hardly a correction on the pages of neat manuscript; and they were exactly the length asked, or had optional cuts carefully marked.

(In the same way, when he became the most distinguished of speakers on radio and television, he invariably arrived punctually in the studio.)

Russell found another source of income through lecture tours in America, a country which he grew to know very well.

In later life, he once remarked that on his tombstone he would have inscribed the words: 'He lived six years in America, and did NOT write a book about it.' In view of the fact that he wrote books on nearly everything else, this may seem a curious and almost discourteous omission. Fortunately it can be repaired by some diligent research among his forgotten journalistic writings, and among scattered references to America in his books. By the time of his six years' residence in the United States, which began a year before the Second World War, familiarity had blunted his original interest in what had struck him as strange at first. But in the course of earlier visits, and especially during his lecture tours in the nineteen twenties, he recorded a number of impressions which are worth collecting here and setting beside his contemporary studies of Russia and China.

His first reports were, as he stressed, merely superficial impressions. But I cannot resist quoting from an early article in the *New Leader*, as an agreeable example of the effortless wit which Russell, like Voltaire, would scatter with the lavish carelessness of a man who knew that there was plenty more where it came from. (When I mentioned Russell's *New Leader* articles to him many years later, he had completely forgotten that he had ever written them.) He wrote after returning from America in 1924:

'There are only two points on which I can speak from adequate experience: one, that the trains are amazingly punctual; the other, that the people have a fondness for lectures which is, to an Englishman, quite unintelligible. In England, if people admire an author they read his books; in America, they want to hear him lecture, but they do not dream of reading him.

'It is impossible to read in America, except in the train, because of the telephone. Everyone has a telephone, and it rings all day and most of the night. This makes conversation, thinking and reading out of the question, and accordingly these activities are somewhat neglected.'

A modern critic of America might say that, in order to bring

K

these remarks up to date, it is only necessary to substitute 'television' for 'telephone'. A more fundamental point was made by Russell some years later when, in *Freedom and Organization*, he traced many American characteristics back to the utilitarian values of a pioneering civilization. The men were so busy making money or fighting the Indians that culture became almost exclusively the concern of women. 'Since most women have not pursued painting or literature or philosophy professionally, but only taken an intelligent interest in all of them, there has come to be a certain superficiality in regard to all such subjects, which, from an early date, was ministered to by lectures . . .'

Russell noticed that 'It has become the thing in America for ladies to read (or seem to read) certain books every month: some read them, some read the first chapter, some read the reviews, but all have these books on their tables.' Since, however, the book clubs never selected *Hamlet* or *King Lear* as the book of the month, 'the reading that is done is entirely of mediocre modern books and never of masterpieces'.

Russell complained that the American male's 'excessive preoccupation with utility' was shown also in the lack of beauty in the American accent. He said most Americans believed that if you made your meaning clear, nothing else mattered. 'The only good thing about the American language is the slang. Fortunately it is just this that the English are most disposed to copy.'

Another impression, noted by Russell on his visit in 1924, was that 'The number and prominence of the Jews in America is astonishing . . . I had the impression that throughout the Eastern states everything that is best in politics, in intellect, and in art, is Jewish. . . . Owing to their merits and their numbers there is a very strong anti-Semitic feeling, which takes an English visitor by surprise.' With regard to the colour problem, Russell wrote that 'The way in which Southerners speak of negroes, to this day, is so horrible that it is difficult to stay in the room with them'.

America, said Russell, was dedicated to democratic equality in theory, but to plutocratic inequality in practice.

Since the social scale in America was continually fluctuating, 'all the snobbish emotions became more restless than they are where the social order is fixed. Moreover, money made is the accepted measure of brains.' American business men became just as worried over the state of the market as students over examinations—'If you lose your money, you're ploughed'. And since 'almost every American would sooner get 8 per cent from a risky investment than 4 per cent from a safe one', the result was continual worry and fret.

'A man,' said Russell, 'may be discontented because of unconscious wants. For instance, Americans need rest, but do not know it. I believe this to be a large part of the explanation of the crime wave in the United States.'

Russell noticed that, whereas on his visit to Harvard in 1914 'pruderies and reticences' had been stronger in America than in England, the position was now reversed owing to the popularity of psycho-analysis in America. On the other hand, the influence of big business on teaching in American Universities had increased. The American intelligentsia thus had 'remarkable social and private freedom, combined with complete public enslavement'.

The Governing Board of Harvard, Russell maintained, had prevented men of liberal views speaking at the Harvard Union. The result was one of the few public controversies in which his opponents scored a point. President Lowell denied 'the malignant control' by big business which Russell had described, and neatly remarked that whereas Russell had lost his job in Cambridge in 1916, Harvard had kept a German on its staff throughout the war.

Russell was one of the first Englishmen to acknowledge, as early as 1922, that America was stronger than any other power; and he predicted that 'America will embark upon a career of imperialism—not so much territorial as economic'. His American audiences were told that 'America is not ruled by the Washington Government. It is oil and Morgan that rule you. The empire of American finance over the whole world, illiberal and cruel to the highest degree, is a nightmare prospect before us.'*

Back in Britain, Russell predicted that capitalist countries

* Russell later stressed how much difference Roosevelt had made in this respect.

like America would treat a Socialist Great Britain in the same
way that Britain had treated Soviet Russia, and would cut off
wheat and other supplies. Therefore Socialism could only come
internationally: 'Suppose we had national socialism, and by it
lost our Empire, we should get no oil, and we should all be
proletarians and have to work for America. . . . At present, and
for an indefinite future, good relations with America are
absolutely necessary.'

Britain must have a strong Navy and six months' supply of
oil stored at home. 'Internationalism is our goal; but we shall be
powerless to reach our goal unless we have an adequate naval
defence against such bodies as Standard Oil and the Comité des
Forges, which will only leave us undisturbed if we are strong.'

It is curious to find Russell demanding a strong British Navy;
evidence that, even in these years, he was neither an orthodox
Pacifist nor an orthodox Socialist. It is even more interesting to
find a speech a little earlier in which, discussing America's place
in the world from a long-term view and from a different
approach, he arrived at a radically different conclusion.

Lecturing to the Fabian Society in October 1923, on the
effects of scientific advances, Russell had said that: 'The best
hope likely to be realised seems to be the forcible victory of one
group (presumably America), leading to a world organization
with America as capitalist and the other nations as proletariat.
If a world organization, however oppressive, were once created,
ordered progress would again become possible.' This was a
line of thought which often reappeared in his writing.

Some of the above pages may have read as though Russell was
always critical of America; but that is because criticism is
always more fun to quote than praise, and is usually more important. There were many points about America which found
Russell's favour; in particular, in spite of his strictures about
American international finance, he admitted that American
diplomacy compared favourably with that of any other power.
In China, for instance, he contrasted the 'shameful' record of
Britain, France, Germany and Russia with the 'generous and
liberal' policy of America. But in China Russell had also seen,
as I myself saw over twenty years later, that the Americans
there seemed incapable of appreciating Chinese civilization. He

put it succinctly: 'What is Americanism? "Clean living, clean thinking, and pep", I think an American would reply. This means, in practice, the substitution of tidiness for art, cleanliness for beauty, moralizing for philosophy, prostitutes for concubines (as being easier to conceal), and a general air of being fearfully busy, for the leisurely calm of the cultured Chinese.'

We may finally note Russell's prescience in forecasting, as early as November 1926, that the world was entering into a new era of intolerant war between the rival philosophies of the 'only two great powers of the times', Russian and America, standing for Communism and Individualism. And he wrote in *Sceptical Essays*, published in 1928, that 'There may be a long period in which the world is virtually divided between America and Russia, the former controlling Western Europe and the self-governing Dominions, the latter controlling all Asia'.

Perhaps the most interesting point which emerges from Russell's writings on America in these years is that his fundamental criticisms are on the same lines as those he made of Soviet Russia. In each case he complained of excessive utilitarianism, and a lack of a love of beauty. He had compared the Bolsheviks with the Puritans, and he often recalled America's Puritan origins. 'America,' he wrote, 'is essentially a country of pious peasants, like Russia.'

In both America and Russia the most serious thing was intolerance. America had 'the tyranny of the herd'; resulting from Puritan ancestry, hard pioneering conditions, and immigration, which had brought defensive mechanisms into play 'to preserve American traditions from being lost like a river in the sand'. Russia, on the other hand, had the tyranny of a minority, based on Marxist theory.

In each country there was boundless belief in man's power, aided by machinery, to shape his environment. Russell sometimes admired this optimism, but feared the mental attitude involved, which he found reflected in national philosophy. He came to criticize Dewey's Instrumentalism for 'cosmic impiety', which was also, in effect, one of his complaints against Marx; and he once greatly annoyed Dewey by telling him how much there was in common between Instrumentalism and Marx's *Theses on Feuerbach*.

Because Russell was a philosopher who did not confine his interests to the lecture room, he went to cinemas to see American films, and found that the ideas of Hollywood were not unconnected with American pragmatic philosophy: 'The object is not to produce something that corresponds to fact, but something that makes you happy by corresponding to daydreams.' He saw the 'immeasurable possibilities' of the cinema as an art form. It was 'perhaps the most heartrending of all examples of artistic barbarism' that films should be made by such 'ignorant and stupid' men, appealing to 'the most ignorant and stupid parts of the population'. Not all Hollywood films in later years were devoted to daydreams on the level of 'nursery tales and fairy stories'; but Russell's criticism was true of Hollywood in the 1920's and early 1930's; and he cannot be blamed if he did not keep up with his film-going after then.

For himself, he confessed that the simplest things in the films he saw gave him pleasure: 'I like to see a race between a motor car and an express train; I enjoy the spectacle of a villain gnashing his teeth because he has just failed to pick off the engine driver; I delight in men tumbling off skyscrapers and saving themselves by telegraph wires.'

CHAPTER XVI

Russell and Relativity

AMONG the traits of Sir Stanley Unwin, as a keen business man, was a disinclination to go out of his way to publicize the wares which a rival publisher had to sell. In practice this meant that the lists of Russell's works, facing the title pages of his books published by Allen and Unwin, sometimes omitted those he wrote when Unwin was not his publisher. *Principia Mathematica* and *The Problems of Philosophy* might need no reminder of their existence, but some other books by Russell tended to be forgotten. Chief among them were books on science which C. K. Ogden persuaded him to write for Kegan Paul—the *ABC of Atoms* and the *ABC of Relativity*, also published as·articles in Brailsford's *New Leader; Icarus, or the future of Science;* and *The Analysis of Matter.* (The last work, after being out of print for many years, appeared again, under the Allen and Unwin imprint, in Britain in 1954.)

In writing about Russell, there is the same difficulty which confronted the Victorian novelists who brought in dozens of different characters, and developed three or four simultaneous plots or subplots, all in the same novel. After describing how one character was getting on, they would continually be dodging back to catch up with the doings of another. Russell was always about a dozen characters at once, all standing in the same pair of shoes; after devoting two or three chapters to Russell as a traveller and sociologist and politician and lecturer, we must now go back to outline the activities, during the same period, of Russell the scientist and Russell the philosopher.

Russell was almost unique among contemporary philosophers in the extent of his knowledge of science: but I think he often regretted he had not devoted more time to it, particularly when he first realized the importance of Einstein's Theory of Relativity. We can date this with some precision.

In May 1919 there occurred the historic eclipse of the sun which provided critical evidence to support Einstein. So delicate were the observations involved that it took some months for the results to be worked out.

During this period Russell was staying at a farmhouse with a party which included J. E. Littlewood, the Cambridge mathematician. Littlewood had just been reading Eddington on the subject of Relativity, and talked about it to Russell. The eagerness and suspense in waiting for the results of the observations of the eclipse were so great that Littlewood sent a telegram to Eddington asking what had happened: Eddington replied that it was too soon to be certain, but the first results seemed favourable.

Listening to Littlewood talking on Relativity, Russell was filled with excitement; and in the characteristic way in which he often disparaged his own achievements and philosophy in general, exclaimed: 'To think that I have been spending all these years on *muck!*'

Russell's mind was soon working on the philosophical implications of Einstein's ideas. During his visit to China, he occupied himself going through the equations of the Theory of Relativity, to familiarize himself with the mathematics of it; and he planned a book with the title *The Analysis of Matter*. When he returned, he was too busy at first with politics and journalism to get much further; but fortunately C. K. Ogden suggested that another way of earning his living would be by writing on popular science. The result was *The ABC of Atoms* and *The ABC of Relativity*.

The ABC of Atoms, published in 1923, is still remarkable for its early predictions of atomic energy. Russell wrote that 'If this source of energy can be utilized commercially, it will probably in time supersede every other. . . . It is impossible to exaggerate the revolutionary effect which it may have both in the practice of industry and in the theory of physics.' And Russell, referring to work on the structure of the atom, said: 'It is probable that it will ultimately be used for making more deadly explosives and projectiles than any yet invented.'

The ABC of Relativity followed in 1925. Littlewood was rather disturbed when he heard that Russell was writing a popular book on Relativity, and cautioned him about some of the difficulties. At the end he agreed that Russell had succeeded in simplifying without falsifying, and in providing what is still the easiest introduction to the subject.

(*The ABC of Relativity* has a particular interest for myself personally, because it was the first book by Russell which I ever read. I can still remember getting it as a boy from the Sydney Municipal Library, and finding myself enraptured by a world which my teachers, with one exception, had never hinted at. About the same time my future wife, as a schoolgirl in Brighton, was reading Russell's books on social questions, by the light of a torch under the blankets after Lights Out. We were rather typical of the fascination which Russell had for many of our generation.)

Russell's fuller philosophical study, *The Analysis of Matter*, was not published until 1927. His custom was to do his popular writing in Chelsea during the winter, and his professional work in Cornwall during the summer; keeping up a continuous output only made possible by his extraordinary gift for concentration—presumably acquired through his early work on mathematics. He would sit writing page after page, turning page after page neatly face downwards as he finished them; he never minded children playing round him while he worked; and once a guest in Cornwall, watching fascinated, saw that Russell did not even notice a wasp circling his head. But he found his attention distracted when his own name was mentioned, and characteristically pointed out that this showed it was not really practicable to 'love one's neighbour as oneself'. (His own realistic advice was: 'Do not attempt to live without vanity, since this is impossible, but choose the right audience from which to seek admiration.')

In *The Analysis of Matter*, following the Theory of Relativity, Russell described 'events' as the raw material out of which the logical constructions of both mind and matter were made. Another development from his position in *The Analysis of Mind* was that he began to abandon the idea of different causal laws for mind and matter; he hoped that such things as memory could be explained by modifications in the brain structure. Thus mind and matter became even more alike than in his previous 'neutral monism'.

Putting his ideas in popular language, Russell said that 'mind and matter are so close that it is hardly worth while to distinguish them'. For instance, adenoids affect mental development; adenoids are caused by bad habits of breathing; and these are caused by mental anxiety—'Everything works round in a circle like that'.

There is a parallel here between Russell's neutral monism and his views on religion, though each was arrived at quite independently. Religious tenets, especially personal immortality, are usually based on an absolute distinction between soul and body; and Russell once said that 'The distinction of mind and matter came into philosophy through religion'. There is also a parallelism with Russell's views on sex: the Victorian outlook he attacked had one of its roots in the Christian tradition that the spirit is noble and the body is base.

Although *The Analysis of Matter* is a very important book, and a very rewarding one to read, I will say little about it here. Many of the most interesting portions are technical; and many of the new philosophical ideas in it are best discussed when we come later to Russell's *Human Knowledge*, where they reached their culmination. For instance, *The Analysis of Matter* admitted that science needs 'postulates', and introduced the 'separable causal lines' which became one of the postulates of *Human Knowledge* in 1948. I think *Human Knowledge* would have been more easily understood but for the accident that *The Analysis of Matter* had gone out of print in the years before it appeared.

Here I will merely add a few rather obvious points.

To begin with, Russell's newer version of 'neutral monism' was in accordance with the viewpoint of modern science as seen by many modern scientists. In fact, what Russell did was to use new scientific theories to clear up centuries of philosophical confusion about mind and matter, idealism and realism; just as, previously, he had used advances in mathematics to clear away muddles in Kant and Hegel.

Next, it is plain that the universe as conceived in *The Analysis of Matter* is a good deal more closely knit together than in Russell's philosophy at the time of his first rebellion against Bradley. In fact, his new views seem at first very like those of Whitehead, who also denied any fundamental dualism between mind and matter.

Russell did not go on, however, as Whitehead did, to a mystical evolutionary philosophy rather like Bergson. In his early days, Whitehead had said that 'It is a safe rule to apply that, when a mathematical or philosophical author writes with a misty profundity, he is talking nonsense': later he seemed to forget this rule. I will not discuss his philosophy here, having two excellent excuses. Firstly, his divergence from Russell began with a technical point; secondly, I have never read right through his *Process and Reality*. I gave up the attempt some years ago when I learnt that neither Russell nor G. E. Moore had read it either. I am content with the views of my valiant friend Professor Weitz, who has studied it in detail and reports that it is very like Leibniz, adapted for modern use; and the views of Miss Anscombe, the leading present day disciple of Wittgenstein, who condemns *Process and Reality* with that greater outspokenness which characterizes a female philosopher.

Yet I have an uneasy feeling that it is a legitimate criticism of Russell's philosophy to say that it is too static; though I have no more idea than anyone else of how to introduce into a philosophy the facts of evolution and process, without the dangers of bringing in an element of mysticism.

It is certainly a curious point about Russell that, when discussing biology and philosophers of evolution whom he disliked, he denied that philosophy should concern itself with the particular results of a particular science; whereas he concerned himself very much with the results of physics and physiology. It was not till *Human Knowledge*, in 1948, that he emphasized any consideration derived from biology.

As mentioned earlier, Russell's neutral monism did a great deal to dispel the ancient philosophical problem of the relation of mind and body. I do not think, though, that he was so successful with the equally ancient problem of free will and determinism, which he had pondered in the garden of Pembroke Lodge; the problem of how, if the body is governed by scientific laws, the mind can be free.

On this question I had various arguments with him in which I, for instance, would point proudly to my having given up smoking as a plain example of free will, and he replied 'I do not deny your moral pride, but I deny you have any occasion for it'. As in most discussions on this subject, we never got much further. I think it is possible he did not understand my point of view; he sometimes seemed to assume that anybody who believed in free will must do so for emotional or moral or theological reasons. I think it is even more likely that, on my side, I failed to understand his position. But it is worth pointing out that he made a distinction between determinism and fatalism. In his later political writings and broadcasts, for instance, he robustly fought the attitude that wars are in some sense inevitable; again and again he stressed that mankind could *choose* between life or destruction.

There is one particularly pleasant aspect of *The Analysis of Matter* to mention in conclusion. It marked something of a reconciliation between Russell and the Trinity authorities, since he used much of the material when he gave the Tarner Lectures on their invitation. And I may also mention here one other famous Cambridge occasion, when Wittgenstein submitted his *Tractatus* as a Ph.D. thesis. Though it was a foregone conclusion that Wittgenstein would get his Doctorate, the formalities had to be observed; so Russell and G. E. Moore, now Professor of Philosophy, were appointed to examine him.

Wittgenstein, recalling the occasion afterwards, said that 'when I went along for it, I was in a funk'. But they began with some pleasant chat as among old friends, and then Russell turned to Moore and said: 'Go on, *you've* got to ask him some questions—*you're* the Professor.' They had a little discussion, in which Russell unsuccessfully tried to persuade Wittgenstein that there was some inconsistency between his doctrine about how little could be said on philosophical subjects, and his claim to have reached unassailable and definite truths on them. The Viva on the *Tractatus* ended amicably with Wittgenstein putting an arm on each of his examiners' shoulders and saying 'Don't worry, I know you'll *never* understand it'.

CHAPTER XVII

Beacon Hill School

🌿

As said earlier, Russell's views during his second marriage were much more conventionally unconventional than before and after. At this time, for instance, he was most militant in the way he expressed his criticisms of orthodox Christianity.

Although he praised some of the precepts in the Gospels, Russell said that Christ was inferior to Buddha and Socrates as regards wisdom and virtue, and complained that Christ had 'a vindictive fury against people who would not listen to his preaching'. He made a special attack on the doctrine of Hell—'I really do not think that a person with a proper degree of kindliness in his nature would have put fears and terrors of that sort into the world'. And Russell thought Christ showed 'a certain pleasure in contemplating wailing and gnashing of teeth, or else it would not occur so often'.

Russell's main interest for many years, however, was concentrated on education. The unorthodox school set up by himself and Dora Russell in 1927, with their two children among the pupils, attracted a good deal of newspaper publicity, which magnified the trivial and obscured the important. A false impression of Russell's views has persisted; partly because of confusion with those of Dora Russell, which were more extreme than his own; and partly because of the practical problems in running the school, which failed for reasons which had nothing to do with the rightness or wrongness of his ideas, and which gave his critics a chance to make up amusing legends.

A typical apocryphal story, circulated in America, told how one day the local rector came to the door of the school, and was greeted by a small girl without any clothes on. The rector spluttered: 'Good God.' The girl retorted, closing the door:

'There *is* no God.'

I will therefore say something about how Russell's interest in education began, and his actual experiences at the school, to clear the ground before trying to assess his theories.

Even before the birth of his children, Russell's attention had been turned to education by the First World War; and he devoted a chapter to the subject in the *Principles of Social Reconstruction*. Both his main arguments against conventional schools, then and later, were based on anti-militarism.

His first argument was that, in effect, wars were so stupid that no sensible man would take part in them; and that therefore the public schools, in order to produce men willing to fight, had to encourage stupidity. He wrote: 'It is intensity of belief in a creed that produces efficiency in fighting: victory comes to those who feel the strongest certainty about matters on which doubt is the only rational attitude.' Therefore 'the child's nature is warped and its free outlook is cramped, to cultivate inhibitions as a check to the growth of new ideas'.

Russell's second argument was derived from his belief that most people enjoyed the war, and his consequent study of psychology. He declared that wars were due, 'in the main, to the insane and destructive impulses which lurk in the unconscious of those who have been unwisely handled in infancy, childhood and adolescence'. He was thus led to criticise the 'old-fashioned' idea of depending on will power to control bad desires. He wrote in almost Freudian language that 'The bad desires, like a river that has been dammed, find some other outlet which has escaped the watchful eye of the will. . . . Theories which justify cruelty almost always have their source in some desire diverted by the will from its natural channel, driven underground, and at last emerging.' By contrast, said Russell, the secret of modern moral education was to make good behaviour a matter of habit, not self-control.

Russell seemed to be advocating, in fact, what can only be called Morality without Tears; because even the acquisition of the good habits was to be a painless process. Discipline, he said, was not necessary to anything like the extent generally believed. 'The child who is in any way coerced,' he maintained, 'tends to respond with hatred, and if, as is usual, he is not able to give free vent to his hatred, it festers inwardly, and may sink into the unconscious with all sorts of strange consequences throughout the rest of life.' Conventional education had 'starved the intellect and the emotions in order to strengthen the will'.

Russell's educational ideas continually fluctuated between theories derived from modern psychologists, and good sense which he provided himself. His leanings towards Freudianism are easily explained by the impact upon him of the First World War; Freud seemed to offer an explanation of what had shocked and puzzled him about men's conduct, and suggested a way of escape. But Russell never really believed it; he would always have had to admit that his own achievements in life were the result of enormous self-control, self-discipline, and will power; and that no amount of habit-forming in infancy could have conditioned him into producing *Principia Mathematica*. Nor did he admire lack of will-power in others. Russell, in fact, wrote in the *Principles of Social Reconstruction* that 'There is a kind of discipline which is necessary to almost all achievement', and that 'Success in producing mental discipline is the chief merit of traditional higher education'.

When, however, he and Dora Russell set up their own 'Beacon Hill School' at Telegraph House near Harting, which they rented from Frank Russell, the main emphasis was on freedom and the avoidance of repressions. At first lessons were compulsory, but later Russell was reluctantly persuaded to abandon even this rule for the children.

'We allow them to be rude,' he said, 'and use any language they like. . . . Otherwise the things they cannot say fester inside them. If they want to call me or their teachers fools, they call us fools . . . there is no check on irreverence towards elders and betters.'

Russell remarked that 'When children are left free as regards their language, they say from time to time such things as Freudian text books assert they must be thinking'. On walks, for instance, they might be heard commenting (in plainer language) that the shape of a tree resembled a phallic symbol, and so on. The alternative 'hush-hush' policy, Russell believed, led to repression and disorders.

One of the features of the school was the play performed each term, with every actor making up his own part. Russell explained that the plays alternated between comedy and high tragedy: 'They used to insist upon everyone dying at the end, but now they are generally content with one murder.' Visitors were sometimes rather taken aback to find ten or twelve year old boys and girls writing and acting in plays which solemnly discussed problems of marriage, free love, and so on. The children also wrote co-operative•poetry, and when someone found this a little odd, Russell replied: 'May I suggest that Homer and the Authorized Version were not products of individual genius, and that the individualism of the artist is perhaps over-emphasized in modern times?'

Probably the leading spirit in setting up the school was Dora Russell, but Russell himself became absorbed in the study of child behaviour. He is certainly the only great philosopher—except perhaps for Locke—who not only devoted an enormous amount of time to teaching a small girl to eat her meals and use her pot, but also recorded his methods in detail, giving extremely useful practical advice on such questions. He wrote triumphantly to the parents of one four-year-old:

'[Jenny] is amazingly well. She eats enormously, and her bowels work every day (often twice) quite satisfactorily without medicine. If I may say so without undue boasting, I regard this as largely a triumph of science. . . .

'At first she used to be *difficile*, but we always accepted at once, at its face value, any reluctance to food that she expressed —often the reluctance was only rhetorical, so soon she changed her tactics. Now she has an idea that we think she eats too much, so she secures all she can. . . .

'As for constipation, we thought it was psychological (*vide* Freudian literature, *passim*). We first gave up letting her have a book while performing, so as to make her wish it sooner over. Then when she said she couldn't do anything, we said she was still too little to be very good at such things—assimilating it to jumping and swimming, in which she had been making rapid progress. The result confirmed our diagnosis, since she put her pride into being successful. It has made a great difference to her health and spirits, which are wonderful. It confirms me . . . in the belief that modern child psychology is sound.'

Results, however, were not always so happy. One of the greatest problems was to get the right staff. The teachers, for instance, might ignore Russell's very sensible ideas about never urging a child to eat; and Dora Russell explained to one visitor that she had just had to dismiss the Matron, because she had caught her giving the children 'a WC complex' by telling them not to use their pots in public.

What really made the school impossible, however, was that it became a natural receptacle for specially difficult children, ejected from more conventional establishments; and with them the attempt to allow free develoment could only lead to pandemonium. Visitors were struck by the contrast between Russell himself, still as fastidiously neat and tidy as ever, and the general impression of uncleanliness and untidiness at Telegraph House. The ceiling of the dining room was spattered with food, as a result of children throwing bits of pudding up and seeing who could make most stick.

The children were warned against starting fires in the gorse, and thereupon two children immediately did so. One of them, a boy, was promptly sent away. It was impossible to follow the same procedure with the other, a girl, because her mother was on her way back from Egypt to England at the time. So Russell put the girl to bed and locked up all her clothes. When the girl objected, Russell said 'If I let you up you might start the fire again, mightn't you?' She admitted 'Yes, I might'. So the girl stayed in bed till her mother got back.

Meanwhile the school was always in financial difficulties; it lost over £1,000 a year. Neither Bertrand nor Dora Russell had had any experience in practical administration; and there was one setback after another. They had rented Telegraph House furnished from Frank Russell, but Frank proceeded to remove most of its furniture. They discovered that the water supply was inadequate, and it had to be expensively increased. Russell had the double burden of trying to run the school—even attending to such domestic details as giving shopkeepers their orders—and making the money to pay for it, by writing articles or going on

L

American lecture tours.

His output remained prodigious. He told an interviewer in 1930: 'I haven't touched a pen since the school started, rather more than three years ago. I dictate at full speed, just as fast as the stenographer can go. I never revise a word. . . . I do three thousand words a day. I plan to work only in the morning. If I haven't done my stint, I sometimes go on working into the afternoon. I plan it all beforehand, so before I start it's all finished . . . when I have a book to write of 60,000 words, I start twenty days before it is due at the publishers. . . .

'I'm writing entirely for money. I don't mind pot-boiling. I have no "lofty feelings".'

The school was plagued by visitors and sightseers: the phrase on the school's notepaper, *Principal at Home Wednesdays 2.30— 5*, was changed to *Visitors by Appointment*. Russell retreated more and more into his room in the tower of Telegraph House, where the children would sometimes come up for lessons. But even today one of those who heard him can still remember the delight of listening to him talking on history.

Russell's connection with the school ended with the breaking up of his second marriage, but Dora carried it on until the beginning of the Second World War.

It was the attitude of the Russells towards sexual education which naturally attracted most attention to the school; I discuss this in the next chapter. So far as other educational problems are concerned, the impression given today by Russell's writings, as opposed to the attempt to work out his ideas in practice, is usually one of moderation and commonsense. As with so many other subjects, he saw that most questions have two sides—both of which he presents himself—and that the truth is never so simple as most theorists think.

He disapproved of punishment, and opposed corporal punishment under any circumstances: 'Every time a child is slapped, a complicated turmoil of conflicting passions is aroused.' But he always recognized that 'some departure from complete liberty is unavoidable if children are to be taught anything'. In his later writings on education, he explicitly listed the ways in which freedom had to be limited—to secure cleanliness, punctuality, respect for other people's property, and enough regular daily routine to give a child a feeling of security. Some interference by adults was always necessary, if only to prevent bigger children bullying the smaller ones. And he described, as an example of a legitimate use of force, how he himself cured a boy of irrational fear of the sea, and taught him to enjoy bathing, by holding him in the water despite struggles, and showing that no harm came from it.

Russell sometimes continued to show an undue deference towards the claims of Freud and modern psychologists, writing that 'I think the study of psychology, and especially of child psychology, makes it really possible to produce virtuous people'. But while he always respected the way in which Freud had encouraged people to talk honestly on sex matters, and agreed with Freud on the unconscious, he did not accept the view that sex is everything in it.* And practical observation of children left him with scant respect for the worst absurdities of the Freudians. He said they had exaggerated the significance of sex in early years; he declared that an Oedipus Complex only existed in 'rare and morbid' cases; he denied that there was anything wrong about parents kissing and fondling their children; and he disagreed with Freudian theories about sexual symbolism in children's play.

Russell was so anxious not to encourage militarism that he said that training in physical courage should come from challenging inanimate forces, and not from competition; he preferred mountaineering to football. Children should not see their parents kill anything, even wasps and snakes: as for human malefactors, they should not be hated but pitied in a detached scientific spirit. In retrospect, these seem curious teachings in a world which contained Hitler, Mussolini and Stalin;† Russell was either behind or ahead of the times. But Hitler was then an obscure agitator: and Russell did not go nearly so far as some other pacifist-minded educationalists of the 1920s. Children, he

* For instance, there is the desire for survival: 'Freud does not take into account the fact that most of us would sooner be alive than dead.' To over-enthusiastic Freudians, who provided detailed descriptions of what went on in the unconscious, he would say characteristically: 'It's all based on hypothesis. You can't *prove* it.'

† Russell commented to me on this passage in draft: 'I did not have a chance to get hold of them as infants.'

said, should not be kept in ignorance of the fact that there is cruelty in the world: and, after a lengthy discussion, he decided that there was nothing wrong about telling them fairy stories with sadistic implications.

It was natural, he said, that children should live in imagination through the life of their remote savage ancestors. The child who delighted in the story of Bluebeard cutting off his wives' heads, and identified himself with Bluebeard, was satisfying his instinct for power; in later life the same instinct could be satisfied in more creative and useful ways. But if the instinct was nipped in the bud in childhood, the child would grow up listless and lazy with 'a kind of milksop goodness'.

This conclusion not only showed admirable common sense, but also showed Russell again veering away from Freudianism: a complete Freudian would presumably deny that a thwarted instinct for power would atrophy, and would say instead that it would find some devious outlet.

Though Russell predicted an increasing tendency for children to be cared for by the state rather than by their fathers, he declared that 'I am not at all sure that this will be a good thing'. He was a strong advocate of nursery schools; but he did not agree with those educational theorists who think that nursery schools should be all play and no work, and that young children should on no account be taught anything. He assumed that a child of five should know how to read and write; and should perhaps have learnt a second language by the age of seven.

In some respects, from the point of view of modern British Socialists, Russell's views would be regarded as reactionary.

He suggested that the children should be picked out for University educations at the age of twelve, with no further competitive examinations. He also urged that exceptionally intelligent children should be sent to special schools. A system which went some way in this direction was introduced in Britain after the Second World War. Grammar Schools were confined to those selected by tests between eleven and twelve; and the Grammar School was almost the only route for poorer children to a University, though there were further competitive examinations on the way. But this system was soon attacked on the grounds that a child's future should not be decided so early;

that to confine Grammar Schools to children with brains was almost as bad as confining them to those whose parents could pay the fees; and that, in the interests of equalitarianism, all children should be mixed up in huge 'comprehensive schools'.

To this sort of argument, Russell had given a devastating reply many years earlier. He wrote in his *Education and the Social Order*:

'A great deal of needless pain and friction would be saved to clever children if they were not compelled to associate intimately with stupid contemporaries. There is an idea that rubbing up against all and sundry in youth is a good preparation for life. This appears to me to be rubbish. No one, in later life, associates with all and sundry. Bookmakers are not obliged to live among clergymen, nor clergymen among bookmakers.'

Russell—writing in 1928—ascribed 'the very small intellectual and artistic achievement in America', compared with France, to the way exceptionally clever boys in France were sent to their own separate schools.

Russell also did not conceal the fact that the children of clever parents are more likely to be clever than the children of stupid ones. In this, again, he was flatly contradictory to the scholarship system introduced in Britain, whereby the sons of professional men had more difficulty getting a University education than the sons of clerks or unskilled labourers.

As the above examples show, Russell's books on education still have an impact and an interest today. Though some of his views are now accepted as a matter of course, other reforms he suggested have still to be carried out. For instance, he criticized too much emphasis on the classics. He once (but not always) went so far as to say that the time he himself had spent on Latin and Greek had been 'almost completely wasted'. In England, at any rate, educational reformers were so busy deciding which children should go to which schools that they paid little attention to what they were taught when they got there; so the classics are still cherished as key subjects for public school and University scholarships.

CHAPTER XVIII

Marriage and Morals

FROM one point of view I approach the subject of this chapter with pleasure: because it is one on which I believe Russell was wrong. The attentive reader may have been pained to discover that on most questions I think (sometimes regretfully) that Russell was right. I know that this is a pity, and that in a book of this kind it is advisable to throw in occasionally a few superior words of criticism and disparagement, to create an impression of impartial aloofness. I am sorry not to oblige in this respect, but I cannot help it. It is unfortunately the case that, on most points, nobody has yet controverted Russell's conclusions, and most of his critics are merely silly. But, when I come to sex and marriage, my views and his are diametrically opposed: I think his ideas are based on two fundamental mistakes.

His writings on sex relations and 'Female Emancipation' form only one small segment of his work, and one at the opposite extreme to his greatest achievements in thought. But nothing he wrote attracted more attention among the general public, or had more immediate influence. More than anyone else, he changed the outlook on sex morality of a whole new generation; and during his lifetime he saw the cause of Women's Rights, once regarded as a crank's crusade, end up as an established part of the laws and customs of the land. A few years ago I was discussing with Gilbert Murray the various progressive causes for which he and Russell had worked in the early part of the twentieth century, ranging from internationalism and Free Trade to the temperance movement; and Dr Murray reached the regretful conclusion that the only one of these causes which had triumphed was Women's Rights.

Another reason for discussing Russell's views on sex and marriage is that they give a striking example of a fault to be found more than once in his philosophy. Whenever he became passionately involved in an argument, he would tend to assume that everything his opponents said was wrong. And though his opponents usually *were* wrong, they were not always wrong about everything.

Russell's first fundamental mistake was to imply that there was nothing strange about sex, and that any atmosphere of mystery was solely due to the obscurantism of the Victorian moralists whom he loathed. They believed that children should be kept in artificial ignorance about sex; Russell went to the other extreme and wrote as though it should be possible to tell children all about it. If the mystery could be taken out of something as marvellous as mathematics, why not out of sex? I cannot make my criticism of Russell stronger than by saying that his attitude became reminiscent of Stalin.

'Marxist philosophical materialism,' wrote Stalin, 'holds that the world and its laws are fully knowable. . . . There are no things in the world which are unknowable, but only things which are still not known, but which will be disclosed and made known by the efforts of science and practice.'

Russell wrote about sex, in words reminiscent of Stalin, that 'The important thing is to produce, as soon as possible, the feeling that the sense of mystery is only due to ignorance, which can be dispelled by patience and mental effort.' Sex, he said, 'should be treated in exactly as matter-of-fact a manner as if you were explaining how the soda-water gets into a siphon'. The way to cure a boy of obscene interests was to bore him with a flood of information, until 'he felt that there was nothing more to know, and that what he did know was uninteresting'. Superstitions based on the fear of death should be combated in the same way: death should be described 'as if it were the most ordinary thing imaginable'. Russell advised parents: 'Do all you can to make the child feel that there is no mystery about it, and to convey the impression that the subject is rather uninteresting.'

The only comment I can make on this attitude is that I think it is impossible. If anyone tells me that there is nothing strange about sex, and that there is nothing more remarkable about the manufacture of a baby than there is about the manufacture of a motor car, I can only reply that I do not believe him. If anyone tries to suggest that life and death are rather dull subjects, I can only say that nobody thinks this for a moment, least of all Russell.

It seems to me self-evident that the secrets of life and death are not only unknown, but may well be unknowable. Russell and others may hope that one day biology and psychology can be reduced to physics, but there is no certain reason for thinking this possible. If Russell implies the contrary, he is in conflict with the undogmatic agnosticism of his whole philosophical outlook. And if he is maintaining that, in spite of all we do not know about life and death, it is right to teach that there is nothing remarkable about them, then he is in conflict with his real beliefs about the correct roles of both teachers and children. For instance, he had written in the *Principles of Social Reconstruction* that a good teacher must have 'reverence', and that such a man 'feels in all that lives, but especially in human beings, and most of all in children, something sacred, indefinable, unlimited, something individual and strangely precious, the growing principle of life, an embodied fragment of the dumb striving of the world'. So far as children are concerned, Russell wrote that 'there must never be discouragement of curiosity'; but it obviously discourages curiosity to imply that a subject is uninteresting.

Now why was it that Russell, by the time he published *On Education* in 1926, had lapsed into an attitude which can be compared—in one respect at least—to that of Stalin? One reason was that, as already remarked, he came closer to conventional progressive opinion during these years. Another reason lay partly, perhaps, in his general philosophical position; he had not yet fully worked out his ideas about the limitations of scientific knowledge. But the main explanation, as is so often the case in both his philosophical and his popular writings, can only be understood by knowing something about his opponents and the nature of the evils he was attacking.

Upon the facts that sex is strange and death is often feared, religion and traditional morality had built a superstructure of superstition, taboo, convention, misery, warped minds and unhappy lives. Russell was so eager to destroy the superstructure that he wanted to deny the existence of the foundations. Because mystery had produced superstition, he wanted to abolish the mystery; because traditional morality could produce misery, he wanted to abolish traditional morality. He sometimes wrote as if the Victorian attitude to sex represented nothing but a phase of mental aberration which could be cured by correct education. He sometimes forgot that sex had been wrapped in conventions and taboos, in all ages and all lands, for the reason that it was something strong and strange, raising problems to which the wisest men did not know the answers, and still do not know the answers.

In Russell's first mistake he agreed with Stalin; in his second he went almost worse and agreed with Bernard Shaw. Shaw expressed it by making one of his characters say that a man is a woman, and a woman is a man, 'with a slight difference that doesn't matter except on special occasions'. Russell said that 'The only difference I know between men and women is one you cannot print'. He never gave any detailed argument for this Russellian remark: in fact contrary statements can be found in his writings. But I think that, like other progressives at the time, he was usually influenced by the idea summed up in that vague phrase, 'the equality of the sexes'.

Now women may be inferior to men; they may be superior; they may be a mixture of both; but the only one thing quite certain is that they are not equal. For instance, there is considerable evidence that women, for anatomical and physiological reasons, are on the average inferior to men in many physical and mental accomplishments. So far as physical strength is concerned, this is confirmed by practical tests; and one might expect this fact to make Feminists feel some doubts about their position. On the contrary, taking advantage of the greater difficulty in measuring intellectual ability, they blandly assert on no evidence whatever that the weaker sex physically are still the equals of men intellectually.

Russell was too honest not to admit that women on the whole show less intelligence than men. As a neutral monist with Behaviourist leanings, he could have found an explanation ready to hand in some sort of correlation of physical and mental capacities. Instead, he produced a curious plea that the main reason why women became less intelligent was that their curiosity about sex was more effectively inhibited in youth. I do not think this is a satisfactory explanation of the relative scarcity of female philosophers, mathematicians, and scientists.

Russell's devotion to the cause of sex equality is an interesting example of how the most independent of thinkers can be influenced subconsciously by the intellectual climate of his age. There was also a long-standing loyalty of principle involved: his father, and his boyhood hero J. S. Mill, had been derided as pioneers of Feminism. It was part of the Liberal tradition in which he had been brought up to champion the weak against the strong. Above all, inequality between the sexes was part and parcel of the whole Victorian outlook against which Russell was in revolt.*

Russell noted that marital infidelity was traditionally greater among husbands than wives. He saw no valid reasons in physiology or psychology for such a difference; it seemed that, to make things all square, wives should be as unfaithful as husbands. He suggested that marriage should not be regarded as excluding outside sexual relations; and that husbands, instead of restraining their inclinations in this regard, should confine themselves to restraining any jealousy at similar infidelities by their wives. Adultery, said Russell, should not in itself be a ground for divorce.

'Many of us believe,' he wrote, 'that the attempt (which has never succeeded) to enforce strict monogamy is a cause of as much preventible misery as any political or economic evil'. . . . 'Of all forms of caution, caution in love is perhaps the most fatal to true happiness.'

This was in accordance with the basic argument of his *Principles of Social Reconstruction*, that creative impulses are to be encouraged and possessive impulses discouraged. He thought that if restraint was necessary, we should not restrain the free

* Russell has emphasized to me that he did not preach equality between men and women, but only equal rights; and that his advocacy of equal rights, moreover, was not derived from any *a priori* principle, but from the utilitarian doctrine of maximization of satisfaction. I do not think this materially affects my argument, because I think I have a similar prejudice against talk of 'equal rights', except in some obvious practical senses.

and delightful emotion of love, but the negative and restrictive emotion of jealousy. But this attractive view failed, I think, to take into account the fact that it is easier to control actions than to control emotions.

It is not impossible for a man who feels sexual attraction to hold back from sexual action, or for a man who suspects his wife of infidelity to refrain from murdering her: such instances of self discipline are occurring every day with ordinary people, and Othello's conduct was the exception rather than the rule. But it requires a very exceptional saint, or a very exceptional state of bloodlessness, not to feel the emotions of sexual attraction or jealousy in the first place. And the only criticism which needs making of the kind of marriages Russell proposed is that they do not work, because jealousy and unhappiness cannot in fact be eliminated where ordinary people are concerned.

It is possible that, on this point, Russell was wrong not because his views were too advanced, but because they were too conventional. In his praise for husbands and wives who could view each other's infidelities with equanimity, he may have been influenced subconsciously by the aristocratic belief that any display of emotion is bad form. The sexual experimentors of the 1920s, who prided themselves on their casual promiscuity and absence of jealousy, thought they were the acme of modern-mindedness and freedom from inhibitions; but in fact they represented the culmination of the old-established aristocratic tradition of self-control.

It is easy and obvious to make the criticism that Russell, when he wrote of human problems, was too much of a logician and a rationalist to understand how irrational people are. As I have already pointed out, the criticism is usually unjustified; but I think it is true that he was incapable of understanding the arguments for conventional marriage, simply because they are irrational and paradoxical, if not mysterious. It is irrational to promise to love one woman for the rest of your existence, when the world is full of other women whom you have not yet met, and may very well prefer; but life goes on as it does because enough people are enough in love to ignore this obvious fact. And the virtue of monogamy lies in the paradox that, precisely to the extent that it is binding, it gives freedom. When fidelity in love is absolutely certain, partners in marriage are free to enjoy any friendships they like with those of the opposite sex; free to travel and to have different interests. Otherwise freedom is confined sooner or later by the shadows of doubt and jealousy.

Russell did not advocate any theory which he was not prepared to see put into practice. He told a married friend that there was no reason why she should not have an outside lover, and he acted on his theories himself. (In fact Gilbert Murray, somewhat characteristically, once gave me his view that Russell departed from monogamy because, having decided by rational argument that he was in favour of free love, he felt he ought to carry it out.) Once somebody asked Russell if he did not think he was being unkind to women who found themselves attracted to him, and in whom he later lost interest. 'Why?' he asked. 'They can find other men too.' It was a remark characteristic of the modesty of which great men can be capable; apparently it simply did not occur to Russell that any other man might be an unsatisfactory substitute for him. And he did not recognize any difference in the speed with which men and women, as a general rule, can change the object of their affections.

At one period during his marriage with Dora Russell, his theories were exemplified to the extent of having one of Dora's lovers living in the same house with them.

There is an honourable rule in British journalism and letters, according to which the reporting of divorce proceedings is reduced to the bare essentials. This tradition I propose to follow, confining what I say about the ending of Russell's second marriage to a short summary of the contemporary account in the columns of *The Times*. The divorce suit brought by Dora alleged Russell's adultery with Marjorie Spence, an Oxford student who had taken a job with the Russells, and subsequently helped Russell with research. It came out during the hearing that, since the marriage, Dora had borne four children, of whom only two were by Russell. (In his writings, Russell had stressed that extra-marital relations should not be allowed to lead to children.) She admitted adultery with two men, but it was stated that 'Both instances of her own adultery . . . were preceded by at least two cases of infidelity on the part of her husband'. There was a technical complication over a *Rose* v. *Rose* clause in a previous deed of separation, which interested the lawyers but which does not interest us; and the marriage was dissolved in 1935. Russell married Patricia* Spence in January 1936; and their only son was born the following year.

One point is perhaps not too obvious to be added. The fact that his own marriage ended in divorce did not in itself prove Russell's theories wrong: any more than any other divorce proves that conventional marriage is wrong.

In the foregoing pages I have criticized what Russell said about marriage; his views on pre-marital sexual experience must be kept separate. It was undesirable, he said, that 'either a man or a woman should enter upon the serious business of a marriage intended to lead to children without having had previous sexual experience'; and this view, though still controversial, became widely accepted in many countries.

Russell applauded a book by Leon Blum, the French Socialist Premier, who urged that young women ought to have as much right to promiscuity as young men; Russell defended this on the grounds of 'justice', regretting that no British Prime Minister would say as much in print. Blum believed that the instincts of both sexes were promiscuous in youth, and became monogamous in the thirties, when marriage should take place. Russell's only criticism was a doubt about whether monogamy would set in at any age.

Russell's own most celebrated proposal was that the life of most University students would be better, 'both intellectually and morally', if they had temporary childless marriages. 'This,' he wrote, 'would afford a solution of the sexual urge neither restless nor surreptitious, neither mercenary nor casual, and of such a nature that it need not take up time which ought to be given to work.' No University authorities have yet looked kindly on this suggestion.

My own instincts are old-fashioned and distrustful of anything so logical as Russell's proposal. But there is not here the

---

* Marjorie Spence changed her name to Patricia by deed poll. Her friends called her 'Peter'. Hence the rather confusing references, in the Prefaces to some of Russell's books, to assistance received from someone variously referred to as 'Peter Spence' or 'Patricia Russell'.

same practical evidence against him. The main reason why there was a reaction against his views on marriage was that they did not lead to happy results. If there was any reaction against his views on pre-marital relations, the cause was mainly economic prosperity after the Second World War. Marriages could take place at a far earlier age than during the years of depression, when Russell was writing.

Changing circumstances also affected Russell's plea that unmarried women should not be debarred from motherhood by the censure of public opinion. At the time he wrote, there were more women than men of marriageable age, so that monogamy meant an unavoidable surplus; in Britain, at any rate, the position became reversed after the Second World War, with more marriageable men than women.

I cannot end this criticism of Russell's views in any other way than by stressing the debt owed to the great work of destruction he carried out. Perhaps the finest tribute to his success is that few people now even realize the nature of the old ideas. Russell, it must be repeated, was fighting a cruel and indefensible state of affairs where sexual ignorance was deliberately fostered, so that a boy might think the changes of puberty were signs of some dreadful disease, and a girl might marry without knowing anything of what lay ahead of her on her bridal night; where women were taught to look on sex, not as a source of joy, but of painful matrimonial duty; where prudery went to the extent of covering the legs of pianos in draperies; where artificial mystery evoked morbid curiosity, and where humbug went hand in hand with unhappiness; where no escape was possible from the misery of an unhappy marriage except by elaborate legal proof of adultery; and where a rigid sexual code was accompanied by the tacit acceptance of prostitution. Russell's revolt did not remove all these things, because I think he did not appreciate all the reasons behind them; and so there has been something of a reaction, and a re-establishment of some of the old conventions. But the relations between men and women can never again suffer from some of the evils he attacked; and on many points at least his views still stand as ideals of tolerance and understanding yet to be attained.

CHAPTER XIX

The Indefatigable Author

SOMETHING of the shyness of Russell's craving for friendship
was shown in a letter he wrote to Charles Sanger in 1929: 'I
am very sorry indeed to hear that you are so ill. . . . Dear
Charlie, I don't think I have ever expressed the deep affection
I have for you, but I suppose you have known of it.' Sanger died
soon after, and Russell somewhat distressed his widow by a
typical refusal to compromise—he would not attend the funeral
because there was going to be a religious service. With the
death of Sanger, Crompton Llewellyn Davies and Lady Ottoline
Morrell, almost all his intimate friends had gone. Lady
Ottoline died in 1938. She became deaf towards the end of her
life; but, with typical kindness, she continued her Thursday
salons, simply to give interesting people the pleasure of meeting
each other, although with her deafness they could have given
little pleasure to herself.

Russell lost philosophical friends too. He could not follow
Wittgenstein in the mysticism shown in the latter parts of the
Tractatus. And one day Wittgenstein solemnly told him: 'We
will not talk together any more.'

Russell's divergence from Whitehead even preceded the parting of their philosophical views. It began, perhaps, on one
occasion when he was arguing with Whitehead and Mrs
Whitehead about Free Love, and I think we can assume that
Russell was putting his views in the most provocative and outrageous way he could. Whitehead grew more and more indignant, and finally exclaimed: 'Bertie, you're an *aristocrat*, not a
gentleman.' Mrs Whitehead once remarked that it was a great
pity for Russell that he had enjoyed an independent income in
his early years, and could thus do as he liked instead of being

tied down by the discipline of an academic post.

Whitehead may have resented the fact that many people gave Russell most of the credit for *Principia Mathematica*. And he thought that, in *Our Knowledge of the External World*, Russell had published some of Whitehead's ideas about 'constructions' prematurely, even though Russell had made full acknowledgment to Whitehead.

There was a further disagreement over pacifism and the First World War: Whitehead's younger son was killed, and Whitehead perhaps never fully recovered from the tragedy. Afterwards he went to America as Professor of Philosophy at Harvard, from which position he looked on Russell's American lecture tours as rather undignified. He was also offended by a ludicrous misunderstanding. He invited Russell to lunch with him at Harvard. The letter was opened by somebody in the firm of agents arranging the lecture tour, and Whitehead was furious to get back a letter quoting a fee for a luncheon engagement with Russell—who, of course, remained ignorant of the whole episode.

There were other losses of friends as well. T. S. Eliot and Russell drifted apart when Eliot changed his interests from philosophy to the Church. Among politicians, Russell disapproved of Clifford Allen supporting Ramsay MacDonald in the formation of the National Government, and accepting a peerage; and though Robert Trevelyan persuaded Russell to go over and talk to him in the hope of a reconciliation, the meeting was not a success, Lady Allen saying after it that she never wanted to meet Russell again. There were others, on the other hand, with whom Russell disagreed because he thought that they were too far to the Left.

He was never very friendly with G. D. H. Cole, at that time the main intellectual force behind the Labour Party. (Russell once remarked, during the First World War, that he hoped he would not have the same effect on Cole as Godwin had on Malthus.) The Webbs, who at first shared Russell's misgivings about Soviet Russia, went there and wrote a book of adulation about it which had a great deal to do with shaping Left Wing opinion. There was a final, irrevocable breach with Bernard Shaw, over a question to do with Shaw's admiration for the

Stalin régime. Russell said that Shaw was 'cruel, narrow-minded and silly', and commented that Shaw 'liked Russia because when he went there it was just as bad as he expected'.

Russell saw little of Charles Trevelyan, who disapproved of his critical attitude to Bolshevism. Meanwhile G. M. Trevelyan disapproved of Russell's views on marriage and morals, perhaps reflecting the lack of human understanding which was his greatest weakness as a historian. That only left Robert Trevelyan, and his wife Elizabeth, who always remained sympathetic. Russell wrote characteristically, after one visit to the Trevelyans at the Shiffolds, their Surrey home near Leith Hill:

'I meant to write to tell you how very much I enjoyed my visit; and then I meant to write and thank you for my pyjamas; and then I meant to write and apologise for not having done any of these things. I shall demand something from the Road Fund for improving the road to Hell.'

For a time Russell and his third wife lived at Telegraph House, but later he and Patricia Russell moved to Kidlington near Oxford, where Russell formed a new friendship.

One of their neighbours was Dr John Baker, the distinguished biologist. Russell, after working hard all day, would always stop in the evening; and after dinner Dr Baker sometimes went over for parlour games. He taught Russell 'Up-Jenkins', which Russell used to play with enormous relish and enjoyment. They also played a game in which everybody had to give everybody else marks, from 0 to 20, for a number of attributes such as intelligence, honesty and so on. As usually played, nobody knows who is responsible for giving the different marks: but Russell had his own version of the game whereby people found out in the end who had given them marks for what.

Baker was once a little disconcerted to find that Russell had given his children higher marks for intelligence than he gave to Baker. Russell gave Baker 20 for sincerity and 0 for tact: explaining that the two were converses, and that therefore the marks for them would have to add up to 20.

During the 1930s Russell still had to earn his living by

M

indefatigable journalism and authorship, despite any worries or bad health. (One of the most practical advantages of his erudition arose when he was critically ill on a trip to Spain, and described his symptoms to the Spanish doctor in Latin.) Among his more 'popular' books in this period may be mentioned *The Conquest of Happiness*, *In Praise of Idleness*, *The Scientific Outlook*, and *Religion and Science*.

Russell had often denied that philosophy could be, or should be, a source of moral guidance or consolation. He once wrote that 'The only "consolations of philosophy" I know are the consolations of *doing* philosophy, which are the same as those of doing anything else'. He said that he had often found himself feeling that all is vanity; but that he never got out of the mood by means of philosophy, but owing to some imperative need for action, like one of his children being ill. He had lived long enough by now, however, to be able to offer experienced advice on some of the problems of life, and this advice was in close conformity with the general bent of his philosophy; and also in conformity, incidentally, with the precepts of many religions.

He urged people to escape from self-preoccupation by the contemplation of greater things. The following, for instance, was very useful and plain advice he gave in *The Conquest of Happiness* to those who cannot stop worrying: 'When some misfortune threatens, consider seriously and deliberately what is the very worst that could happen. Having looked this possible misfortune in the face, give yourself sound reasons for thinking that after all it would be no such very terrible disaster. Such reasons always exist, since at the worst nothing that happens to oneself has any cosmic importance. When you have looked for some time steadily at the worst possibility and have said to yourself with real conviction, "Well, after all, that would not matter so very much," you will find that your worry diminishes to a quite extraordinary extent.'

Russell's writings often refer to the insignificance of man in comparison with the Universe. He carried the same point of view a bit further—I think too far—in his *Religion and Science*. He wrote: 'If it is the purpose of the Cosmos to evolve mind, we should regard it as rather incompetent in having produced so little in such a long time. . . . It may seem odd that life should occur by accident, but in such a large universe accidents will happen.' There may be good reasons for denying cosmic purpose and belittling the importance of human life, but I do not think this is a good one. Nature has never heard of Occam's Razor; a female codfish lays about 9,000,000 eggs a year, of which only one or two come to maturity; but nobody deduces from this that the purpose of the eggs is not to produce a new generation of codfish. (One can imagine a modest-minded codfish, who had read Bertrand Russell, deciding that its own existence was the kind of unimportant accident only to be expected among such large numbers; and that if nature had meant the eggs to produce codfish, nature would never have set about it in such a wasteful and incompetent way.) Frank Ramsey once wrote that 'I don't feel the least humble before the vastness of the heavens. The stars may be large, but they cannot think or love; and these are qualities which impress me far more than size does. I take no credit for weighing nearly seventeen stone.' I agree, at least in part, with Ramsey's point of view; and I think that Russell would really agree in part too. (His considered view on two ways of looking at man and the universe can be found at the beginning of Part III of *Human Knowledge*.)

As I said earlier, it is impossible to divide Russell's life into convenient compartments; he always tended to be interested in everything. In 1936, for instance, there appeared his article on *The Limits of Empiricism*, representing an important step towards the philosophical position he finally reached in *Human Knowledge*. And he returned for a time to mathematical philosophy, writing an Introduction to the second edition of *The Principles of Mathematics*, published in 1937. In this he accepted a modification of his Theory of Types suggested by Frank Ramsey. But he still insisted on his fundamental thesis, the identity of mathematics and logic, against the rival views of the Formalists and Intuitionists.

Broadly speaking, however, Russell's main interests during these years were in economics, political theory and history. It is interesting to note that, in his *In Praise of Idleness*, he anticipated Keynes by challenging the orthodox economists who always applauded saving and deplored spending. He wrote 'As long as a man spends his income, he puts bread into people's mouths. . . . The real villain, from this point of view, is the man who saves.' What he once called 'the detestable vice of thrift' could lead to unemployment.

On the whole, said Russell, it would be much better if savers were to spend their money, even on drink or gambling, or in giving parties for their friends. This, at the time, was sheer heresy: and the Professors of Economics dismissed Russell's ideas lightly as the amusing fallacies of a philosopher straying out of his own field. But in 1936 Keynes developed a detailed argument, in his *General Theory of Interest, Employment and Money*, to the effect that unemployment could result from people trying to save too much; and this idea became part of established economic doctrine.

Much of Russell's work was devoted to a systematic study of the causes of historical development. He characteristically decided that no systematic explanation is possible, and that historians tend to falsify things through trying to show that history makes sense. Ever since 1896, he had always rejected the over-simplification of the Marxist attempts to explain everything in terms of economic forces. He once pointed out, for instance, that 'The really important scientific discoveries . . . have very seldom been the result of economic motives'; and that 'Everyone knows that bad pictures and bad books bring in more money than good ones; nevertheless many artists and writers do the best work of which they are capable'. As another illustration, Russell wrote that 'No one ever heard of a civil servant being sacked for laziness, so that any work done by a civil servant must be done for non-economic motives. Nevertheless some of them sometimes work. Why? Partly from love of honour, partly from love of power.'

If human history was not governed solely or dominantly by economics, what were the causal factors at work? To answer this question, Russell wrote *Freedom and Organization*, 1814–1914, a historical study which remains one of the most valuable and readable of his non-philosophical books. His scope embraced both Europe and America. Historical events, he said, resulted from a complicated tangle of causes, grouped under three headings: economic techniques, political theories, and important individuals. Illustrating his thesis, he described doctrines such as Nationalism, Philosophical Radicalism, Marxism, and American democracy; and he gave vivid sketches of the personalities and work of such men as Malthus, Bentham, Marx, Jefferson, Jackson, Rockefeller, and Carnegie.

Like all good portraits, these sketches tell us something about the man who painted them as well as about the subjects. Russell, for instance, was grossly unfair to the Reverend T. R. Malthus. No one would ever guess, from his description, that Malthus was a cheerful and kindly man who exalted 'the pleasures of pure love', advocated shorter hours and higher wages, and challenged Christian orthodoxy by rejecting the idea of eternal punishment in Hell as unworthy of a 'merciful and righteous God'.

But one feels that, so long as Russell had any life in him at all, he could not help being hostile to a clergyman who urged the 'moral restraint' of a natural and delightful impulse. The vitality in the writing of *Freedom and Organization* more than counter-balanced an occasional bias, which can easily be corrected by anyone knowing the bent of Russell's mind.

Russell wrote *Freedom and Organization* at the suggestion of his American publisher at the time, W. W. Norton, and had the idea from the start that it would show the defeat of nineteenth century Liberal theories. They had been defeated by Bismarck, who had allied Nationalism with Conservatism instead of Liberalism; and by Rockefeller, who had shown how free competition could lead to industrial concentration and monopoly. (This was the point which, as early as 1896, Russell had noted as the most important argument in Marx.)

Russell decided that such monopolies should at least be under public control. He wrote:

'The Radical who believes in competition is doomed to defeat in any contest with modern corporations. Their power is analogous to that of armies, and to leave them in private hands is just as disastrous as it is to leave armies in private hands. The large-scale economic organizations of modern times are an inevitable outcome of modern technique, and technique tends increasingly to make competition wasteful. The solution, for those who do not wish to be oppressed, lies in public ownership of the organizations.'

In an essay on *The Case for Socialism*, he demanded the State ownership of ultimate economic power, 'which involves, as a minimum, land and minerals, capital, banking, credit and foreign trade'.

Russell had thus become a supporter of nationalization on a wide scale. The reason, I think, was that he had over-estimated the advantages of large-scale organization, and under-estimated the sheer administrative difficulties in running a huge bureaucratic machine, concerned with industrial affairs as well as the ordinary business of Government. But if Russell was wrong in this, every other Socialist theorist was wrong too; it was many years after a Socialist Government had actually come to power, in Britain in 1945, before anyone began to see the extent of the problems involved.

Another difficulty was one which Russell saw clearly. His whole argument as a Socialist now led to the conclusion that the powers and activities of the State should be enormously increased. But, especially since the war and his visit to Soviet Russia, he had stressed the dangers of 'too much organization in the realm of thought, and too much strenuousness in action'. He said once that 'Love of power does far more harm than love of drink'.

In 1938 he published his book *Power*, devoted to the thesis that 'Love of power is the chief motive producing the changes which social science has to study'. Russell argued that economic needs were finite and could therefore be satisfied; but the craving for power had no limits.

He stressed that Socialism had to be safeguarded by a more thorough-going democracy than any known before, including special measures to safeguard liberties; otherwise the result might be 'a new tyranny at once economic and political, more drastic and more terrible than any previously known'. He said that 'To suppose that irresponsible power, just because it is called Socialist or Communist, will be freed miraculously from the bad qualities of all arbitrary power in the past, is mere childish nursery psychology'.

This problem of 'the taming of power'—whether under Socialism or Capitalism—was one which Russell always recognized, and to which he continually returned. He had discussed it in *The Prospects of Industrial Civilization*. It was reflected in the title *Freedom and Organization* (and still more in the title used in America, *Freedom versus Organization*). It was described again many years afterwards in *Authority and the Individual*. Russell never found a really satisfactory answer to it; but his various suggestions are at least as good a compromise as any others yet offered.

CHAPTER XX

Pacifism and the Second World War

IT is somewhat unfair to Russell's reputation, though easily understandable, that books like *Freedom and Organization* and *Power* attracted less public attention than his pacifist propaganda during the same years.

Russell was so far from being an orthodox pacifist that, as we have seen, he had advocated a strong British Navy, as a condition for a socialist Britain surviving in a capitalistic world. What changed his mind was air power, which he saw was making sea power obsolete; and he predicted that another war would be fought by aeroplanes spreading poison gas and perhaps disease germs.

He wrote in 1933: 'If either side wins the next war (which is unlikely), it will be the side whose young men have shown the most intelligence in chemistry and bacteriology.' Lecturing to the Fabian Society in 1935, he prophesied that air attacks on big cities would mean destruction and panic, 'involving a total breakdown of our food supplies, and the launching of millions of starving desperate nomads from the ruined towns on the countryside.' These predictions were developed in detail in his book *Which Way to Peace?*, written for Michael Joseph and published in October 1936. He forecast tremendous loss of life, and he added in a newspaper interview that he was afraid the war would go on until Europe was in chaos, industrialism and ordinary government had disappeared, and there were widespread epidemics.

In *Which Way to Peace?* he argued that the chaos caused by air raids would make martial law essential: 'A war in defence of democracy would necessarily begin with a military despotism, and there is no reason to doubt that it would end with one.' . . .

'The end of all the death and destruction will be the substitution of an English Hitler for the German one.' The British would become like the Nazis in the process of fighting them; so that even if they won, their character would be changed, making them cruel and ruthless.

In these circumstances, said Russell, pacifism was the only sensible policy. 'If, under a Pacifist Government, Hitler were to attack this country, he and his German troops should be welcomed like tourists and greeted in a friendly way.' . . . 'If the Germans were allowed to walk in without fighting, it would alter the mood of average Germans and make militarism seem silly.'

He urged individuals to refuse to fight, and said that pacifists were justified in emigrating to a neutral country. He discussed with his friends whether it was not his duty to take his three children to America.

In his campaign for pacifism, Russell even spoke to the House of Lords. He had not a very high opinion of that august but somewhat soporific assembly. On it being remarked to him about this time that the peers on their red benches looked rather like goldfish in a bowl, he replied: 'But the goldfish sometimes move.' Though he inherited his title in 1931, it was not till 1937 that he made his maiden speech, declaring that 'I believe—I may say I hope—that in all the countries engaged in the next war, the civil populations, after they have had some experience, will refuse to continue the fighting, and will show thereby that they have more sense than their rulers'.

I imagine that, of all his books, *Which Way to Peace?* was the one which Russell would be least disposed to defend. It was certainly far from his best; and, perhaps as a natural corollary, it was one which many reviewers praised most. Russell's opinions were not individual idiosyncrasies; they were shared by, and largely derived from, those held by many intelligent people. Similar predictions about destruction by air raids had been made for years, for instance, by H. G. Wells and Aldous Huxley; they had often been voiced in the *New Statesman*, a left-wing weekly which used to have considerable influence. Its review of *Which Way to Peace?* said that 'If we do get into a war it will not be a war "against Fascism". . . . Those who oppose militarism should welcome a strong pacifist movement in this country'. This was less than three years before Britain found itself at war against all the forces of Nazi Germany.

It is a sad fact that, in the years immediately before the Second World War, many of the most intelligent people in England were hopelessly wrong, and the Colonel Blimps were right. I think Hitler would never have come to power in Germany if the advice given by the intelligent people had been taken earlier, and the Blimps had not had their way after 1918. But the fact remains that, even when Hitler was firmly established and obviously bent on conquest, the intelligentsia either went on preaching pacifism and opposing re-armament, or else predicted a kind of war quite different from the one for which Britain should have been preparing. Civilization was saved by the stupid young men who believed that victory would still depend on the kind of courage and discipline needed in personal combat, and who went into the Army or spent their weekends learning to fly fighter planes.

The glaring mistakes of the intelligentsia suggest some fundamental fault in their reasoning: but it need be no part of my purpose to discuss why, in these years, so many Socialist intellectuals were such idiots. (I tactfully refrain from any discussion of whether some of them are still idiots.) The only points of fundamental importance in theory were their worship of Soviet Russia, and their Marxist views about political morality; and many of them have themselves explained, in orgies of autobiographical self-analysis, exactly why they admired Communism in the 1930s, and why they changed their minds when admiration for Communism went out of fashion. I do not know whether anybody else is particularly interested, and it need not interest us; since, as we have seen, Russell was remarkably free from this fault. We need only concern ourselves with his mistake about pacifism; which I think we shall find was based on two technical errors, and not on any important issue of principle.

In the first place, he over-estimated the importance of the bomber as a purveyor of poison gas. Secondly, he under-estimated the evil of which the Nazis were capable. From these two errors, everything else in *Which Way to Peace?* followed automatically.

The first was not only shared by others on the Left, but by military experts whom Russell quoted and studied,* and it came to be accepted by Whitehall. Anyone who was in England in 1938 and 1939 will remember the hasty distribution of gas masks, and the 'gas drill' in the Army. What is less familiar is the fact that skeleton plans were made for Britain to be governed on a regional basis, on the assumption that air raids on London might well lead to a breakdown of the central Government. And, as it turned out, Russell was merely wise a little too early; had the atom bomb been discovered on both sides a few months sooner, his forecasts of destruction would have been underestimates.

Russell's second error, about the Nazis, might seem to result from a fundamentally false view of human nature. It might be said, that just as he had failed to realize before 1914 the way in which ordinary people could get vicarious enjoyment out of war, so he failed to realize before 1939 the extremes of sadism to which abnormal perverts could reach. But the Nazis were no worse, for instance, than Genghis Khan, whose atrocities Russell described in the *Problem of China*. What he did not realize was the way that modern means of mass propaganda, like broadcasting and the cinema, and the enlistment of science in the service of secret police, could allow perverts to enforce their opinions on a whole nation. Genghis Khan could not scream hatred into a microphone, to be heard by millions; he could not have telephone wires tapped when his enemies were plotting. Born in an age of modern science, Genghis Khan might have been very like Hitler; and it is to this extent that Russell's mistake can be called a technical one.

The only moral to be drawn, therefore, is the rather obvious one that it is wrong to regard a philosopher as an authority on poison gas and techniques of mass propaganda.

It was a natural mistake to make when so much journalism, advertising and publicity have conspired to convince us that the

* For instance, Major-General Fuller: 'London, for several days, will be one vast raving bedlam, the hospitals will be stormed, traffic will cease, the homeless will shriek for help, the city will be a pandemonium. What of the Government of Westminster? It will be swept away by an avalanche of terror.'

Throughout the time Russell was writing *Which Way to Peace?* he regularly subscribed to and read the *Army, Navy and Air Force Gazette* and the *Aeroplane*.

best people to express an opinion on any particular subject are those who know nothing about it. We grew accustomed to a playwright like Shaw setting himself up as an authority on Bergson's philosophy, a scientist like Jeans discussion theological questions, and a theologian like Dean Inge explaining the Second Law of Thermodynamics. In more modern times, we take it for granted that a cricketer is an expert on hair cream, and that a television celebrity should advise us about ball-point pens. So far as Russell was concerned, he was always writing articles on everything under the sun, with one curious exception. After diligent years spent searching through press cuttings and newspapers, after reading his views on politics and pacifism and war and international affairs and socialism and marriage and education and science, I can think of only one subject on which almost no newspaper seems to have solicited his opinions. That subject is philosophy.

The marvel is that, among this profusion of writing, Russell did not make more mistakes. He rarely went wrong when he was seeing and judging for himself, as in Germany and Russia and China. When he erred, it was often because he paid too much attention to the expert opinion of others. The real danger about the intelligent amateur is that he may have too much deference for the professional. Russell modestly assumed that, if he was writing about any subject on which he was not an authority, he should be guided by people who were: he said afterwards that in *Which Way to Peace?* he had taken his facts from the experts, 'in the way that a man who is not an expert should'. Apparently he did not always distinguish how subjects should be arranged in a kind of hierarchy—for instance, Mathematics, Physics, Biology, Economics, Politics, Psychology—in which experts are more and more likely to be wrong.

One might almost lay down the principle that no eminent person should write about anything outside his own sphere unless he *disagrees* with the experts. If he is right in disagreeing it will do good; and if he is wrong it will not matter.

It is fair to add that *Which Way to Peace?*, considered as a book in which the main conclusion was wrong, included an extraordinary number of points which were right. For instance, Russell was right in saying that he was more consistent than the

Labour Party, which had opposed rearmament while demanding resistance to Fascist aggression. And he had no illusions about the future: 'The momentum of events certainly points to war in the very near future.' He wrote with complete realism that 'Germany . . . has built up a terrifying war machine, which is evidently intended to be used when a suitable moment arrives. . . . It is argued that, if Germany's just claims are met in a friendly spirit, the militaristic temper which is now dominant will gradually become softened. . . . [But] the treatment of defenceless opponents within the Reich suggests the mentality of the bully who grows worse, not better, through success.'

In this, of course, Russell was candid enough to conflict with what he had written elsewhere about the Nazis; and he was candid enough to confess that 'the old Adam within me boils with rage at the thought of what may happen if we sit still'. He did not, like some other prominent British pacifists, go to meet Hitler and the Nazi leaders: the ordinary courtesies involved in calling on such men, he said afterwards, 'would have stuck in my throat'.

He also annoyed out-and-out pacifists by stressing that the use of force would be permissible for a World Government.

Perhaps, in retrospect, one of the most interesting passages in the book is where Russell noted that 'the Germans would like to be let alone while they attack Russia'; and he argued that, if they did, Britain should be neutral. He wrote: 'Napoleon attacked Russia as a step towards the conquest of England; perhaps Hitler would find a similar policy equally disastrous.' This view of Russell's particularly horrified orthodox Socialist opinion, as something of which only a Tory reactionary would approve. One can imagine future historians not feeling quite so certain, in view of Stalin's subsequent tactics, that Russell and the Tory reactionaries were wrong.

Finally, we may note how Russell pointed out that, 'of all the danger points of Europe, Poland is now perhaps the most exposed. . . . There is no impossibility in an alliance between Germany and Russia, leading to a new partition. . . . Everything possible is being done by Stalin to show that no question of principle divides him from Hitler, and I cannot doubt that he would be glad if the differences between the two countries could be composed at the expense of the traditional victim.'

This slur on Stalin, once again, particularly infuriated his British admirers.

It is now ancient history to recall how the Soviet-German Pact of 1939 preluded the invasion of Poland, and how this started the Second World War. Remembering how the Pact came as a complete shock to all shades of British political opinion at the time, Russell's forecast was an extraordinary one to have made as early as 1936. It emphasizes, once again, that he was at his best as a political commentator when he was alone, and at his worst in a crowd.

I think the fact is that, as in so many of his political books, Russell was caught in two minds when writing *Which Way to Peace?*, though this was not so obvious as in other cases. Something of the inner conflict between his pacifism and his realism can be seen in quotations already given; and he prefaced the book with the significant remark that 'I have long been myself in genuine doubt as to the right policy'. But, once he had committed himself to pacifism, he was caught up in the momentum of his own pacifist pleading, and gave another illustration of the danger of an intellectual acquiring loyalty to a political cause; he could not let his followers down by voicing any doubts. In view of his belief that war was virtually inevitable, and his belief about the nature of another war, he felt that there was nothing useful which he as an individual could do in any case. (Beatrice Webb described him in 1937 as 'physically worn out', and worried over money.) He devoted himself more and more to philosophy and academic work, lecturing at Oxford and accepting invitations to conduct seminars at the University of Chicago and the University of California.

In 1938 Russell was still enough of a pacifist to support Munich, writing that: 'Here in America, nine people out of ten think that we ought to have fought, but America ought to have remained neutral—an opinion which annoys me.' He said it was odd that the very people in England who had protested in 1919 against the unjust frontiers of Czechoslovakia, were now the most anxious to defend them. But after war broke out, and Britain was threatened with invasion, Russell announced that he was renouncing his pacifism, and that he would have fought himself if he had been of military age. 'I am still a pacifist,' he said, 'in the sense that I think peace the most important thing in the world. But I do not think there can be any peace in the world while Hitler prospers. . . . His defeat, if at all possible, is a necessary prelude to anything good. . . . If we lose it will be hell, probably for a long time to come.' And he wrote to a friend in July 1940: 'We constantly wish we were in England—it is like being absent when someone whom one loves very much is dangerously ill. But the children and the need for earning money make it impossible.' About this time he finished his *Inquiry into Meaning and Truth*, commenting that 'I feel the only thing I can do for the world for the moment is to try to preserve as much as possible of our perishing civilization, in the hope of a Renaissance in a thousand years'.

CHAPTER XXI

An Outcast in America

THE war years in America were probably the most unhappy in Russell's life. To begin with, there was the fear of Hitler winning the war. Those who regard Russell as nothing by a dry and dispassionate logician could find the strongest evidence to the contrary in the way in which, during both the First and Second World Wars, his moods would alternate between utter despair and eager hopes of an early peace. Worse still was being away from England at such a time: he wrote that 'Sometimes the longing for home is almost unbearable', and that 'one feels ashamed of comfort and safety'. He wrote asking Mrs Trevelyan at the Shiffolds whether the peacefulness of the Surrey woods he knew so well was now spoilt by the noise of aeroplanes, and whether it was true that the trees on Leith Hill had been cut down: 'I am haunted by the thought of disappearing beauty.' He confessed that 'Physical and mental depression is very hard to avoid. We find ourselves falling into it, largely from the baulked impulse to be in some way useful. It is horrible to do nothing to help, but difficult here to do much.'

In addition to these worries, he found himself faced with acute financial anxieties. To begin with it was impossible, under war-time financial regulations, to get his earnings from British royalties remitted to America, apart from a small and insufficient allowance for his three children's education. Then he was the victim of a Roman Catholic agitation in New York, the details of which are still little known in England, as the case was barely reported in the restricted war-time newspapers.

In February 1940, when Russell was still at the University of California, he was invited to join the staff of the College of the City of New York. He had already agreed to give the William

James lectures at Harvard in the autumn of 1940. So the Board
of Higher Education in New York appointed him Professor of
Philosophy as from February 1, 1941. The appointment was to
run till June 30, 1942—by which date he would have reached
the retiring age of seventy.

Accepting this position, Russell resigned his Professorship in
California. But a protest against his New York appointment
came immediately from a bishop of the Anglican Church,
William T. Manning, on the ground that Russell was 'a
recognized propagandist against religion and morality . . . who
specifically defends adultery'. The next step was the filing of a
taxpayer's suit in the New York Supreme Court to anull the
appointment. It was brought by a dentist's wife, a Mrs Jean
Kay of Brooklyn, whose lawyer, Joseph Goldstein, described
Russell's books as 'lecherous, salacious, libidinous, lustful,
venerous, erotomaniac, aphrodisiac, atheistic, irreverent,
narrow-minded, untruthful and bereft of moral fibre'. Russell,
he maintained, had also written salacious poetry, conducted a
nudist colony in England, and condoned homosexuality: moreover, he was not an American citizen. So far as Russell's philosophy was concerned, continued Goldstein,

'He is a sophist. . . . By cunning contrivances, tricks, and
devices, and by mere quibbling, he puts forth fallacious arguments. . . . All his alleged doctrines which he calls philosophy
are just cheap, tawdry, worn out, patched up fetishes and propositions, devices for the purpose of misleading the people.'

The judge who heard the suit was a Roman Catholic, John E.
McGeehan; and on March 30, 1940, he delivered his historic
verdict. Russell's appointment was annulled on three grounds.
In the first place, Russell was not an American. 'Other Universities and colleges,' complained McGeehan, 'seem to be able
to find American citizens to employ. . . .' In the second place,
Russell had not been made to sit for a competitive examination
as a condition for the appointment. In the third place, McGeehan
denounced the 'immoral and salacious doctrines' and the 'filth'
contained in Russell's books, citing the advocacy of companion-
ate marriages for university students, and the advice that sexual

N

experience should precede marriage.

Referring to the argument that, after all, Russell would only be teaching mathematics, logic and philosophy, McGeehan made a valid reply from his point of view: 'The personality of the teacher has more to do with forming a student's opinions than many syllogisms. It is contended that Bertrand Russell is extraordinary. That makes him the more dangerous. . . . The more he is able to charm [students] and impress them with his personal presence, the more potent will grow his influence in all spheres of their lives.'

Finally Justice McGeehan summed up by saying that the Board of Higher Education, in appointing Russell, were in effect establishing 'a Chair of Indecency', and had 'acted arbitrarily, capriciously, and in direct violation of the public health, safety, and morals of the people'.

The petition brought before Justice McGeehan simply took the form of a lawsuit between a taxpayer and the New York Corporation. So that he could reply to the charges made against himself, Russell applied to be made a party to the proceedings; but McGeehan refused.

It was assumed at first, by all concerned, that there would be an appeal against McGeehan's verdict. But Mayor La Guardia decided that it would be politically convenient to let the affair drop, so Russell was left without any means of reply or redress.

The *New York Times* declared that Russell should have withdrawn from the appointment 'as soon as its harmful effects became evident'. Russell replied that he would have done so if he had considered only his own interests and inclinations. But this would have been 'cowardly and selfish', because 'a great many people who realized that their own interests and the principles of toleration and free speech were at stake were anxious from the start to continue the controversy. If I had retired I should have robbed them of their *casus belli*, and tacitly assented to the proposition that substantial groups should be allowed to drive out of public office individuals whose opinions, race, or nationality they find repugnant.'

Pressure was next brought on Harvard to cancel its invitation to Russell to give his William James lectures; but the President and Fellows stood firm. A. N. Whitehead was now Professor

Emeritus at Harvard. As mentioned, his philosophical views had diverged considerably from Russell's: in fact he was accustomed to telling his students 'Gentlemen, Bertie Russell says I am muddle-headed. Well, I say that *he* is simple-minded.' But he joined with Dewey, Einstein and others in championing Russell's cause in the controversy over the New York Professorship.

Russell, however, still faced unemployment after his Harvard lectures were finished. The insinuations and slander in the court case started a full flood of rumour and gossip; especially about things alleged to have happened at his school in England. He felt compelled to issue a denial: 'I have never felt I should be ashamed of anything God created, but that does not mean that either my children or I run about naked.' And he said that, though he had a record of adultery in England, 'that country's law is more to blame than I', since at the time it allowed virtually no other ground for divorce.

Russell was rescued from financial embarrassment for a time by an eccentric millionaire, Dr Albert Barnes, who engaged him to lecture on the history of philosophy at the Barnes Foundation in Pennsylvania. Russell and his family moved to an old farm-house, known at Little Datchet Farm, about twenty-five miles west of Philadelphia. There he found that 'people in the Eastern States are passionately pro-English, and everyone is kind to us because of our nationality'. He was able to enjoy the visits of friends from England, including Julian Huxley; and he went over to see G. E. Moore, who had been invited to lecture at Princeton. He reported that Moore was 'exactly as usual, very charming, and very unperturbed'.

Unhappily, there were further troubles ahead. Russell had a severe illness, an infected sinus slowing down his reactions to such an extent that he was warned that it would not be safe for him to cross a road on his own. Then, in January 1943, his contract at the Barnes Foundation was abruptly terminated on three days' notice.

According to Barnes, Russell 'failed to meet the standard of personal and professional conduct inherent to his position'. One reported complaint was that Patricia Russell had distracted the students by attending her husband's lectures in slacks, and busily clicking knitting needles as she knitted garments to be sent to bombed-out children in Britain. Another trouble may have been that Russell, in a debate with Louis Fischer, had criticized Gandhi's attitude to the war, and said that India would be worse off if the Japanese were allowed to conquer it. Barnes regarded this as 'defending British Imperialism'.

Thus at the age of seventy, when most men have retired, Russell was left with a family to support, three children to educate, and no job. *Time* called him 'the philosophical hot potato of US campuses'. He had been so besmirched by the attacks and gossip against him that no University would offer him a position, and few newspapers would publish his articles. The strength of the feeling about him can be judged from one incident. Gilbert Murray wrote to an American friend, a man of the highest standing, asking if he could help Russell. The reply came back that, much as the man in question would like to oblige Gilbert Murray, asking him to have anything to do with Russell was going a bit too far.

Russell hit back by bringing a lawsuit against Barnes for wrongful dismissal: but though he won his case, there were so many delays that it was three years before the money was paid. During the hearing Russell said that his total earnings during the previous eight months had only been £781, and when the Judge suggested that perhaps he had not tried to get work, he retorted: 'Do you suppose I don't try to get money? I'm not *that* kind of philosopher.'

Even in his desperate position, pressed for money and isolated in a foreign country, Russell's spirit remained undaunted. He cheerfully informed a reporter: 'At the present time my income is less than my income tax. It will be interesting to see how the Government handles this situation.' He wrote to Sir Stanley Unwin in England, who had an estimate made of the likely future royalties from Russell's books, and advanced him this amount, so that his two elder children could complete their University educations in America. Next, Russell secured an advance from an American publisher for a book which he proceeded to make out of his Barnes Foundation lectures.

This book, a masterpiece to emerge under such turbulent and unhappy circumstances, was published as *A History of Western Philosophy*, with the subtitle 'and its connection with political and social circumstances'. The book was the first of its kind ever written by a philosopher who was himself in the first rank; it was also one of the very rare attempts to write a comprehensive history based on a conscientious reading or re-reading at first hand of the philosophers discussed. Patricia Russell told afterwards of her journeys in search of complete editions of different philosophers, and how she had the greatest difficulty in making it understood that the kind of 'selections' popular in America would not be good enough.

For the middle section of the book, Russell delved into mediaeval Catholic philosophers rarely studied at length: remarking that, though dull, they were much better than he expected. Naturally enough, what he said about them did not entirely meet with Catholic approval. So it is interesting to mention that, when I criticized this section of the book as being too long, Russell vehemently disagreed, and insisted on the importance and value of some of the work done in the Middle Ages.

The *History of Western Philosophy* has so many virtues that it would be presumptuous to praise it: I shall therefore confine myself to mentioning its faults.

A book of such massive proportions was bound to contain a few slips. There was a unanimous verdict, among admirers of Kant, that the chapter on Kant was the worst in the book. Russell, writing of Kant's maxim that the test of rightness of an action is whether we would like everyone to behave in the same way, said 'Kant gives as an illustration . . . that it is wrong to borrow money, because if we all tried to do so there would be no money left to borrow'. A chorus of Kantians promptly protested that this particular example was one which Kant never used. I am quite prepared to take their word for it, for nothing would induce me to read Kant again in order to find out.

A more interesting mistake was in the chapter on Bergson. As mentioned earlier, this was simply Russell's famous lecture to the Heretics, inserted into the book virtually without alteration. For instance the chapter was divided into two parts simply because, when addressing the Heretics in 1911, there had been a break half way through so that the lecturer could recover his breath, and the audience could pause and think. In this lecture, Russell criticized Bergson severely for 'the confusion of subject and object', and 'the confusion between the act of knowing and that which is known'. Russell had changed his mind on this question when adopting neutral monism, but his criticism of Bergson was reprinted verbatim in the *History of Western Philosophy;* although, in the next chapter, he praised William James for denying a fundamental distinction between subject and object. *

The discrepancy was an interesting illustration of one of Russell's weaknesses, considered purely as an author. He was a stylist who wrote passages which deserve a place in any anthology of English prose; but his books tend to be collections of disconnected chapters, instead of adding up to a complete whole. This, of course, is a natural enough corollary to his analytical and piecemeal approach to any problem, and his rejection of monism. In view of the subtitle, one might have expected his *History of Western Philosophy* to be centred on the relation between the views of philosophers and the times in which they lived. On this he reached no general conclusions whatever; he rightly rejected the extreme Marxist theories about philosophers being the product of economic forces, and rightly said that historically they are both causes and effects. But even this somewhat inconclusive conclusion was not kept in mind throughout as the theme of the book, with each chapter related to it.

In fact, though he had many illuminating comments about philosophers and their times, he did not really write the book he set out to write; and with some philosophers he forgot to discuss their surrounding circumstances altogether. What Russell did succeed in writing was the most illuminating history of philosophy which has ever been brought together in one volume. It was quite unnecessary modesty which made him feel that this was not enough, and that his book needed the justification of serving some other purpose. And its weaknesses as a book increased its virtues as a history: his summaries and criticisms of different philosophies would have suffered if, in the interests of artistic unity, he had tried to turn them into neat exemplifications of some theory. His critics used to argue that

* This point, however, does not affect the validity of Russell's criticism of Bergson's views on memory.

analysis means falsification; it is more often the case that unity means falsification.

Early in 1944 Russell got the chance of returning to war-time England for which he had longed. His old college, Trinity, invited him back to Cambridge, and he managed to get a passage home on a cargo boat. One of his first acts on reaching England was to visit the Trevelyans at the Shiffolds. He walked outside on the terrace, openly relishing the delight of seeing the Surrey hills again, and the beauty of the beech trees. He relished, too, the chance of good talk with English friends again: it was not long before he was out on a walk with Bob Trevelyan, and they began discussing theology.

'The trouble is,' said Trevelyan, in his quiet ruminative way, 'I just don't seem . . . to be able . . . to get *interested* in God.'

'Perhaps it's reciprocal,' said Russell promptly, and their laughter was heard over the hills.

The invitation back to Cambridge seems an obvious step, seen in retrospect; so it is extraordinary to realize that even at this time, even in England, Russell was still sometimes regarded as rather an outrageous person. Professor Littlewood had sounded out earlier the possibility of his being made an Honorary Fellow of Trinity, but was surprised to meet strong opposition. Shortly afterwards, however, came the invitation to return as a Fellow and give lectures.

Disapproval of Russell was also shared for a time by the BBC, which showed some reluctance at first to ask him to broadcast. He wrote that 'The BBC doesn't want me, but I am to lecture at Trinity, which I prefer'.

By way of lighter relief to end this chapter, we may mention one change which Russell noticed on his return to England. The philosopher whom he found most in the public eye was C. E. M. Joad.

One of the most surprising but common characteristics of great men is their capacity for being annoyed by little men. The future historian will wonder, for instance, why Winston Churchill should ever have bothered about being criticized by a politician named Shinwell. And future generations will, I think, be delighted to recall Russell's violent hostility to minor figures like J. A. Smith and C. E. M. Joad, as evidence that genius did not stop him being human.

Joad was a man of many virtues who might, if he had been born at a different time, have been remembered as a sincere thinker and a lucid teacher. Unfortunately he came to epitomize all that was worst in a section of British left-wing intellectuals of his particular period. He was a pacifist during the First World War; but he did not endure prison and hardship, finding a satisfactory compromise by working in the Civil Service. Like Russell, he recanted his pacifism during the Second World War; but whereas Russell thought he should refrain from exhorting young men to fight when he was too old to fight himself, Joad embarked on such activities as speaking at War Loan rallies. He received a rich reward following his renunciation of pacifism. Previously he had been known to a few people as a typical writer of the kind of advanced nonsense admired by the *New Statesman*, and as a philosophical popularizer who sought attention by growing a beard and talking about sex. Now the BBC started featuring him in a discussion programme called the 'Brains Trust', and showed its curious knack of taking a second-rate personality and turning him into a national celebrity. Joad also wrote weekly articles for the *Sunday Dispatch*, which described him as 'Britain's leading philosopher'.

It was hard not to feel some sympathy for Joad. He was a clear-headed but unoriginal thinker who had suddenly been thrust into the limelight, given a platform, and exposed as a man with nothing to say; for his philosophy of life was a secondhand repetition of ideas picked up from Russell and Bernard Shaw. Even so, he deserved much credit for arousing interest in philosophy among many people who had never thought about it before. But Russell would give Joad neither sympathy nor credit. He detested Joad with all his detestation for the counterfeit in any man. He called Joad 'a humbug and a plagiarist'; the latter epithet referring to Joad's occasional practice of taking ideas from Russell's books and incorporating them, without acknowledgment, in his own. One of the most concentrated examples of Russell's wit came when he was asked to contribute a complimentary Preface to a book by Joad. Russell replied: 'Modesty forbids.'

Joad fell from the grace and favour of the BBC when he was caught travelling without a railway ticket, and tried to mislead the Inspector about where he had got on the train. Towards the end of his life he recanted more and more of his left-wing views, and ended by joining the Church of England. Russell's comment on these proceedings was that 'Joad found his God after he had lost his railway ticket'; and he was moved to the most emphatic fury when he heard of a rumour reaching America that he himself had returned to orthodox religion, having been converted by Joad.

CHAPTER XXII

The Rebel Becomes Revered

RUSSELL received a hero-worshipping welcome back to Cambridge. The largest lecture-room was taken for his lectures, but there were still queues of students outside who could not get in. He was able to meet again his old friends like Moore and Broad and Hardy and Littlewood. Perhaps the one man who was not altogether glad to see Russell back was Wittgenstein, who had succeeded Moore as Professor of Philosophy at Cambridge; a post for which he was somewhat handicapped by his disinterest in the teaching of philosophies other than his own. Wittgenstein seemed violently hostile to Russell. For instance, when he saw the volume on Russell in the American 'Library of Living Philosophers', he was disgusted to notice a facsimile of Russell's signature on the cover. Though every volume in the same series had the philosopher's signature in exactly the same harmless way, apparently Wittgenstein thought the whole series involved undignified display. It was not a very reasonable objection; but Wittgenstein was not always reasonable in his objections to people or things. For instance, he formed an explosive hatred of Sir Arthur Eddington, calling his 'insincere', and saying he would rather be in Hell with himself than be in Heaven with Eddington; but nobody could understand what his objection to Eddington was based on. Once, walking in the Fellows' Garden at Trinity, he flew into a quite inexplicable rage because he saw some tulips among rough grass, declaring that they looked 'artificial'.

At one time Wittgenstein had no chairs in his rooms, so that everyone had to stand or recline on couches; and he dined at Lyons or in early Hall, because he said he could not bear the company of the other Fellows.

Russell not only taught at Trinity but came to London for debates in the House of Lords, sometimes spending the night with Julian Huxley in Hampstead. On one such occasion they amused themselves with the idea of compiling texts from the Old Testament to illustrate the contradictions in its moral precepts. Husley commented afterwards that it was curious that, in modern times, the only people who seem to have studied the Bible thoroughly are Rationalists; he himself knew a good deal about the Old Testament, but he had to admit that he did not know nearly as much as Russell.

Russell was filled with rejoicing by the Labour Party's victory over Churchill in the election of 1945; but he did not, after the petty fashion of party politics, proceed to belittle Churchill's achievements. 'There's no doubt', he would say, 'that Churchill's a great man. A very great man. . . . I have an enormous affection for him.' This admiration for Churchill, of course, only dated from the Second World War.* But in spite of Russell's criticism throughout of Churchill as a Conservative, he always recognized that he was sincere—'not a slippery slimy scoundrel like Baldwin'.

When Churchill's War Memoirs came out, Russell commented that Churchill was 'Inoffensively egotistical, and not offensively egotistical, if you see what I mean. . . . He claimed no more than he had a right to, which great men so often do.'

Russell's period of delight, after the return to power of the Labour Government, was ended by the atomic bomb on Hiroshima. He wrote: 'In the little interval between the general election and the atomic bomb I had been feeling rather happy; but at the crack of Truman's whip the British Government will have to relinquish all its projects. . . .

'The atomic bomb makes one . . . reconsider all sorts of things. I have never, not even in 1940, felt the outlook as gloomy as now. Everything is working up for a war between the USA and the USSR, with us a satellite of the USA; both sides will use

* In a lecture in 1927 on 'Why I am not a Christian', Russell combated the argument that the Universe could only be the result of some divine design by saying: 'Do you think that, if you were granted omnipotence and omniscience over millions of years in which to perfect your world, you could produce nothing better than the Ku Klux Klan, the Fascisti and Mr Winston Churchill?' [Russell deleted this reference to Churchill on reprinting the lecture.]

atomic bombs, and very little will be left at the end.'

When he returned to England he had found the country in a mood of unqualified admiration for Stalinist Russia—he had heard the sailors on his cargo boat across the Atlantic lustily singing *The Red Flag*—and he was one of the first to predict the post-war rupture. As early as August 1944, in an interview with Mary Seaton Wood, he said that 'I am afraid there is likely to be another world war'. In November 1945, referring to events in Eastern Europe, he said that the Communists had committed atrocities 'very much on the same scale and the same magnitude' as the Nazis.

In these circumstances, Russell felt that the only chance lay in the policy followed by Bevin, the new Labour Foreign Secretary. He told the House of Lords that 'I am a whole-hearted supporter of the present Government, both in their foreign policy and in their home policy'. (Truman's Government did not interfere in British domestic affairs to the extent Russell had feared, partly because of American fears of Russia.) Russell said that 'I do not think that the way to secure Russian co-operation is merely to express a desire for it. I think it is absolutely necessary to be firm on what we consider to be our vital interests.'

Russell prophesied the hydrogen bomb as early as 1945. He told the House of Lords how the existing atom bomb could be used to set off a hydrogen bomb, which would be 'practicable in time'. He opposed suggestions that Russia should be told the secrets of making the atom bomb, but he warned that 'The secret is a short-term one. Within a few years the Russians will no doubt have bombs every bit as good as those which are at present being made in the United States.'

Writing in the *Manchester Guardian* in the same year, Russell said that everything possible should be done to increase the American preponderance of strength, 'in the hope of making it so great that the necessary monopoly of armed force may be brought about without another great war.' He was still obviously hankering after the idea that the most certain way to world Government was the supremacy of one nation; and he kept this hope until it was made impossible by Soviet Russia obtaining nuclear weapons too.

At the time of the Korean war, Russell supported Western rearmament and the rearmament of Western Germany, saying that Germany could never again be a world menace. The best chance of peace lay in remaining 'obviously stronger' than Russia. 'The only thing to do is to prevent an explosion somehow, in the hope that time will bring wisdom.'

On the main point, Russell now had no doubts.

'If I had to choose between Russian Communism and American capitalism,' he said, 'I should without a moment's hesitation choose the latter . . . because it is combined with democracy, and with a measure of personal liberty.' He added that the best argument for capitalism was that it kept political and economic power apart—an emphasis opposite to when he wrote *Freedom and Organization*. And Russell went farther than before in defending the American way of life.

'I do not think,' he said, 'that Americans are in any degree more materialistic, in the popular sense of that word, than . . . other nations. We think they worship the almighty dollar because they succeed in getting it. But a needy aristocrat or a French peasant will do things for the sake of money that shock every decent American . . .'

This did not prevent him being severely critical of American policy. The Chinese, he said, would never have become Communist but for America leaving them no alternative between Communism and the 'corrupt and reactionary' government of Chiang Kai-shek. The Americans were 'twenty times more ignorant' than the British in foreign affairs, making mistakes through inexperience comparable to those of the British in the eighteenth century: 'We must and can control the Americans through the United Nations. They will always want to save their moral faces—they are descendants of the Pilgrim Fathers, after all.'

He was also staunch in standing out against 'the reign of terror' of McCarthyism. He remarked in 1950 that 'America is getting very hysterical. We should show ourselves a cut above that.'

His resoluteness in criticising America, as well as Russia, did not save him from Communist attacks; particularly when he was reported as advocating a 'preventative' war against Communism—a report which Russell promptly denied. Moscow radio called him 'this philosophizing wolf, whose dinner jacket conceals all the brutal instincts of a beast. Hatred, murder, the eat-one-another state, seems to be the fundamental ethical principle preached by this beast in philosopher's robes.' According to the *Cominform Journal*, he was 'A British ideologist of cannibals'.

Russell also had to face attacks nearer home. Besides the full-blooded invective of Stalin's propagandists, there was a sneer in the *New Statesman*, saying that Russell had decided 'that it would be both good morals and good politics to start dropping bombs on Moscow.' Russell called on the *New Statesman*, taking his lawyer with him, and it published a long letter from him giving extracts from what he had actually said about Russia.

It was only to be expected that former left-wing friends, in their bitterness, should accuse Russell of changing his views to make them closer to public opinion. I do not think anyone could believe this who realized how Russell had criticized Marxism as early as 1896, and who had studied the gradual evolution of his opinions from *German Social Democracy* onwards. He had become more and more convinced of the evils of fanaticism, and of the success with which evil men could mould the minds of a whole nation to suit their devices. So, though he had opposed rearmament against Hitler, he did not oppose it against Stalin.

There was a genuine change of opinion; but this means that, although it is ridiculous to suggest that Russell was seeking popularity, it is also wrong to claim that his views were always the same.

It was certainly something of a change that the Foreign Office, which had refused him a visa to go to America in 1916, now urged him to give lectures in Berlin and elsewhere abroad. During these years Russell travelled tirelessly and interminably, with the vigour of a man half his years. The most dramatic episode came in October 1948, when he survived a flying boat crash in Norway at the age of 76.

Going aboard the plane, he had been told that smoking was only permitted in the back compartment. He said 'I'll die if I can't smoke', and went behind. Russell was feeling airsick as they came in to land, and loosened his safety belt. There was a sudden gust of wind: the plane hit the water with a jolt and went on one side, letting in enough water to submerge it. Russell found himself sitting on the floor, with hats and coats floating all around him. At first he merely thought that a wave had broken in at a window, and did not realize that it was serious. He said to himself: 'Well, well,' started looking for his hat, but could not find it.

Passengers were hurried out into the sea through the rear door. Already there was a boat standing by about twenty yards away, and Russell swam to it. But it was discovered afterwards that nineteen people in the front compartment had been drowned.

Russell was driven to his hotel, given brandy and coffee, and went to bed because he had no clothes. The British Consul arrived with socks and a shirt, and the Vice-Consul lent him a suit. The next arrivals were journalists. He told them 'I don't suppose I was swimming for more than about a minute. For one who has been swimming regularly for about seventy years, it wasn't much.'

One journalist telephoned from Copenhagen to ask what Russell had thought about when he was in the water. He replied that he had thought that the water was cold.

'Didn't you think,' pressed the journalist, 'about Mysticism and Logic?'

'No,' said Russell, and rang off.

Gilbert Murray wrote to Russell commenting on his feat in being able to swim in freezing water at such an age, and adding that Russell must owe his life to the habits of temperance which they had both championed in the old days. Murray said that he was glad to see Russell's teachings getting their reward in this way. Russell replied that, on the contrary, he owed his life to the brandy he had been given after he reached shore.

Describing his activities during these years, Russell wrote that 'six days in the week I dictate to secretaries, and on Sundays I speak somewhere—I wish Stalin would disarm, and then I would have leisure'. Not all his travels, however, were on business. Once he and Patricia Russell took a holiday at Taormina in Sicily with Julian Trevelyan the artist, the son of Robert Trevelyan. One evening Russell, with Julian and Julian's future wife Mary Fedden, went out in a fisherman's boat, and then had supper on a beach. They ate fish cooked over a fire, drank wine which they had buried in the wet sand to cool, and Julian went a little way off, sat on a rock, and played the oboe to them. Russell sat—as erect as ever—on an upturned fisherman's basket, enjoying it enormously; he said the evening had given him more happiness than he had known for years. 'I'm as drunk as a Lord' he said (with considerable exaggeration), 'but then I *am* a Lord, so it's all right, isn't it?'

At this time came the final parting from Patricia Russell, who went back to England alone. A divorce followed.

The breaking-up of each of Russell's marriages brought its own pain and hurt; it was characteristic that, outwardly, he would cover his feelings with jests. Once somebody said he was surprised to hear of one of Russell's children getting engaged, because he thought that Russell did not believe in marriage. 'Don't be silly,' said Russell. 'Look how many times I've been married.'

During all this period Russell's eminence in British life was rising steadily. In the winter of 1948 he had been invited to give the first BBC 'Reith Lectures', on *Authority and the Individual*. In these he supported the Labour Party's nationalization of key industries, but on the whole was more concerned to defend the individual against authority. He said that the powers of a World Government should be limited to those essential for eliminating war; that national Governments should leave as many powers as possible to regional authorities; and so on down the scale. He praised experiments in industrial democracy like the Lewis Partnership.

In June 1950 came the Order of Merit, the most exclusive honour which it is in the King's power to bestow.

When Russell went to Buckingham Palace to receive this award, it was obvious that George VI was not very much at his ease. It must have been the first time that a King of England had found himself conferring a supreme honour on a man who had once been an inmate of one of His Majesty's prisons, and whose views and conduct were abhorred by the Established Church of which the King was the head. George VI remarked to Russell:

'They tell me you have led a very adventurous life. But it would not do if everyone tried to lead such a life, would it?' Russell with an effort checked himself from replying: 'No, as your brother the Duke of Windsor discovered.'

Instead he said: 'Postmen go about knocking on doors, even though it would not do if everyone went about knocking on doors.' His Majesty changed the subject.

Altogether one feels a certain sympathy with the King, because not long afterwards he was also called upon to bestow an OM on G. E. Moore. The King obviously had great labour in keeping the conversation going. Moore tried to help him out by mentioning other Cambridge men whom he thought the King might know, like Russell and Wittgenstein; but the King was forced to confess that he had never heard of Wittgenstein.

On Russell, his only comment was: 'Queer looking man.'

CHAPTER XXIII

Australia Felix

ONE of Russell's most interesting journeys, as showing the continued liveliness of his interests, was his visit to Australia in 1950. Unlike Kant, who spent his whole life in Königsberg, he was a philosopher who was always ready for new travels and new experiences, as a good empiricist should be. He always loved any adventure into the unknown: 'Isn't it wonderful,' he once said, 'to *find out* things?'

A wealthy Melbourne business man, Edward Dyason, had set up a Trust Fund so that distinguished men from overseas could give lectures in Australia. Russell accepted this invitation to a strenuous tour in a new land with alacrity, although he was then already seventy-eight.

Since nobody quite like Russell had ever been to Australia before, his arrival caused a certain amount of anxious preparation. There had recently been trouble with Communist demonstrations; so two policemen, Sergeant Lanighan and Detective Lightbottom, were provided for his protection. A senior representative of the Department of External Affairs, Richard Greenish, went to Sydney to meet him, and was later detailed to accompany Russell throughout his travels. Actual arrangements for his journey were in the hands of the Australian Institute of International Affairs, the official concerned solemnly heralding Russell's approach by sending out these instructions:

'In reply to questions from various branches, the following additional information on B. Russell's likes and dislikes has been received:
  'He would prefer not to be a guest of Governors.
  'He would rather not have mayoral receptions and such

functions.

'He would like a bathroom, which I presume has already been arranged.'

The Australian newspapers plainly hoped to entice Russell into outrageous remarks, and Sydney journalists gathered eagerly for a press conference on his arrival by Qantas in June. He showed himself, however, far too adroit when they tried to draw him out on the question of free love. He was asked: 'We have a lot of single young women in Australia. We have heard something about your views: would you care to suggest what they can do, in view of certain social prejudices, to lead fuller lives?'

Russell thought for a moment, and then replied cheerfully: 'I think I should advocate a policy of mass emigration for them.'

As well as fending off the journalists, Russell showed himself —no doubt through long practice—to have a ready answer to most of the other worries which beset a celebrity. Autograph hunters were told that he disliked signing his name on loose slips of paper, but that he never minded autographing one of his own books. When overdressed elderly ladies gushed over him at parties, and said how much they admired everything he had written, he had a standard reply. He would ask them if they had liked his *Introduction to Mathematical Philosophy*, and sometimes they would blink and say 'Yes'. Whereupon Russell would remark casually 'I wrote it when I was in prison', and watch their faces.

Experience in America even helped him with the problem of avoiding damage to his hand by all the people who wanted to shake it. When somebody suggested that the best technique for a celebrity was to let the hand go limp, Russell characteristically retorted that, on the contrary, what he did was to get in first, and 'squeeze *their* hands till they yelp'.

From Sydney, Russell flew to Queensland, to Canberra, Melbourne, Adelaide, and Perth—he was in Australia altogether for over two months. Everywhere he not only gave his public lectures and broadcasts, but wanted to see and learn all he could. 'I am ashamed to say,' he remarked, 'that this is my first visit to Australia. As I have wasted seventy-eight years of my life in other parts of the world, I am very glad indeed to have the opportunity of rectifying this omission.'

He went to Green Island in Queensland, where he sent back postcards to his grandchildren inscribed 'Grandpa was here today'. He had a very successful meeting in Canberra with William McKell, a former boiler-maker and boxing champion who, after being Labour Premier of New South Wales, had become Governor-General of Australia. Russell went to morning tea with him and stayed much longer than the scheduled time, having become absorbed in a model which McKell showed him of the Snowy River Scheme, the project for boring tunnels through a mountain range to turn a river round inland instead of flowing straight down to the sea.

Russell, in fact, seemed to have the knack of getting on with most people he met. There was a slight contretemps when a dignified Melbourne club asked him to become an honorary member, addressing the invitation to 'Earl Russell. Esquire': but Russell merely commented that 'Evidently they think that I'm another of these Americans'. When a journalist said that Russell looked like 'a sophisticated koala bear who has just thought of a funny story', Russell promptly went off to the Melbourne Zoo to see what a koala bear looked like. He came back saying that they were most engaging creatures, and that he felt extremely flattered.

Determined to see everything, Russell got much nearer to the heart of Australia than most visitors, flying up from Adelaide over the gibber plains and red sandhills to Alice Springs. He bought some paintings by aborigine artists of the Arunta tribe, and went out to the Flying Doctor Centre, where he heard the wireless messages from outback stations, asking for diagnosis and treatment by radio-telephone, or for the doctor to call. He listened fascinated, and was asked to speak over the wireless; but he modestly refused, saying 'They wouldn't want to hear me—just say that I have been listening with very great interest and admiration'.

In spite of the ceaseless pressure of all the people in Australia who wanted to meet him, Russell was always ready to see some-one new. One day he received a parcel of books in his hotel in Adelaide. They were from an old man named Arthur Gasc, a

Fabian Socialist who had gone out to Australia in 1898, and who wrote novels lampooning some of the more pompous citizens of Adelaide. Russell liked the books so much that he insisted on going to see Gasc, and the two men struck up an immediate and touching friendship. Russell was delighted to be transported back in reminiscence to the outlook of nineteenth century radicalism, and to the campaigns against the Church in the days when the Church was strong. He called Gasc the most impressive person he had met in Australia, and he gave Gasc the happiest days he had known. When Russell had to leave Adelaide, Gasc wrote to him:

My Dear Master,
    You came like a flash of lightning into my life, and now the sky is very dark and empty. . . .

Russell also found time to help the young. At Melbourne, an inexperienced junior journalist arrived late and missed his press conference; Russell saw his distress and gave him a special interview on his own. In another city, Russell heard that the young secretary of an organization concerned with his lectures had just learnt that his wife had cancer. Russell sought him out, and talked to him alone; and somehow he managed to give him courage.

One of his hosts was Professor Macmahon Ball, of Melbourne University. One day Macmahon Ball had arranged to leave Russell alone before lunch, thinking he might like to rest. But, seeing Russell was obviously in the mood for conversation, Macmahon Ball asked his young daughter Jenny, then thirteen, to go and talk to him. Jenny went in with barely concealed awe. A little later Macmahon Ball returned to find Jenny listening delighted, completely at her ease, as Russell entertained her with a sparkling succession of stories, beginning with the one about how he had drunk port with Mr Gladstone.

Yet another person with reason to remember Russell's visit was Richard Greenish, his guide from the Department of External Affairs. They got to know each other well, developing a code word 'Humph' which was used on occasions of too much pomp or pomposity at receptions; and at nights Russell would sometimes regale Greenish by reciting indelicate limericks—some of which, he was disconcerted to observe, Greenish would jot down on the backs of cigarette cartons.

The Universities naturally took advantage of Russell's presence to stage seminars, in which he could discuss philosophical questions with the Professors and a few selected students. These occasions were not always successful. There was one Professor who arrived in a somewhat unshaved condition. It was soon obvious that Russell was getting ruffled by the Professor's insistence on doing most of the talking, and his evident failure to comprehend what Russell said in reply. Russell went away muttering angrily 'The man doesn't even *begin* to understand me—and he needs a wash, anyhow'. There was another unsuccessful seminar at a University which does not charge any fees for its students. Russell's comment afterwards was 'No wonder it's a free University'.

It is fair to mention that the criticism may not have been entirely one-sided. One lecturer at an Australian University was heard to say, in criticizing the *History of Western Philosophy*, that: 'To be frank, Russell doesn't *know* enough. . . . When original scholarship is needed, he's completely at a loss. . . .'

Perhaps Russell was a little disappointed at not causing more controversy in Australia. Undoubtedly one of the things which pleased him most was his rare feat in eliciting a public apology from a Roman Catholic Archbishop. The celebrated Archbishop Mannix of Melbourne attacked Russell's visit, saying that he should not have been allowed to come in and propound his 'atheistic theories' in Australia, and that America had known better.

The Archbishop was startled to receive a pungent telegram from Russell, concocted by him and Greenish, which read: 'I demand that you make an immediate public apology for untrue statement that the US Government refused me permission to enter the United States of America.' Mannix immediately complied, explaining that he had spoken in good faith, but on 'unreliable information'.

The journalists of Australia, if they hoped that Russell himself would go out of the way to make provocative remarks, remained disappointed. One of the few points he found to criticize was the treatment of the aborigines. He was shocked to find, on talking to some of them, that though an aborigine could be accepted as a volunteer for the Australian Forces in Korea, the same man could be excluded from a pub on account of the colour of his skin. 'Both popular feeling and the police,' he said, 'seem unwilling to grant to the aborigines elementary rights of justice. Their tribal organization is largely dissolved, their past masters have been taken from them, and many of them are left homeless and helpless through no fault of their own.'

The Korean War broke out soon after Russell began his tour, and it was against this sombre background that his main impressions of Australia were formed. For a time he was so afraid that Korea might be the beginning of a world war that he wanted to fly straight back to be with his grandchildren, and he cabled instructions for a house to be found for them well away from London. He was reported as telling an interviewer that 'I think Russia will go to war, and I think World War Three will last ten years. . . . Anybody who lives in London would probably not be able to survive, if [the war] happens in the way I think it might.' But Russell added 'I think there will be people still living in Tierra del Fuego after the next war—and in Alice Springs'.

So far as Australia was concerned, even if the immediate danger of war was averted, there was still the long-term threat of invasion from Asia. He reminded Australians that China and India had a hundred times as many people as Australia, and said that 'The time has passed when Australia can acquiesce in a desert'.

Australians, he said, should spend a hundred times as much on development: 'You must make rain. You must get water. Somehow you must get people into the empty lands.' He predicted that scientists, with sufficient Government encouragement, could find a way of increasing total rainfall.

Given a vigorous development policy, the population of Australia could rise from 8,000,000 to 50,000,000 in thirty years, and perhaps to 100,000,000 by the end of the century.

Large-scale development would obviously need Government action. In Australia, as in Germany in 1895, and in Russia and China and America, Russell showed his curious gift for picking out essentials. He said the trouble was that the things in Australia which most needed doing had to be done in the country; but politicians were more influenced by the cities, where most of the voters were. And he pointed out the conflict in Australia between individualistic convictions and collectivist necessities, which is the key to understanding Australian politics.

He drew an illuminating contrast between Australia and America as it had been a hundred years earlier. Rugged individualism had been possible at first in America, because there was plenty of timber and water: a man could build his own log cabin, and grow crops as soon as the ground was cleared. But in the Australian outback water often needed big capital expenditure, and timber for building might have to be brought from far away.

Before going to Australia, Russell remarked that he had always thought of Australians as being 'rather like Americans, only more so'. Now he said that he was more struck by the differences. Australians were happier than Americans, without 'the same restless itch to be always doing something else, or being somewhere else'. When Australians found their circumstances were fortunate, they sat down and enjoyed them. Most Americans, strenuously engaged in seeking something better still, had no time to enjoy what they had got.

'No doubt,' said Russell, 'American restlessness is bound up with American energy and enterprise, and it is possible that if Australia were inhabited by Americans, its resources would be developed more rapidly. But, if so, this result would be surely purchased at the price of universal discontent.'

Russell ended up full of praise for Australia; and, though a courteous guest cannot be held to be on oath when saying things which will please his hosts, what he said is at least worth quoting as showing the continued youthfulness of his outlook, and his refusal to lapse into looking backwards. He declared that: 'If I had my choice of being born again, I would rather be born an Australian than a Western European. The greatness of Australia lies ahead—the greatness of Western Europe lies behind. To live with the past is deadening and depressing, but to live with a vision of the future brings hope and vigour and happiness. . . .

'The culture of England and France is infected with a certain weariness, with the theory that everything has been done already—that the books a man may hope to write are not so good as those written in earlier times, that if he composes music it will not be as good as Beethoven, and that if he paints pictures they will not be as good as the Old Masters.

'Beyond all this he feels in his bones the political discouragement that comes of being no longer in the centre of growing power. If the old culture of Europe can be transplanted into the environment of an expansive economy, a new vigour and a new renaissance are to be expected.'

But the vigour, Russell characteristically added, must be tempered by tolerance. He pointed out to Australians, who sometimes lack this quality, that 'The men who make artistic or cultural inventions seldom conform to the behaviour considered proper for a responsible citizen, and usually have something anarchic in their disposition. They are likely to be men of whom their neighbours disapprove. If a country is to produce great individuals it must add to the Four Freedoms a fifth—the freedom to be eccentric.'

Therefore, said Russell, if he were a young Australian without the physical strength to be a pioneer, or the scientific ability to be a research worker, he would devote himself to inculcating tolerance—'probably by means of novels'.

On this parting note, Russell flew back to England, declaring that his only disappointment about Australia was that it had been too cold for him to swim. Arriving in England after an exhausting twelve thousand mile flight on top of all his previous travelling, he only rested a few weeks before setting off again on a lecture tour of America because, he said, 'one has to do *something*'.

Soon afterwards another great honour came upon him; the award of the Nobel Prize. From Greenish in Australia came a congratulatory cable including the word 'Humph'.

CHAPTER XXIV

The Unfinished Philosophy

WITTGENSTEIN, in one of his sudden moments of penetration and insight, once remarked that the trouble with Russell in his later years was 'loss of problems'. It was a striking phrase: and, if my view of philosophy is right, it was the most fundamental criticism that can be made of any philosopher. Wittgenstein meant that, in a sense, Russell had begun to find philosophy too easy and straightforward: his mind had become too precise: he was no longer vaguely perplexed by unexpected doubts and strange questions coming into his mind.

To some extent, I think, the criticism is true. Thirty years of strain and stress in a world which grew madder every day, thirty years of political activity and personal worries and re-current financial anxiety, had taken some of the freshness out of Russell's mind; particularly after the way he had drawn on every reserve of strength in writing *Principia Mathematica*. During these thirty years, with little chance of mental relaxation and recuperation, he had few of those illuminating flashes of doubt in which he had questioned the axioms of Euclid, or questioned whether every word or phrase in a sentence must stand for some-thing. He contented himself, for the most part, with working away at problems which had occurred to him already; for which he had the reasonable justification that he had not yet solved these problems, and that no one else had solved them either.

The fullest statement of his conclusions was given in his *Human Knowledge: Its Scope and Limits*, published in 1948, when he was 76. I believe it is one of the most important of Russell's books, and a landmark in the history of philosophy; but I confess that I know hardly anyone who agrees with me. The fact that the book was underestimated was mainly, I think,

Russell's own fault. To begin with, it was far too long and dis-connected, with too much repetition of what he had already said in the *Analysis of Matter* and *An Inquiry into Meaning and Truth*. This was because he meant it to be a definitive summing up of his views. But another trouble was that Russell, for some unknown Russellian reason, prefaced the book by saying that it was not addressed primarily to professional philosophers, but to general readers interested in philosophy. The book contained, in fact, long and strenuous technical arguments, just as difficult as those in the *Inquiry into Meaning and Truth*, and in some chapters much more difficult.

It is easy to understand, therefore, the reaction of the average professional philosopher to the book. He began by disparaging it as something written for the edification of mere amateurs. He then ploughed his way through the first four Parts, finding a great deal that he had read before. Thereupon he arrived at Part V, noticing with dismay that it was spattered with mathematical symbols, and that it was a technical discussion of one of the most baffling of all unsolved problems, the Theory of Probability. This, to the professional philosopher, was the final insult and humiliation. He had been told that *Human Knowledge* was a simple book written for ordinary people to understand; and now he found that he could not understand it himself. He either put it down there and then in a bad temper, or else arrived in a highly disgruntled frame of mind at Part VI, the concluding part, on the 'Postulates of Scientific Inference'. It was this Part which contained most of what was original in the book. (I say 'most', because earlier passages included important technical discussions.)

In 1912, at the beginning of his *Problems of Philosophy*, Russell had asked 'Is there any knowledge in the world which is so certain that no reasonable man could doubt it?' In 1948, on the last page of *Human Knowledge* he came to the conclusion that 'All human knowledge is uncertain, inexact, and partial. To this doctrine we have not found any limitation whatever.'

Why did he reach this somewhat disheartening result?

To begin with, there was his realization of how little know-ledge could be obtained by logical *deduction*. I have earlier mentioned this as one of Russell's most important contributions to philosophical thinking, but it was an opinion at which he arrived gradually, helped by Wittgenstein. When he wrote the *Problems of Philosophy*, he still argued that deduction could give us new knowledge. In *Human Knowledge* he wrote that 'deduction has turned out to be much less powerful than was formerly supposed; it does not give new knowledge, except as to new forms of words for stating truths in some sense already known'.

It therefore became even more important to find some justification for accepting *induction* as a source of knowledge. (Induction can be roughly described as the problem of how you can infer, from the fact that the sun has risen every day of your life, that it will rise tomorrow.) Some philosophers thought that there might be an answer in the Mathematical Theory of Probability: it was the purpose of Part V of *Human Knowledge* to dispose of this idea by discussing various theories on the subject.

Even though Russell had written little about induction, he had called it a 'scandal' that no one had found an answer to the difficulties first pointed out by Hume. For a long time he thought that there must be *some* justification of induction to be found, better than the obviously fallacious ones put forward. He wrote in 1927:

'When men began to reason, they tried to justify the inferences that they had drawn unthinkingly in earlier days. A great deal of bad philosophy and bad science resulted from this propensity. "Great principles" such as "the uniformity of nature", the "law of universal causation", and so on are attempts to bolster up our belief that what has often happened before will happen again, which is no better founded than the horse's belief that you will take the turning you usually take. It is not altogether easy to see what is to replace these pseudo-principles in the practice of science; but perhaps the Theory of Relativity gives us a glimpse of the kind of thing we may expect.'

Human Knowledge, in 1948, was Russell's formal admission that he could not find anything, either in the Theory of Relativity or anywhere else, to replace these 'pseudo-principles' in the way he had hoped. All he could do was to base his philosophy on the kind of 'animal faith', or horse sense, which he had previously decried.

Moreover, induction was only part of another larger problem. I have called induction the problem of how you can infer that the sun is going to rise tomorrow. The other problem is how you can infer, from certain perceptions called 'seeing the sun', that the sun is there at all. It is essential, of course, to solve both problems if we are to have certainty in accepting the truth of science.

Russell had hoped to meet the second problem by regarding the sun as a 'logical construction' based on sense data. He abandoned this idea, and admitted that it is quite impossible to arrive at the world of science from the little bits and pieces of knowledge given in experience, unless you can put them together by some principles known independently of experience.

In my more technical book on Russell's philosophy I trace in detail the steps whereby, over the years, he reached this conclusion that empiricism is not enough. In *Human Knowledge* he set out to examine exactly what it was we needed in addition. He found the answer in five rather complicated 'postulates'. Having more fellow feeling than Russell for the general reader, I will not quote them in full. The first, the 'Postulate of Quasi-Permanence', will do as an example: 'Given an event A, it happens very frequently that, at any neighbouring time, there is in some neighbouring place an event very similar to A.' In other words, to put it in popular language, if you look at the sun one minute, and then look again a minute later, it is very likely that there will be a very similar 'event': you will see the sun is still there. 'Events' often seem to go together in this way. This postulate is designed to replace the old idea of 'substance'. *Something* was needed to replace it; Russell could not simply cut it out completely with Occam's Razor.

The postulates also involved reinstating the notion of cause, which Russell thought at one time could be reduced to invariable (or nearly invariable) antecedence.

In his later philosophy he was still a neutral monist in the sense of stressing that all constituents of the world are the same in kind so far as we know; beyond that we cannot say whether physical 'events' are the same or different from thoughts and feelings. All we know about them is through causal laws allowing us to infer structure.

Why should we accept the postulates of *Human Knowledge*? Russell, in effect, gave three reasons.

To begin with, if we reject them we shall be reduced to solipsism, the belief that nothing exists except yourself—or, rather, the 'events' you call yourself—and nobody really believes this. In fact, you can really only believe in the experience you are having at this moment. This is a typical example of what I have called Russell's philosophic technique of reaching a positive result by a negative method. He destroyed all the comfortable halfway houses between his postulates and solipsism of the moment.

Secondly, without something like the postulates, we cannot believe in the broad general truth of science, and nobody seriously doubts it.

Finally, if our belief in the postulates was wrong, the human race would not have survived. When we climb a ladder, we assume that its rungs will have enough 'quasi-permanence' not to dissolve suddenly into thin air; if we are wrong, we would fall and break our necks. If we had been mistaken in believing in 'quasi-permanence' and induction, the human race would by now have died out, and been replaced by other beings with more accurate beliefs about the nature of reality. In fact, our beliefs have probably arisen as a result of biological adaptation to environment; we think that way because the world is made that way.

These three points are interesting as showing Russell's growing impatience with philosophers who spin out arguments by professing doubts about things which no one could doubt sincerely. They show him adopting a much more commonsense and practical philosophy. They show a great change, however, from the days when Russell had hoped to find some *certain* ground for believing in science, and had derided the claims of common sense. He still denied, of course, that common sense is infallible; but he now admitted that there was sometimes nothing better to act on in practice.

Human Knowledge can therefore be regarded from one point

of view as a confession of failure. Russell had been unable to find the certain knowledge which had been his quest throughout his philosophical life; his new philosophy was based on 'postulates' and an appeal to practical results which could not be justified by the kind of critical criteria he had laid down earlier. But there was much more to *Human Knowledge* than this.

Any recognition of a failure can often be fruitful; and Russell's failure to be a complete empiricist was fruitful in this kind of way. In his detailed working out of the postulates, he went much further than anyone before to define exactly *what* knowledge must be accepted *a priori* in order to construct science on an empirical basis; and by this work he added to our understanding of the nature of the universe.

Consider, for instance, the way his postulate of 'quasi-permanence' emphasized the way in which 'events' are found to go together.

I mentioned before that one of the difficulties of his earlier construction programme was to explain why the aspects of a table are collected so as to form a table. Russell now answered this question, even though the best answer he could find was 'It just happens that way'. I also remarked that one of the difficulties of the method of analysis is that, having chopped the universe up into very small pieces, it is hard for an analytical philosopher to put it together again. So one of Russell's critics might now say: 'Why not choose the other approach, and start with things as they are, considered as unities?' But it is worth noting that the philosophical procedure of Russell is more in accordance with the ideas of present-day cosmogonists; for instance, Mr Fred Hoyle's discussion of how diffuse hydrogen atoms collect themselves to form stars. Again we have a case where philosophy prompts a question which it cannot answer— why are 'events' and collections of 'events' found together?— and can give renewed stimulus to scientific thought.

The justification for dissection in philosophy remains the same as in anatomy. It increases knowledge, even it it does not explain everything; and it focuses attention on what it leaves unexplained.

Reading through the postulates, and Russell's arguments in reaching them, one is struck by the recurrence of the word

'structure'—the importance of which he had already stressed—
and also of such words as 'continuity' and 'similar'. I believe that
what Russell succeeded in doing, in *Human Knowledge*, was in
making explicit certain assumptions which had been implicit in
his writings before. In the *Problems of Philosophy*, for instance,
he had discussed the 'idealist' view that a cat in a room goes out
of existence when no one is looking at it. Russell, on some
vague grounds of continuity, said it was natural to assume that
the cat was there the whole time, particularly if it had got
hungry since last seen. But neither he, nor anyone else, inquired
just how valid this argument was; the principle of continuity was
based on some subconscious assumption of the old idea of
substance. In fact Russell did not even mention the word
'continuity'; he appealed vaguely to 'every principle of simplicity'; but what he meant, I think, was that it is simpler to
believe in a continuous cat than in an intermittent cat. Later on,
in his technical writing about *sensibilia*, he appealed directly to
'continuity', but I believe he did so without consciously thinking
about it. Now he prompted the question as to what sort of
'continuity' is involved.

If I am right, then, Wittgenstein was wrong in disparaging
Russell's later philosophical writings. In *Human Knowledge* and
the books which led up to it, as in his work on mathematical
philosophy and the Theory of Descriptions, Russell performed
the supreme philosophical task of questioning assumptions previously taken for granted, and making them explicit.

Particularly interesting is the idea of similarity. Russell had
also been led to emphasize the word 'similar' by the technique of
'minimum vocabularies'. This was the surviving relic of his
belief that we can get knowledge about the structure of reality
by studying the structure of sentences. His idea, put in simple
language, was this: Try to find how few words you need to
describe the Universe; if you cannot describe it without using
some particular word, then there must be something in the
Universe corresponding to that word. In this way, for instance,
he tried to see whether he could find a vocabulary which dis-
pensed with words standing for 'universals'; and he found that
he could not dispense with the word 'similar'. He came to the
conclusion that:

'The fact that we need the word "similar" indicates some fact about the world, and not only about language. What fact it indicates about the world, I do not know.'

It is certainly a curious fact that the world has similar things in it. It is much easier, when you come to think of it, to imagine a world in which things are all different, or all exactly the same, or a mixture of both; like the nineteenth century scientific picture of the world as built up of about ninety different sorts of atoms, the atoms of each sort being identical. But it is very puzzling to have a world in which things are similar; in which elements have isotopes; in which one blade of grass is very like another blade of grass, but not quite the same. It was Russell's merit that he made us think of this question; or, at least, that he should have made us think of it. The fact that he did not offer any explanation of it himself is much less important. Philosophers exist to ask questions, not to answer them. We might have expected *Human Knowledge* to provide a mature rounded summary of Russell's conclusions; the remarkable thing is that instead he was still drawing attention to more problems than he could solve, resulting in a book with the untidiness which so often characterizes original thinking. His work was never so much a complete philosophy as a philosophy Under Construction. His vitality was such that his philosophy was still Under Construction when he was seventy-six.

Unfortunately there is little sign yet of anyone building some great new philosophy in continuation of Russell's work (or as a reaction to it.) Hundreds of years may elapse before this happens; for big philosophical advances are often a matter of centuries. Among contemporaries, the man who has done most to carry on Russell's ideas is Professor Ayer. Other British philosophers, owing to their admiration for Wittgenstein, belittled Russell's work after the time that he and Wittgenstein began to disagree; so they took their starting point from Russell's earlier views rather than his later ones. In these earlier days, as we have mentioned, Russell hoped to cut out all *a priori* principles of knowledge, apart from logical principles, and to deny that we have any other knowledge except empirical knowledge. From this, and Wittgenstein's *Tractatus*, arose the

P

Logical Positivist doctrine that, since we know about nothing but observable facts, the metaphysical discussions of traditional philosophy are meaningless. In the early days Russell also saw much more importance in linguistic analysis than he saw later; and the emphasis on the linguistic approach was reinforced by the stress which Wittgenstein laid in his Cambridge lectures, and in his posthumous *Philosophical Investigations*, on the way in which words are actually used in ordinary speech. These two beliefs—that metaphysical discussions are pointless, while language is all-important—were the guiding rules of Russell's immediate successors.

I will not say much about these philosophers, because I think their work was rather artificial. It was artificial for much the same reasons as some contemporary artists and writers were artificial; because they had found themselves out of a job.

For centuries artists had tried to depict reality; and because they were absorbed in this aim, devoted to something outside themselves, they could produce great art. The invention of the camera meant that their work could be done better by a box with a lens in it, and the artists had to do something else to earn a living. So they started painting things which did not exist, and talking self-consciously about their subjective visions of the world; the result being a hundred bogus artists for every experimenter of genuine inspiration. The same thing happened with poets and writers after the invention of films, which can portray a landscape, or reveal a human character, or inspire emotion, far better than by words alone. Poets were reduced to playing with words for their own sakes; and thus became self-conscious, introvert, barren and futile.

Something analogous happened with philosophers who followed the Logical Positivists. It was no longer their business to discuss the real world and find answers to the real problems which bother men and women, because they had declared that all these problems were either meaningless, insoluble, or only capable-of solution by scientists or logicians. But, like the unemployed artists and the poets, they had to do *something*; so they plunged into an orgy of clever talk and word-splitting. They were asking pernickety questions about the use of words, not always because of some deep-rooted desire for knowledge, but to exercise their brains and justify their existence. They spent their time thinking about their own thoughts.

It was this, I believe, which was the reason for Russell's low opinion of them. It was this which led C. D. Broad to characterize certain contemporary philosophers, in a phrase reminiscent of Disraeli, as 'clever sillies'. Perhaps Russell was a little unfair in his repeated attacks on Oxford philosophers; some of them never entered this phase, and others soon began to emerge from it: but Russell did not realize this because he had stopped reading them.* In some moods he even despaired of philosophy altogether, describing it as 'a dud subject', and advising young men not to waste their time on it. 'Oxford philosophers,' he said, 'have shown philosophy is nonsense. I am now left regretting my ill-spent youth.'

He declared that 'I have been painfully forced to the belief that nine-tenths of what is regarded as philosophy is humbug. The only part that is at all definite is logic, and since it is logic, it is not philosophy.' When Russell talked like this, one began to sympathize with his critics. It is quite true that every time a philosophical problem is solved definitely it ceases to be part of philosophy, and becomes part of science. This has happened with many ideas which philosophers first put forward, like planetary motion and biological evolution and the atomic composition of matter; but it does not prove they were wrong in speculating about them; and it does not prove they are wrong in thinking about unsolved problems today. Their talk is often vague and muddled; but this follows inevitably from the fact that they are searching for solutions which no one has yet found. I would define philosophy as something which I would defend to the death: the right to talk about things which you do not understand.

What Russell should have said was not that most philosophy is humbug, but that most philosophers are humbugs. I think this was what he really meant, but he was too polite to say so; and it is a much more tenable argument. If we were to arrange the human race in order of average intellectual integrity, I would give first place to professional cricketers, put scientists some way

---

* Russell informed me (March 1956) that he had just read some Oxford philosophers again, without changing his opinion of them.

after them, and put professional philosophers a good deal lower down. It is impossible for a cricketer to be a humbug; if he pretends to be a better batsman than he is, he will probably be found out first ball. A scientist who puts forward a theory usually knows that it can be proved or disproved by a practical test. But a philosopher need only write a book which nobody understands, and for the rest of his life nobody can be quite sure whether he is a genius or a charlatan; so it is understandable that the ranks of philosophers contain a proportion of the latter. But this does not prove that philosophy, in itself, is an inferior pursuit to science or cricket.

CHAPTER XXV

'While Still at Work'

RUSSELL'S *Human Society in Ethics and Politics* was not published till 1954. But it is convenient to discuss it here, because most of it was originally meant for inclusion in *Human Knowledge*, and was written at the same time.

Human Society was remarkable for the candour with which Russell confessed his dislike of his own subjective theory of ethics. 'I find it quite intolerable,' he wrote, 'to suppose that when I say "Cruelty is bad" I am merely saying that I dislike cruelty.' He therefore laboured to find some objective foundation for ethical theory, deciding that 'Right desires will be those that are capable of being compossible with as many other desires as possible'. The word 'compossible' was due to an analogy from Leibniz's philosophy; what Russell meant was a repetition of an argument, in his *Principles of Social Reconstruction*, that creative impulses are good because the pleasure they give is not at the expense of any one else; while possessive impulses can only be satisfied by depriving others. If two people both want to possess the same thing, their desires are not 'compossible'.

To put it simply, it is all right to do what you want if it makes you happy, and doesn't do anybody else any harm. Russell even carried this to the logical extreme of saying that, if one man is filled with hatred of another, it may be a good thing for him to have the pleasure of a false belief that the other man is suffering.

Russell's teaching was, in effect, that of the greatest good (or pleasure) of the greatest number. If a schoolboy with a box of chocolates passes them round, he causes greater total satisfaction than if he eats them all himself and makes himself sick. Therefore benevolence is good, selfishness is bad. And Russell added to traditional Utilitarianism a way of measuring a pleasure against a pain; they are equal if you don't mind whether you have both or neither.

To call Russell's moral philosophy 'utilitarian' can be misleading; perhaps 'hedonism' comes closer to it. He was certainly not a utilitarian in the everyday sense of the word, as was shown by his criticism of excessive 'utilitarianism' in Russia and America. Unlike some of his predecessors, he allowed for different intellectual and aesthetic capacities; and he believed in eugenics, which is based on the fact that people are *not* equal mentally or physically.* He even came to stress a significant difference between men and women, because many of his most promising women students abandoned their intellectual ambitions sooner or later.

The importance of Russell's idea of 'compossible desires' was not so much pedantic as practical: he once put it that 'The wish to harmonize desires is the chief motive of my political and social beliefs, from the nursery to the international state'. At the end of his discussion in *Human Society* Russell decided that he had merely found some guiding principles for use in practice, not objective knowledge. The basis of ethics was 'still one of emotion and feeling'. This was why he did not include what he wrote in his book on *Human Knowledge*.

Unfortunately Russell did not leave things at that: he showed his recurrent fault of paying too much attention to foolish critics. Philosophers like C. E. M. Joad accused him of destroying the authority of traditional religion and morality, which could have important effects on people's conduct. Russell should obviously have admitted the accusation, but denied the implication that philosophers should sacrifice their intellectual integrity to avoid destructive conclusions. But Russell could not bear Joad, or bear any excuse for a revival of organized religion; and he maintained that the destructive side of his teaching was not of much practical importance.

He said in a broadcast:

'Philosophers are fond of endless puzzles about ultimate

---

* He wrote about the secret of a happy old age that 'My first advice would be to choose your ancestors carefully', pointing out that three out of his own four grandparents had lived to over eighty.

ethical values and the basis of morals. My own belief is that so far as politics and practical living are concerned we can sweep aside all these puzzles, and use common sense principles. We all desire and need food and shelter and clothing; security from injury, happiness, joy of living, freedom. . . .'

Or, as he put it in *Human Society*, 'In political arguments, it is seldom necessary to appeal to ethical considerations, since enlightened self-interest affords a sufficient motive for action in accordance with the general good.'

But immediately he had to qualify this view. Russell had often pointed out that self-interest is not so strong a motive as often thought—and hoped; nor had he always praised 'prudence'. As he himself recognized, we cannot go through life deciding our every action with a calculating machine, trying to work out possible consequences.

I think it is better to say plainly that in ethics, as in some other subjects, Russell's questions outran his answers. His great merit was that he forced us to see that we must either find some acceptable answers, or else learn to live without them, using such general principles as are to be found in his sayings: 'Inspired by love, and guided by reason.' He brought precisely into focus the dilemma of an age when science has given almost unlimited power for good or evil, and simultaneously destroyed belief in previous faiths by which it had been thought that good and evil could be definitely distinguished. Nor can science put anything in their place. Russell's typically honest conclusion was that we have nothing approaching certain knowledge about the world except through the methods of science, and that science cannot prove anything is right or wrong; it cannot prove, for instance, that it is wrong to enjoy the infliction of cruelty.

Russell wrote in 1943 that 'while my own conclusions as to ethics do not satisfy me, other people's satisfy me even less'. I confess to agreeing with him on the second point as well as the first.

So far, subsequent philosophers have not done any better with ethics than with the other awkward problems which Russell left on their hands. Many of them, abandoning the austere doctrine that we can only know the truth of logical and scientific statements, developed the theory that different departments of human knowledge each have their own special kind of truth; that the statements of science and ethics and aesthetics and economics and theology can all be true in their own different ways. This has obvious difficulties. On this theory, it is hard to see what we mean when we say, for instance, that 'The laws enunciated by physicists are more often accurate than those enunciated by economists'; but this seems almost certainly true, and it seems to imply some general standard of truth.

One thing, at any rate, certainly followed from Russell's views on ethics. If ethical beliefs were matters of feeling and emotion, then he should do all he could to influence people's feelings and emotions in the right direction. This had been his constant concern ever since 1914; and in his later years he became more and more of a preacher, using the word in the best but not the conventional sense. He surprised some of his hearers on his lecture tour of Australia, for instance, by saying that:

'The root of the matter is a very simple and old-fashioned thing—a thing so simple that I am almost ashamed to mention it, for fear of the derisive smile with which wise cynics will greet my words. The thing I mean, please forgive me for mentioning it, is love—Christian love or compassion.'

There was no need for surprise: it was not a conventional case of a sceptic softening with advancing years. Russell was merely repeating in different words what he had preached in *A Free Man's Worship* in 1902, and in his *Principles of Social Reconstruction* in 1916. What was new was that he should emphasize that an old-fashioned idea might be true. He had finally shaken himself free from the assumption, derived in the first place from the Victorian belief in progress, and reinforced by the intellectual *avant-garde* of the 1920's, that new moralities are bound to be better than old ones.

The reference to Christianity did not mean that he had come any closer to orthodoxy; he remarked about this time that 'I am not sure whether I am atheist or an agnostic, so I sometimes call myself one thing and sometimes the other'. He defined a religion as 'the desire to believe a lot of nonsense in order to make yourself comfortable'. . . . 'I mean any form of belief designed as a sop to cowardice. It is the dishonesty and cowardice I mind.' Saying prayers, according to Russell, was equivalent to believing that the Universe is governed by a being who changes his mind if you ask him to.

He said in 1950: 'The only thing I see in which Catholicism is better than Communism is that it is older. Religion is like wine—it improves with age.'

Russell worried a little about the new-found respectability of his later years, and wondered whether he was getting *too* respectable: 'I have always thought respectable people scoundrels, and I look anxiously at my face every morning for signs of my becoming a scoundrel.' The explanation, however, was probably the way in which the British, like the Chinese, venerate age: however outrageous a rebel may be, by the time he is eighty the British public will decide that it is safe to admire him. In America, by way of contrast, Russell remained suspect for many years. When the NBC recorded a television interview for his eightieth birthday, a Customs official seized the film when it reached New York, and was reported as remarking: 'Russell? He's the guy who wrote about sex, isn't he? Then it will have to be censored.'

In Britain, even Bernard Shaw ended his days as a venerated figure. With Russell there was also the fact that, on many subjects, British public opinion had come round to agreeing with him.

But he himself had also mellowed a little in these later years, when he returned for a time to live in Richmond, in a big Victorian house only a mile or so from the gardens of the Pembroke Lodge where he had played as a boy. 'The world,' he wrote, 'takes a lot of getting used to, and I have only lately begun to feel more or less at home in it.'

In 1952 came his happy marriage to Miss Edith Finch, author of the biography of Wilfrid Scawen Blunt. Miss Finch was a member of an old-established New England family, which had gone over to America in the seventeenth century, and she had taught at Bryn Mawr. But she had many other interests besides academic work; including the somewhat unusual experience, while a student in Paris, of riding a horse bareback in a circus.

Russell still made occasional incursions into philosophy, with book reviews and articles, in which his wit could be as devastating as ever. Discussing the fondness of Oxford philosophers at one time for investigating the 'common usage' of words, he remarked that 'To discuss endlessly what silly people mean when they say silly things may be amusing, but can hardly be important'. And he satirized the attitude of some modern philosophers by telling a story of a shopkeeper whom he had once asked the shortest way to Winchester:

'He called out to a man in the back premises:
' "Gentleman wants to know the shortest way to Winchester."
' "Winchester?" an unseen voice replied.
' "Aye."
' "Way to Winchester?"
' "Aye."
' "Shortest way?"
' "Aye."
' "Dunno." '

'He wanted,' said Russell, 'to get the nature of the question clear, but took no interest in answering it. This is exactly what modern philosophy does for the earnest seeker after truth. Is it surprising that young people turn to other studies?'

Russell never stopped working. He wrote that 'I should like to die while still at work, knowing that others will carry on what I can no longer do, and content in the thought that what was possible has been done'. His output of broadcast talks and newspaper articles seemed unending. In politics, he still criticized both Russia and America. He told the Archbishop of York that he prayed every night 'Help me to love the Americans', but that his prayers had not been answered yet. And he wrote to Greenish in Australia that 'I spend most of my time having fun finding fault with the Yanks. They enjoy it.'

Not content with all these activities he turned to a completely new vocation, the writing of fiction. He wanted to publish his short stories under a pseudonym, building up a new separate reputation at the age of eighty; but editors refused to take his stories without his name on them. Eventually *The Corsican*

Adventures of Miss X was published anonymously in the magazine *Go*, with a prize of £25 for anyone who could guess who had written it. Nobody succeeded in doing so.

His first stories appeared in book form as *Satan in the Suburbs*, and Russell announced cheerfully that 'I have devoted the first eighty years of my life to philosophy. I propose to devote the next eighty years to another branch of fiction.'

Satan in the Suburbs won some high praise: Angus Wilson, for instance, called it 'an exceedingly entertaining collection', in which 'the formal eighteenth-century syntax and language add delightfully to the general ironic mood'. Personally I preferred the following volume of stories, *Nightmares of Eminent Persons*; the secret was, I think, that while writing them Russell had the relish of thinking how they would annoy different people he disliked. One story in particular in this volume—*Zahatopolk*—has a savagery and bite reminiscent of Swift.

In the intervals of writing, Russell still read voluminously, taking *The Times*, *Manchester Guardian* and *New York Herald Tribune* regularly; and getting through, in addition to more serious books, about one detective novel a day. He once pointed out that anyone who wanted to abolish war should find harmless ways of satisfying the instincts inherited from generations of savages. He said that he himself found such an outlet in detective stories, 'where I alternately identify myself with the murderer and the huntsman-detective'.

He still liked having someone to read aloud to him, the only trouble being that Edith Russell was as fond of smoking as himself; so they would take turn and turn about, Russell reading at intervals so that his wife could have a cigarette.

Russell himself kept to his pipe, with a regular order for a quarter-pound tin each week of Fribourg and Treyer's Golden Mixture. He remarked that 'When I was young I was told that smoking would shorten my life: after sixty years of smoking, it hasn't shortened much. . . . Anyway I get much more pleasure from smoking than I would from a few more years in decrepitude. I smoke heavily and only stop to sleep or eat.'

He would claim, in one of his frequent moments of mischief, that he had once given up tobacco, and could thus go on smoking with a good conscience, having proved he could do without it.

It would then transpire that the last time he had stopped smoking was over thirty years earlier, when he was in China in 1921.

No philosopher ever had more sensible views about physical fitness. 'I have never yet,' he said, 'done anything on the ground that it is good for my health. I smoke what I like. I eat what I like. I drink what I like. I have always found that to forget about oneself is the best way to keep your health, if you are as naturally healthy as I am.' In later years, however, he made one concession to what the doctors said was good for him. He usually drank whisky in place of wine, because it was less acid.

He had more illnesses than might be supposed from the way he talked, but his resilience carried him over them all. He nearly died from pneumonia in the summer of 1953, but was back from hospital in a week. Then, at the beginning of 1954, he had an operation which was bound to be serious at the age of eighty-one. He faced it with the same attitude of cheerful disrespect as in his Peking illness, protesting that 'I'd be quite all right except for the doctors'.

A few days before, my wife and I spent an evening with him and Lady Russell, and the talk turned by chance to personal immortality. Though nothing was said about his forthcoming operation, it was inevitably in our minds; and I could not help recalling how Socrates, before taking the hemlock, had comforted his friends by giving them fallacious proofs that his soul would survive after death.

Russell was just as uncompromising as ever in denying immortality, and in keeping to the 'neutral monist' doctrine that a personality is a collection of 'events'. My wife said that, despite her agnosticism, she found it hard to accept the complete end of the individual. Russell replied that 'A personality is an aggregate, or an organization, like a cricket club. I can accept the dissolution of the MCC.' My wife then spoke of young men who had been killed in the war; and said that it seemed monstrously unjust that they should not, somehow or somewhere, have a second chance of happiness and achievement. 'But the universe *is* unjust,' said Russell.

In this, I think, lay the essence of Russell's practical wisdom: to the end he remained true to the faith—preached long before in *A Free Man's Worship*, and intensified by the horrors the world had known since—that the beginning of any worthwhile creed of living must be a recognition of harsh and unpleasant truths. He said that 'the secret of happiness is to face the fact that the world is horrible, horrible, *horrible.* . . . You must feel it deeply, and not brush it aside. . . . You must feel it right in here'—hitting his breast—'and then you can start being happy again.' Russell went beyond Christian morality in not only stressing man's insignificance compared with the universe, but in saying that the universe has no principle of justice at work in it. I call this practical wisdom because, if you can give up believing in cosmic justice, then nothing can make you have a grievance against the world; and there is nothing so sterile and profitless as having a grievance. Russell, unlike many philosophers, seemed to find in the fundamental point of his philosophy of life a practical help in his own living. I do not think he could possibly have kept up his courage and cheerfulness, in the face of so much recurring sorrow and anxiety, if he had not come to learn by experience the knack of not feeling sorry for himself. Energy which he might have wasted on feeling sorry for himself was diverted into feeling angry with other people: which I think is much more healthy. He once said 'I don't believe in meekness'.

This, perhaps, was one of his sharpest departures in practice from Christian precepts. But only in practice, because, of course, his theories did not allow him to be angry with anybody. An evil man was not to be hated, but studied and cured by scientific methods: 'It is a waste of energy to be angry with a man who behaves badly, just as it is to be angry with a car that won't go.' But the truth is that a life based strictly on Russell's principles, without occasional deviations, is as difficult as one based strictly on Christian teachings, except for a few exceptional saints. And even Christ himself (as Russell pointed out) was capable at times of unloving remarks to his enemies.

'Hatred of some sort,' Russell once wrote, 'is quite necessary —it needn't be towards people. But without some admixture of hatred one becomes soft and loses energy.'

Speaking of Russell's practical wisdon, I cannot resist adding here some of the aphorisms among his innumerable newspaper articles. They include 'Never try to stop people thinking, because you will certainly succeed', 'It is better to do a little good than a great deal of harm,' and 'Never feel absolutely sure of anything'. I think the last is most important, being the summing up of his philosophical position. It should not only be interpreted as advocating universal scepticism, but as pointing out that you cannot expect to live without taking risks. It is not only a gospel of tolerance in thinking, but also of courage in action.

Russell's operation in 1954 proved even more serious than expected. But within two weeks he was sitting up in bed smoking his pipe as vigorously as ever, and within two months he was resuming his round of broadcasting and writing.

There was now a significant change in his attitude to international affairs. In the years immediately after the Second World War he had stressed that he would prefer an atomic war to world conquest by Soviet Russia. He said in 1950 that 'In spite of some alarmists, it is hardly likely that our species will completely exterminate itself'. The position was now changed by the hydrogen bomb, which he himself had predicted. Here at last, he thought, there should be a chance for enlightened self-interest, now that international politics had come down to an elemental choice between survival and suicide.

And so, in December 1954, Russell made one of his most moving broadcasts, on the subject of the hydrogen bomb. He ended: 'I appeal as a human being to human beings: remember your humanity, and forget the rest. If you can do so the way lies open to a new paradise; if you cannot, nothing lies before you but universal death.'

No one who heard him will forget the passionate sincerity with which he spoke. The response was immediate; Russell found himself looked upon as the standard bearer of the mute mass of people throughout the world who dreaded another war. He took up one of his greatest crusades. He conceived the idea, only possible for a man with his international standing, of getting Communist and anti-Communist scientists to issue a joint statement warning the world of the dangers of the hydrogen bomb.

First he asked Einstein, who agreed and suggested that Russell should draft the statement. The draft was sent to Einstein at Princeton. Then, when Russell was flying back after speaking at a conference on World Government in Rome, the pilot came back from the cockpit with a news item just picked up by the wireless operator: Einstein had died. Russell had lost a personal friend, and he thought it would also mean losing Einstein's support for his appeal. But when the plane reached Paris, he found a letter waiting for him. It was one of the last Einstein ever wrote, and in it he agreed to sign Russell's statement.

Russell, taking on with his wife immense labours of correspondence and negotiation, got other signatures: Bridgman of Harvard, Infeld of Warsaw, Muller of Indiana, Powell of Bristol, Rotblat of London University, Yukawa of Kyoto, Max Born, Linus Pauling and Joliot Curie. Early in July 1955, at the age of eighty-three, Russell called a press conference in the Caxton Hall in London. For over an hour, with the blinding lights of the newsreel cameramen shining on his white hair, he stood answering the questions of two hundred journalists. Then he repeated his speech for television. His words went round the world, carrying unanswerable conviction. His was a voice that was heard and answered.

He even won praise from old Sir Charles Trevelyan; who, at the time when Russell was most prominent as a critic of Soviet Russia, had growled that 'any decent Government would shoot McCarthy and Bertie Russell'. Now Sir Charles was heard to say, in his Northumberland fastness, that 'Bertie's the only great man in the world today who is talking sense'.

On June 23, 1950, Russell had said that there was a half chance of avoiding war in the next five years, and that the Russians would not provoke a war after five years 'because the Western Powers will be well prepared by then'. In July 1955, almost exactly five years after this prediction, the heads of Governments began the meeting at Geneva which led to a new hope in international affairs. Russell said soon afterwards that never since 1914 had he felt so cheerful about the prospects before the world; it seemed that, for at least a time, sanity had been given a chance to prevail.

CHAPTER XXVI

The Young Octogenarian

ANY biographical study written during the lifetime of the subject must necessarily be incomplete; it can only be rounded off by prophecy, notoriously a risky business. I propose to take the risk.

Russell was nearly eighty when I first started work on this book; but even then it could easily be foreseen that he had many more years of active life still in front of him. England after the Second World War was a land of Grand Old Men; in which, if you wanted an interesting and stimulating discussion on some subject, you often had to go to one of the octogenarians to get it. They included Russell himself, G. E. Moore, Bernard Shaw, Winston Churchill, Gilbert Murray, H. N. Brailsford; and they formed a group which, I think, may always remain somewhat unique. Their early lives had been spent in the serene golden age before the First World War, and their later years were prolonged by advances in medical science. The generation before them had died younger; the generation after them had grown up in a world of nervous strain and tension, a world full of wars and the fear of wars and recurrent economic anxiety. No one of more modern times, one felt, however long they lived, would carry forward into old age that atmosphere of serene and gentle scholarship of which one was always conscious, for instance, in the presence of Gilbert Murray.

The octogenarians were all, of course, exceptional men. I am not suggesting that sulpha drugs and penicillin had anything to do with the greatness of Winston Churchill; though without them he might well have died in 1943. These men owed their vigour in old age not only to the accident of the time they were born, but to some innate vitality inside them. Both Churchill and Russell exemplify the view that all great human achievement can be resolved, in the last resort, to some superabundant source of energy. I can remember going to see Russell with a young American Professor who, after two hours' intense philosophical argument, was much the most exhausted; I can remember seeing Russell full of vigour after midnight, when he had come home from spending five hours at the BBC rehearsing and taking part in a television discussion, and had spent the early part of the afternoon going for a long walk in Richmond Park. Perhaps my most vivid recollection is of going to the theatre with him, going on to a late supper at which he recalled with precision some Greek tags which he had learnt as a boy, and then driving him home to Richmond at half past one in the morning, with Russell talking the whole time about the exact reasons why he was led to reject Hegelianism in the 1890s, and myself torn between a fascinated desire to give my whole attention to what he was saying, and the need to remember my responsibilities as the driver of the car. (Unlike most elderly people, Russell disliked driving slowly.)

He never lost his boyish zest in baiting people: I can remember him gravely assuring Mr Michael Curtis, the young editor of one highly respected British newspaper, that 'Of course the *News of the World* is the only paper which honestly sets out to give the true facts about what is really going on'.* Lady Russell leant across to Mr Curtis and said 'Don't rise to him'. Another characteristic Russellian remark on this occasion, containing an element of truth put in the most provocative way possible, was that 'The only things I believe in the newspapers are the cricket scores and the Stock Exchange prices'.

Russell had none of that horrible and unnatural inhibition which stops some Englishmen enjoying their own jokes. The jests would come swift and free in sparkling profusion; there would be a quick look round to make sure that everyone had seen the point, and then he would laugh with the rest.

What of his reputation in the years to come? Here again I am

---

* For readers outside Britain, it may be explained that the *News of the World* is a Sunday paper which specializes in full and detailed reports of murders, divorce cases, etc.

Q

bold enough to say that this can be predicted with some precision.

It is almost inevitable that there will be a first period of reaction and denigration, as there was against Bernard Shaw. Russell is an easy target for anyone who wants to write a debunking book. Because his thought continually developed, he often proved himself wrong by saying things different from what he had said before; I am sometimes tempted to think that there is no single subject on which, from the vast corpus of his writings over the years, I could not produce two opposing quotations. Again, his ideas are so intertwined with those of other men of the age that a clever detractor could easily deny him much originality; perhaps the only important things to which nobody else could make some sort of a claim are his work on the Logic of Relations, the Theory of Descriptions, and the postulates of *Human Knowledge*.

Above all, Russell suffers from the disadvantage that his later work was overpraised, while his earlier work was often forgotten. No one can read through all he wrote before the First World War without realizing the greatness of his sheer intellectual vigour and vitality; but some of these massive and diverse writings were buried in obscure periodicals, and many of them will always be completely unintelligible to everyone except a few specialists. Paradoxically enough, he was accused of lack of profundity because his best work was so difficult that few people could understand it. All these factors point to some reaction against the veneration in which he came to be held. In fact the reaction is already well under way in academic circles in Britain, though it has not yet spread to the general public.

What of his standing, in the long run, in the history of philosophy? Here again he is under a grave handicap. The surest way to philosophical immortality is to put forward some striking doctrine which is subsequently shown to be completely wrong. The names of most philosophers live in the refutations of their successors. As Professor Austin once put it, 'to be a great philosopher you have to make a great mistake'. It is doubtful whether Russell has made any great mistake in this sense; and, where he has been wrong, he has spoilt the fun of following generations by pointing out the errors himself. In spite of all the logical and philosophical advances for which he is responsible, and in spite of all the dark places which he has made plain, one is tempted to say that his immortality depends on somebody finding some fundamental fault in his work. Or, to put it more accurately, his assured place in the history of philosophy partly lies in the fact that any subsequent philosopher has to begin where he left off, because—as with Hume—it is impossible to be satisfied with things as he has left them.

I doubt whether Russell would accept this view himself. He only asked philosophical questions because he genuinely wanted to know answers, so I fancy he would consider himself a failure in so far as he had left problems unsolved. When, at one time, I thought of sub-titling this book 'The Great Questioner', he pointed out that he had done something to answer questions too; and that is a typically English understatement. But my own view is that many questions which philosophers ask may well be unanswerable; and Russell himself once wrote that the value of philosophy lies largely in the questions themselves. I think that the conclusions at which a philosopher arrives are often less important than the discussions which lead up to them, and the spirit of inquiry in which he approaches them. Stevenson said that 'to travel hopefully is better than to arrive'. The same thing applies to philosophy, which is often not a matter of getting anywhere—if it was, we should sometimes be sadly disappointed—but a matter of pursuing a worthwhile objective in the best possible company. That is why it is always more rewarding to read a great philosopher in the original, and follow the workings of his mind, than to read the most lucid modern summary of his conclusions. That is why Russell's work will always be read.

It comes down, I suppose, to saying that there are no great philosophies; there are only great philosophers, which is one good reason for my including so much in this book about Russell as a man. The same applies even more to his writings on politics and sociology, where definite knowledge is even more elusive. They contain at least one point of permanent importance: his emphasis on the love of power, and his rejection of the over-simplifications of Marxists and Freudians. He laid himself open to criticism on some other points because of mistakes which it is easy for anyone to see in retrospect. Yet we would not think higher of Russell if he had stood aloof from the day-to-day struggles and agonies of his fellow human beings.

If we set out to read through all his journalistic and non-philosophical writings, the first impression is one of bewilderment at their sheer voluminousness and variety of viewpoint. As Dr Johnson remarked of Burke: '[He] *is* an extraordinary man. His stream of mind is perpetual.' I do not say that every word which Russell wrote, including all his popular writing, is worth reading. But I do say, on the basis of my own research, that every word he wrote should be read, at least by anyone attempting any estimate of his stature. Even in the most ephemeral newspaper article, even in the most obvious pot-boiler, there may be some interesting idea or little-known fact, not to be found anywhere else.

When we make our way through this vast mass of wordage—he himself once called it 'logorrhoea'—I do not think we discover at the end, as some earnest Americans seem to believe, a number of oracular political and social theories to be studied at length in solemn books. I think we end by finding an extraordinary man; a man of immense erudition who also had a delight in teaching; a man of warm human understanding who started many others thinking on lines which could lead to happiness; a man with a passionate hatred of folly and cruelty, and the power to give hope and heart in the fight against them. We find a rationalist who, in his final summing up, asked whether the human race could survive; and who replied 'Beyond all reason, I am unconquerably persuaded that they will'.

To a world crying for a Faith, religious or political, Russell replied with his uncompromising conclusion that nothing is absolutely certain: but at the same time he showed how an agnostic can be unafraid. While cynical scepticism is sterile, a passionate sceptic can live a life of courage and achievement.

As it happens, the point I am making was perhaps best illustrated by a comment in the Sydney *Bulletin* after Russell had given a press conference in Australia. There was, said the *Bulletin*, something pathetic and even tragic about the interview: 'In times of grave anxiety people turn to the Wise Old Men of the tribe; but even a man as wise as Bertrand Russell did not really know how to be an incorrigible Socialist and yet defend the individual; how to be a Liberal when the Communists have forced on us an age of tyranny; how to be a Pacifist and yet stand up to the Soviet. . . . He didn't really know whether there would be a war or not; or how, except by arming, you could stop it coming.'

And yet, concluded the *Bulletin*, 'at the same time he was heartening, simply because of his own unquenchable vitality and cheerfulness. If the world has the atomic bomb in it, it also has the valiant human spirit.'

That was how Russell impressed one of the more critical of his contemporaries. That was how he impressed me. It is a shocking confession to make in an age which delights in disparagement, and it may shatter any remaining faith in my impartiality; but I have not the slightest doubt about Russell being a great man of the kind only counted in terms of centuries; and I do not think anyone could have any close knowledge of him without coming to the same conclusion. It may be easy for anyone in the years to come to attack him from a distance, aided by ignorance; just as it will be easy for any future scribbler to belittle Winston Churchill. We in this generation can only reply, in each case: 'You did not know him.' If this book serves any purpose, it is to allow people to know a little more about one of those rare and valiant human spirits who, throughout the ages, have inspired their fellow men by reaching their thoughts into the furthermost realms of truth.

INDEX

About the Author

A native Australian, Alan Wood was graduated from Sydney University, where his father was Professor of History. He went on to Oxford to study philosophy, was the first Australian to become President of the Union, and later returned to Oxford for a period during the course of his work on Bertrand Russell. The fruits of his studies and his close acquaintanceship with Russell are the present biography and a forthcoming book, Russell's Philosophy: A Study of Its Development.

Mr. Wood did not, however, confine his interests to philosophy. He first became well known to the English public as a correspondent with the airborne forces at Arnhem during World War II. His varied books include Islands in Danger (*with Mary Wood*), *the history of the German occupation of the Channel Islands.*

As this book was going to press, word arrived from London of the death there of Mr. Wood at the age of 43.